REA's *interactive* *flashcards*™

GERMAN

**Staff of Research and Education Association,
Dr. M. Fogiel, Director**

D0558402

Research & Education Association
61 Ethel Road West
Piscataway, New Jersey 08854

REA's INTERACTIVE FLASHCARDS™ GERMAN

Printed in the United States of America

Library of Congress Catalog Card Number 98-67200

International Standard Book Number 0-87891-160-X

Research & Education Association, Piscataway, New Jersey 08854

REA's Interactive Flashcards

What they're for

How to use them

They come in a book, not in a box of hundreds of loose cards.

They are most useful as test time approaches to help you check your test readiness.

They are a good tool for self-study and also for group study. They can even be used as a competitive game to see who scores best.

They work with any text.

The interactive feature is a unique learning tool. With it, you can write in your own answer to each question which you can then check against the correct answer provided on the flip side of each card.

You will find that the flashcards in a book have several advantages over flashcards in a box.

You don't have to cope with hundreds of loose cards. Whenever you want to study, you don't have to decide beforehand which cards you are likely to need; you don't have to pull them out of a box (and later return them in their proper place). You can just open the book and get going without ado.

A very detailed index will guide you to whatever topics you want to cover.

A number of blank card pages is included, in case you want to construct some of your own Q's and A's.

You can take along REA's Flashcard book anywhere, ready for use when you are. You don't need to tote along the box or a bunch of loose cards.

REA's Flashcard books have been carefully put together with REA's customary concern for quality. We believe you will find them an excellent review and study tool.

Dr. M. Fogiel
Program Director

P.S. As you could tell, you could see all the flashcards in the book while you were in the store; they aren't sealed in shrink-wrap.

HOW TO USE THE FLASHCARDS IN THIS BOOK

You will encounter several types of questions in this book. They include fill-in-the blank questions and true-or-false questions.

In addition, you will find some questions in German with an English or German word in parentheses. These questions require you to translate and / or conjugate the word in parentheses to accurately and grammatically complete the sentence. Here is an example:

Question:

_____ *des Weines trinke ich das Bier.* (instead of)

Answer:

(An) statt

In some other instances, you will find an English word in parentheses with conjugation instructions (in parentheses) at the end of the sentence. Here is an example:

Question:

Darf ich (your) *Buch lesen?* (informal singular)

Answer:

dein

Questions

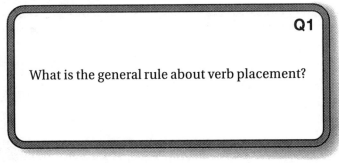

Q1

What is the general rule about verb placement?

*Your Own Answer*_____

_____

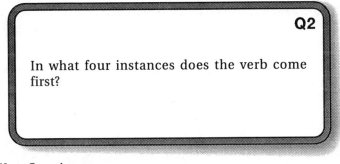

Q2

In what four instances does the verb come first?

*Your Own Answer*_____

_____

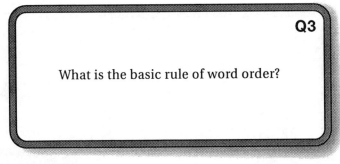

Q3

What is the basic rule of word order?

*Your Own Answer*_____

_____

Correct Answers

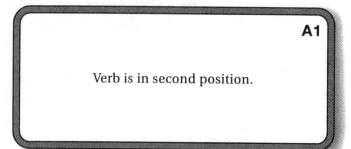

A1

Verb is in second position.

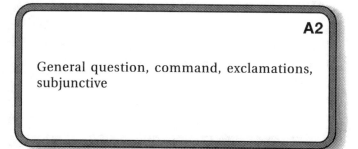

A2

General question, command, exclamations, subjunctive

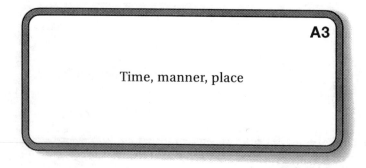

A3

Time, manner, place

Questions

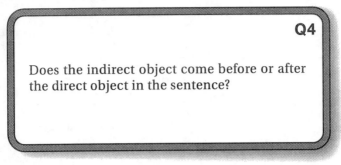

Q4

Does the indirect object come before or after the direct object in the sentence?

*Your Own Answer*_____

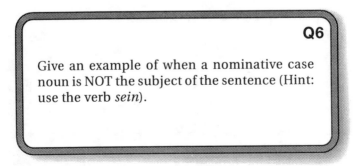

Q5

If a noun is in the nominative case, what position does it usually hold in the sentence?

*Your Own Answer*_____

Q6

Give an example of when a nominative case noun is NOT the subject of the sentence (Hint: use the verb *sein*).

*Your Own Answer*_____

Correct Answers

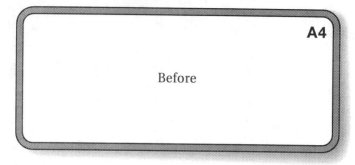

A4

Before

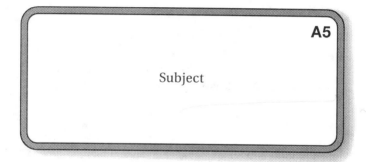

A5

Subject

A6

Er ist der Burgermeister.

Questions

Q7

Do the following sentences mean the same thing? Why or why not?

Der Hund hat den Mann gebissen.
Den Mann hat der Hund gebissen.

Your Own Answer_____

_____

Q8

What parts of speech can nouns in the accusative case be?

Your Own Answer_____

_____

Q9

What parts of speech can nouns in the dative case be?

Your Own Answer_____

_____

Correct Answers

A7

Yes. The article indicates the case. Change in word order does not change basic meaning.

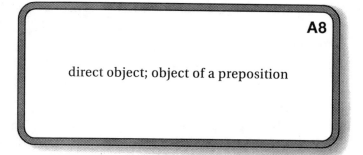

A8

direct object; object of a preposition

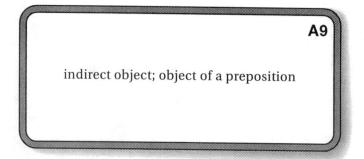

A9

indirect object; object of a preposition

Questions

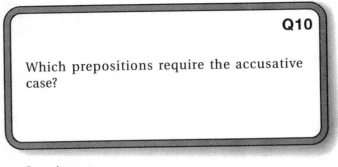

Q10

Which prepositions require the accusative case?

*Your Own Answer*_____

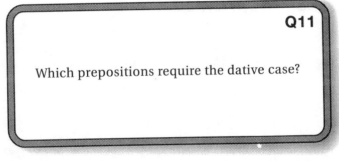

Q11

Which prepositions require the dative case?

*Your Own Answer*_____

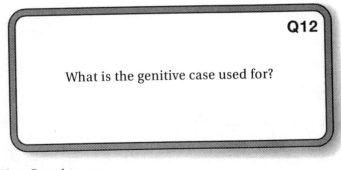

Q12

What is the genitive case used for?

*Your Own Answer*_____

Correct Answers

bis, für, ohne, gegen, and *um*

aus, außer, bei, mit, nach, seit, von, zu, gegenüber

To show possession or the relationship between two objects

Questions

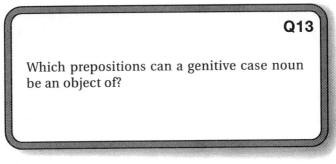

Q13

Which prepositions can a genitive case noun be an object of?

*Your Own Answer*_____

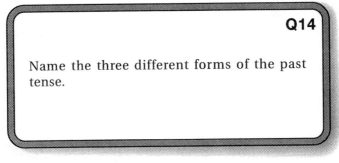

Q14

Name the three different forms of the past tense.

*Your Own Answer*_____

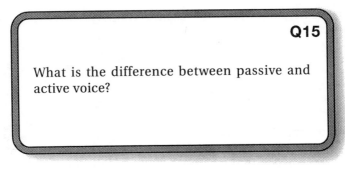

Q15

What is the difference between passive and active voice?

*Your Own Answer*_____

Correct Answers

A13

(an)statt, trotz, während, wegen

A14

simple (narrative) past, present perfect (conversational past), past perfect

---

A15

With passive voice, the emphasis is on WHAT is being acted on. With active voice, the emphasis is on WHO is doing the action.

Questions

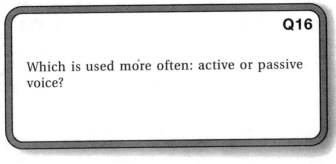

Q16

Which is used more often: active or passive voice?

*Your Own Answer*_____

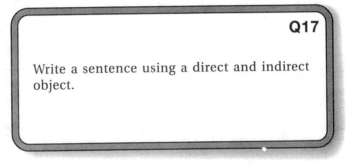

Q17

Write a sentence using a direct and indirect object.

*Your Own Answer*_____

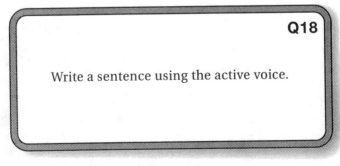

Q18

Write a sentence using the active voice.

*Your Own Answer*_____

Correct Answers

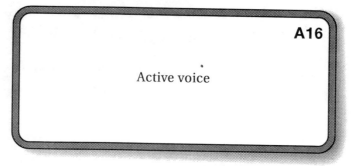

A16

Active voice

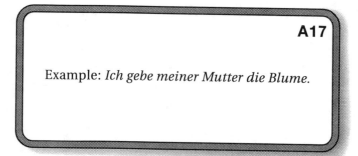

A17

Example: *Ich gebe meiner Mutter die Blume.*

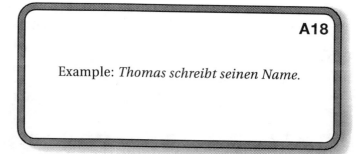

A18

Example: *Thomas schreibt seinen Name.*

Questions

Q19

Write a sentence in which the verb comes first.

*Your Own Answer*_____

Q20

Make a sentence using the following words:

Katja / mit dem Bus / fahren / in die Stadt / heute Nachmittag

*Your Own Answer*_____

Q21

What are the three ways to form questions?

*Your Own Answer*_____

Correct Answers

A19

Example: *Gehen wir nach Hause!*

A20

Katja fährt heute Nachmittag mit dem Bus in die Stadt.

A21

Invert subject and verb; use a question word; add *nicht wahr?* to the end of a statement.

Questions

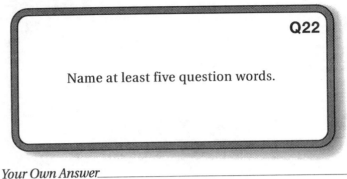

Q22

Name at least five question words.

*Your Own Answer*_____

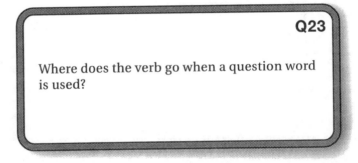

Q23

Where does the verb go when a question word is used?

*Your Own Answer*_____

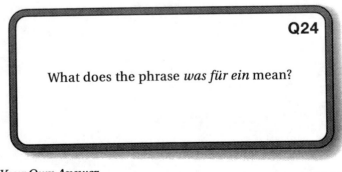

Q24

What does the phrase *was für ein* mean?

*Your Own Answer*_____

Correct Answers

A22

wann, warum, wie lange, was, wie, wie viele, wieviel, was für ein, wo, wer, wohin, woher

A23

second position

A24

What kind of?

Questions

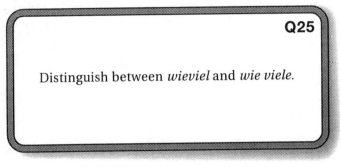

Q25

Distinguish between *wieviel* and *wie viele*.

*Your Own Answer*_____

_____

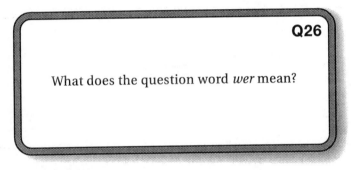

Q26

What does the question word *wer* mean?

*Your Own Answer*_____

_____

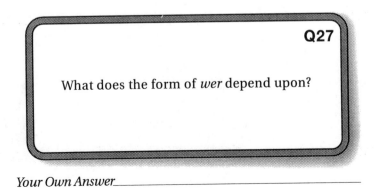

Q27

What does the form of *wer* depend upon?

*Your Own Answer*_____

_____

Correct Answers

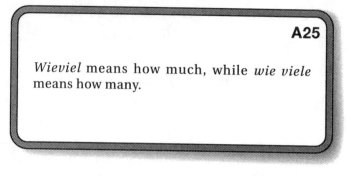

A25

Wieviel means how much, while *wie viele* means how many.

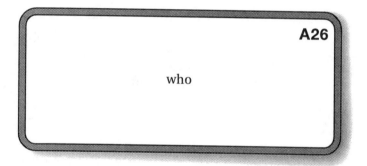

A26

who

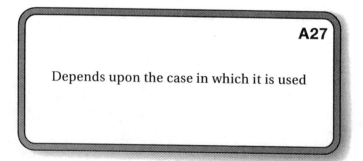

A27

Depends upon the case in which it is used

Questions

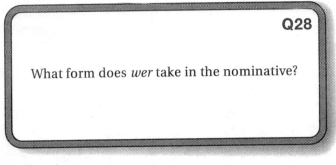

Q28

What form does *wer* take in the nominative?

*Your Own Answer*_____

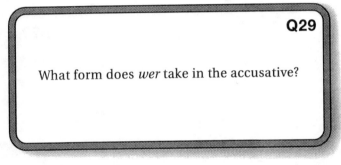

Q29

What form does *wer* take in the accusative?

*Your Own Answer*_____

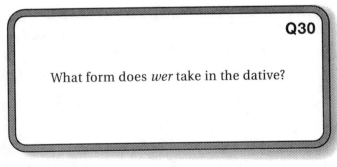

Q30

What form does *wer* take in the dative?

*Your Own Answer*_____

Correct Answers

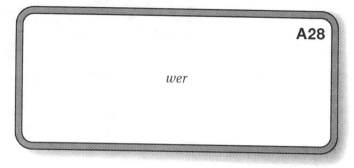

A28

wer

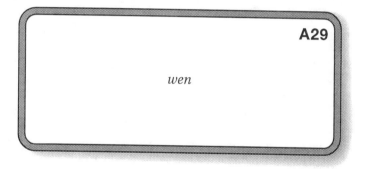

A29

wen

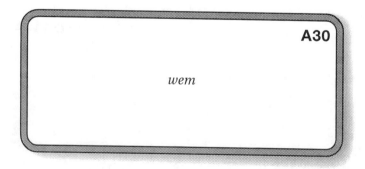

A30

wem

Questions

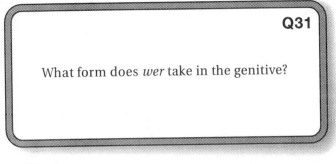

Q31

What form does *wer* take in the genitive?

*Your Own Answer*_____

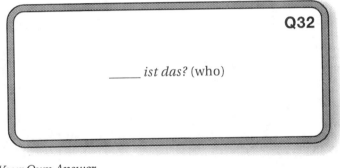

Q32

_____ *ist das?* (who)

*Your Own Answer*_____

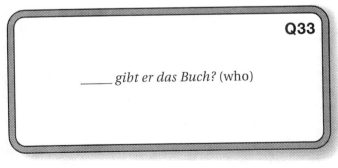

Q33

_____ *gibt er das Buch?* (who)

*Your Own Answer*_____

Correct Answers

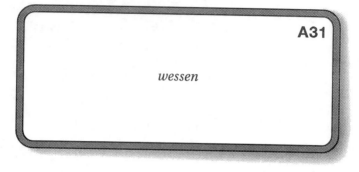

A31

wessen

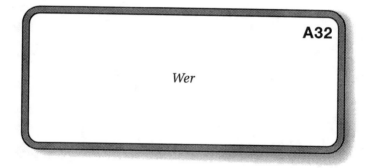

A32

Wer

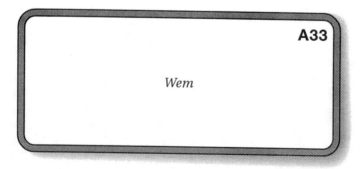

A33

Wem

Questions

Q34

_____ *siehst du?* (who)

Your Own Answer_____

Q35

_____ *Buch ist das?* (whose)

Your Own Answer_____

Q36

Which three German words correspond to where?

Your Own Answer_____

Correct Answers

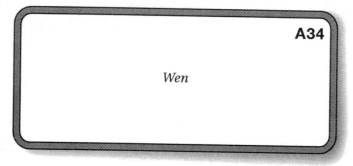

A34

Wen

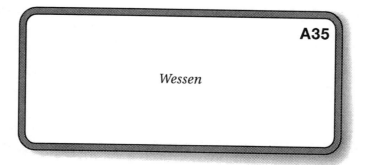

A35

Wessen

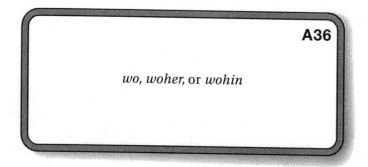

A36

wo, woher, or *wohin*

Questions

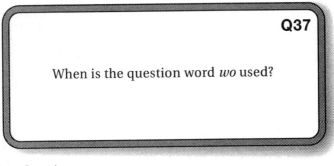

Q37

When is the question word *wo* used?

*Your Own Answer*_____

_____

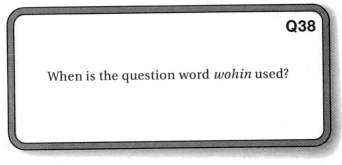

Q38

When is the question word *wohin* used?

*Your Own Answer*_____

_____

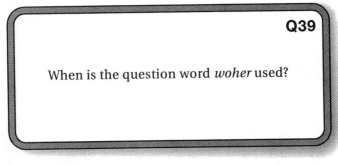

Q39

When is the question word *woher* used?

*Your Own Answer*_____

_____

Correct Answers

A37

to ask about location

A38

Used with verbs of motion; indicates motion **away** from the speaker

A39

Used with verbs of motion; indicates motion **toward** the speaker

Questions

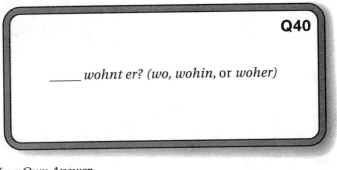

Q40

_____ wohnt er? (*wo, wohin,* or *woher*)

Your Own Answer_____

_____

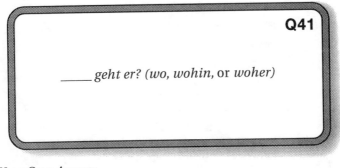

Q41

_____ geht er? (*wo, wohin,* or *woher*)

Your Own Answer_____

_____

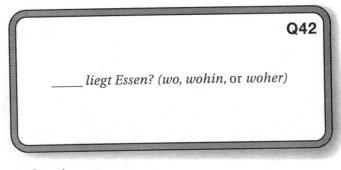

Q42

_____ liegt Essen? (*wo, wohin,* or *woher*)

Your Own Answer_____

_____

Correct Answers

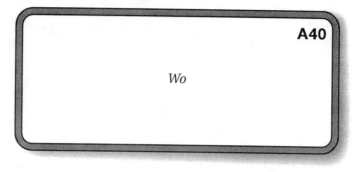

A40

Wo

A41

Wohin

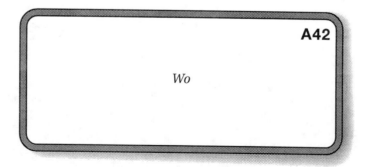

A42

Wo

Questions

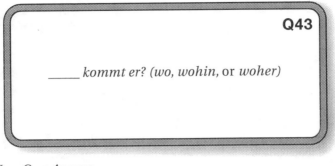

Q43

_____ kommt er? *(wo, wohin,* or *woher)*

*Your Own Answer*_____

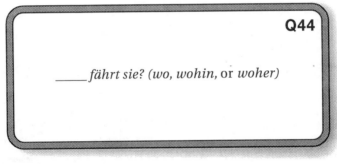

Q44

_____ fährt sie? *(wo, wohin,* or *woher)*

*Your Own Answer*_____

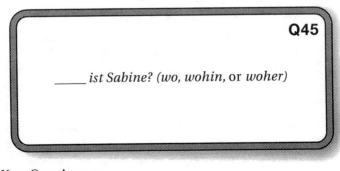

Q45

_____ ist Sabine? *(wo, wohin,* or *woher)*

*Your Own Answer*_____

Correct Answers

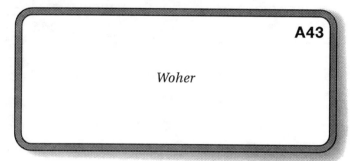

A43

Woher

A44

Wohin

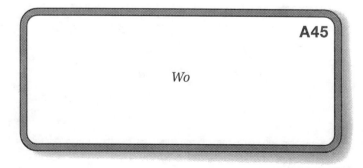

A45

Wo

Questions

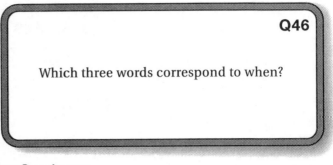

Q46

Which three words correspond to when?

*Your Own Answer*_____

_____

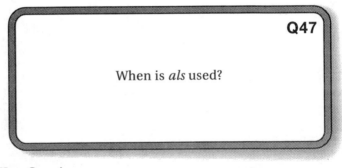

Q47

When is *als* used?

*Your Own Answer*_____

_____

Q48

When is *wenn* used?

*Your Own Answer*_____

_____

Correct Answers

A46

als, wenn, wann

A47

In statements about a past event

A48

Corresponds to whenever; often implies the future

Questions

Q49

When is *wann* used?

*Your Own Answer*_____

Q50

_____ *ich vor kurzem mit ihm sprach, war er freundlich. (als, wenn,* or *wann)*

*Your Own Answer*_____

Q51

_____ *fängt die Vorstellung an? (als, wenn,* or *wann)*

*Your Own Answer*_____

Correct Answers

A49

For direct and indirect questions

A50

Als

A51

Wann

Questions

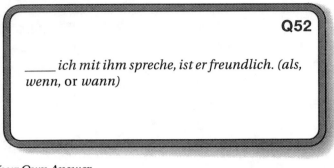

Q52

_____ ich mit ihm spreche, ist er freundlich. *(als, wenn,* or *wann)*

_Your Own Answer_____

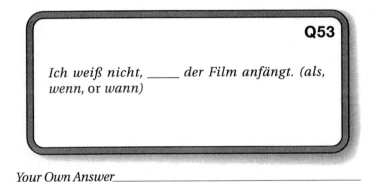

Q53

Ich weiß nicht, _____ *der Film anfängt.* *(als, wenn,* or *wann)*

_Your Own Answer_____

Q54

_____ *ich jung war, spielte ich mit ihm.* *(als, wenn,* or *wann)*

_Your Own Answer_____

Correct Answers

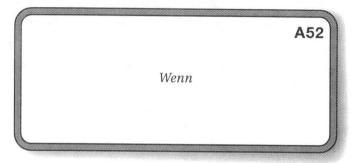

A52

Wenn

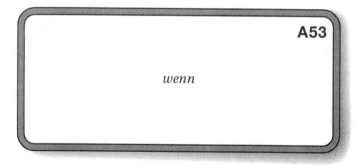

A53

wenn

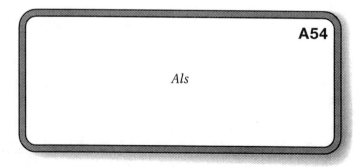

A54

Als

Questions

_____ ich Tennis spiele, verliere ich immer. (als, wenn, or wann)

Your Own Answer_____

What does the question word *welcher* mean?

Your Own Answer_____

What makes *welcher* different from other question words?

Your Own Answer_____

Correct Answers

A55

Wenn

A56

which

A57

It is declined like the definite article.

Questions

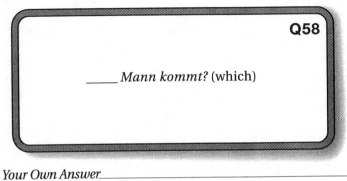

Q58

_____ *Mann kommt?* (which)

*Your Own Answer*_____

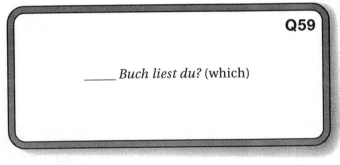

Q59

_____ *Buch liest du?* (which)

*Your Own Answer*_____

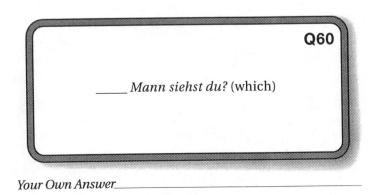

Q60

_____ *Mann siehst du?* (which)

*Your Own Answer*_____

Correct Answers

A58

Welcher

A59

Welches

A60

Welchen

Questions

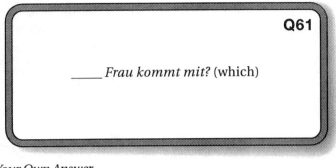

Q61

_____ *Frau kommt mit?* (which)

*Your Own Answer*_____

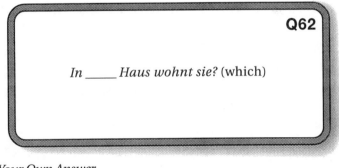

Q62

In _____ Haus wohnt sie? (which)

*Your Own Answer*_____

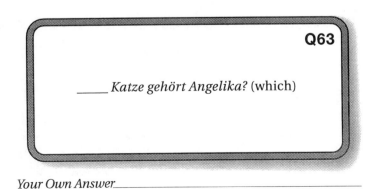

Q63

_____ *Katze gehört Angelika?* (which)

*Your Own Answer*_____

Correct Answers

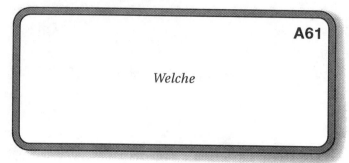

A61

Welche

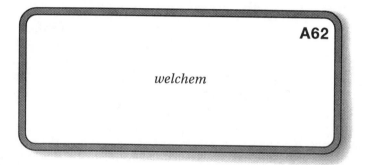

A62

welchem

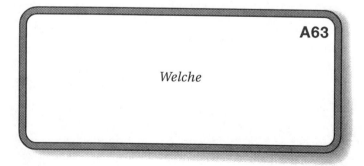

A63

Welche

Questions

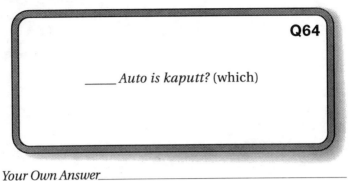

Q64

_____ *Auto is kaputt?* (which)

Your Own Answer _____

_____

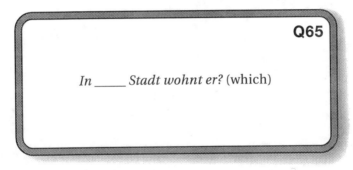

Q65

In _____ *Stadt wohnt er?* (which)

Your Own Answer _____

_____

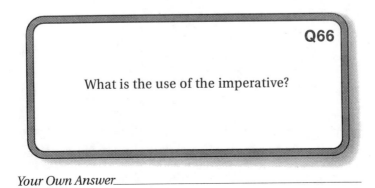

Q66

What is the use of the imperative?

Your Own Answer _____

_____

Correct Answers

A64

Welches

A65

welcher

A66

Used as commands

Questions

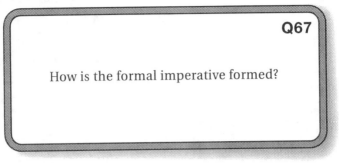

Q67

How is the formal imperative formed?

*Your Own Answer*_____

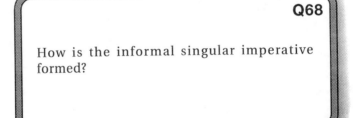

Q68

How is the informal singular imperative formed?

*Your Own Answer*_____

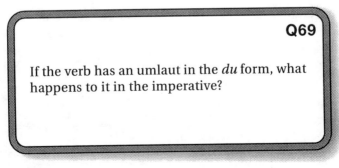

Q69

If the verb has an umlaut in the *du* form, what happens to it in the imperative?

*Your Own Answer*_____

Correct Answers

A67

infinitive + *Sie*

A68

No pronoun used; the *du* form of the verb is used without an ending *(Geh!)* or with an *-e* ending *(Gehe!)*

A69

It is dropped.

Questions

Q70

How is the informal plural imperative formed?

*Your Own Answer*_____

Q71

What is the informal singular imperative of the verb *gehen*?

*Your Own Answer*_____

Q72

What is the informal plural imperative of the verb *gehen*?

*Your Own Answer*_____

Correct Answers

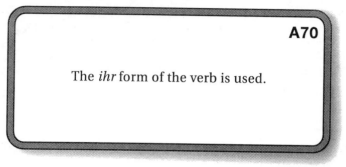

A70

The *ihr* form of the verb is used.

A71

Geh(e)!

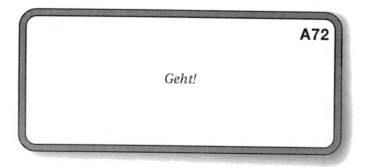

A72

Geht!

Questions

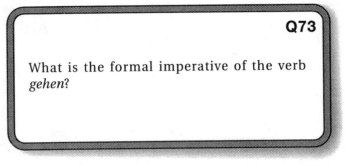

Q73

What is the formal imperative of the verb *gehen*?

*Your Own Answer*_____

_____

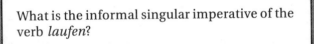

Q74

What is the informal singular imperative of the verb *laufen*?

*Your Own Answer*_____

_____

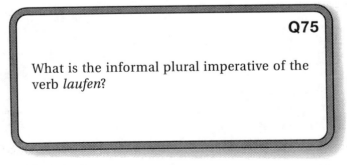

Q75

What is the informal plural imperative of the verb *laufen*?

*Your Own Answer*_____

_____

Correct Answers

Gehen Sie!

Lauf(e)!

Lauft!

Questions

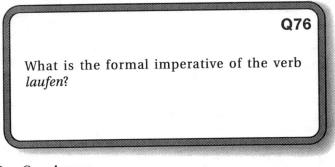

Q76

What is the formal imperative of the verb *laufen*?

*Your Own Answer*_____

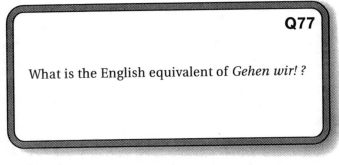

Q77

What is the English equivalent of *Gehen wir! ?*

*Your Own Answer*_____

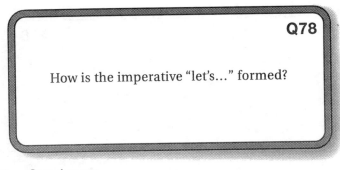

Q78

How is the imperative "let's..." formed?

*Your Own Answer*_____

Correct Answers

A76

Laufen Sie!

A77

Let's go!

A78

infinitive + *wir*

Questions

Q79

Why is the exclamation point especially important in written German?

*Your Own Answer*_____

Q80

Go home! (informal singular)

*Your Own Answer*_____

Q81

Run fast! (informal plural)

*Your Own Answer*_____

Correct Answers

A79

It's the only thing that distinguishes it from being a question.

A80

Geh(e) nach Hause!

A81

Lauft schnell!

Questions

Come! (formal)

*Your Own Answer*_____

Let's talk!

*Your Own Answer*_____

Drive slowly! (informal singular)

*Your Own Answer*_____

Correct Answers

A82

Kommen Sie!

A83

Sprechen wir!

A84

Fahr(e) langsam!

Questions

Q85

Stand up! (informal plural)

*Your Own Answer*_____

Q86

Name the singular masculine articles for all the cases.

*Your Own Answer*_____

Q87

_____ *Mann trägt einen Mantel.* (the)

*Your Own Answer*_____

Correct Answers

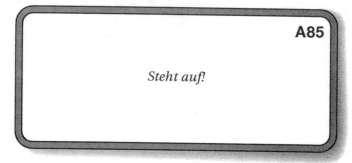

A85

Steht auf!

A86

der, den, dem, des

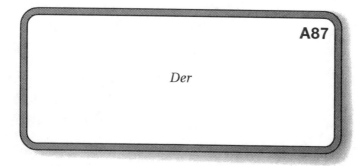

A87

Der

Questions

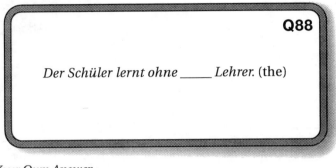

Q88

Der Schüler lernt ohne _____ Lehrer. (the)

Your Own Answer_____

_____

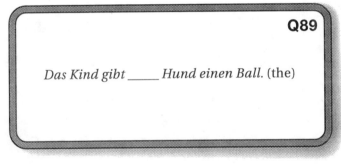

Q89

Das Kind gibt _____ Hund einen Ball. (the)

Your Own Answer_____

_____

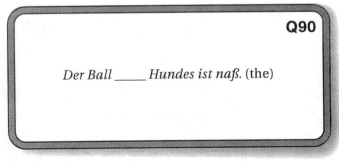

Q90

Der Ball _____ Hundes ist naß. (the)

Your Own Answer_____

_____

Correct Answers

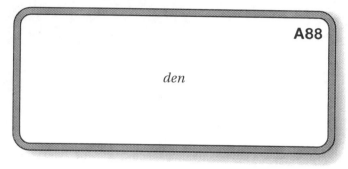

A88

den

A89

dem

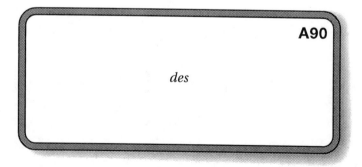

A90

des

Questions

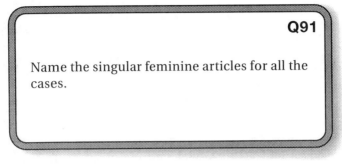

Q91

Name the singular feminine articles for all the cases.

*Your Own Answer*_____

Q92

_____ *Frau trägt ein Kleid.* (the)

*Your Own Answer*_____

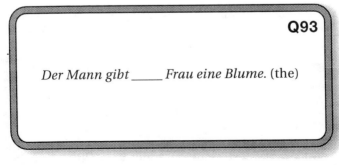

Q93

Der Mann gibt _____ *Frau eine Blume.* (the)

*Your Own Answer*_____

Correct Answers

A91

die, die, der, der

A92

Die

A93

der

Questions

Q94

Ich fahre in _____ *Stadt.* (the)

*Your Own Answer*_____

Q95

Die Bluse _____ *Frau ist gelb.* (the)

*Your Own Answer*_____

Q96

Name the singular neuter articles for all the cases.

*Your Own Answer*_____

Correct Answers

A94

die

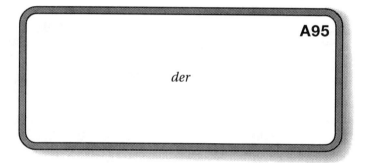

A95

der

A96

das, das, dem, des

Questions

Q97

Ich trage _____ Kleid. (the)

Your Own Answer_____

_____

Q98

_____ Kind ist neun Jahre alt. (the)

Your Own Answer_____

_____

Q99

Die Katze spielt mit _____ Maus. (the)

Your Own Answer_____

_____

Correct Answers

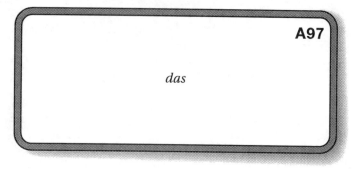

A97

das

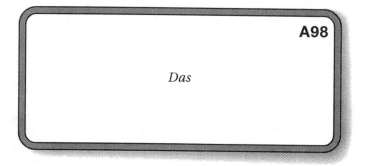

A98

Das

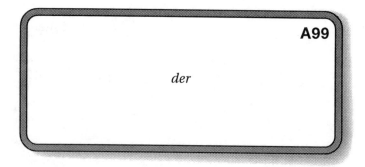

A99

der

Questions

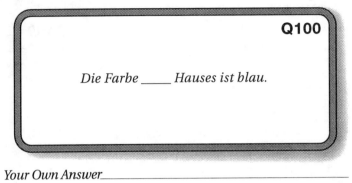

Q100

Die Farbe _____ Hauses ist blau.

*Your Own Answer*_____

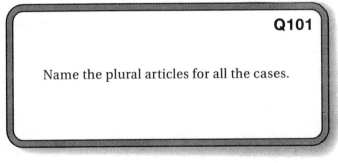

Q101

Name the plural articles for all the cases.

*Your Own Answer*_____

Q102

Monika trägt _____ Socken. (the)

*Your Own Answer*_____

Correct Answers

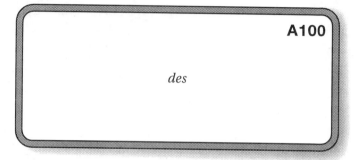

A100

des

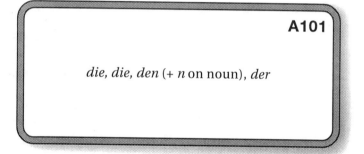

A101

die, die, den (+ *n* on noun), *der*

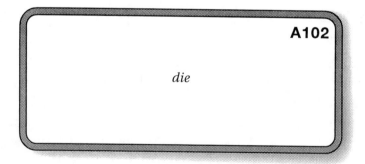

A102

die

Questions

_____ *Blumen sind frisch.* (the)

Your Own Answer_____

Thomas geht mit _____ *Frauen ins Theater.* (the)

Your Own Answer_____

Der Ball _____ *Kinder ist kaputt.* (the)

Your Own Answer_____

Correct Answers

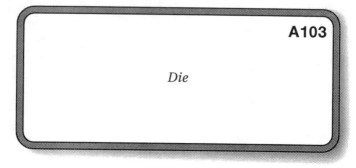

A103

Die

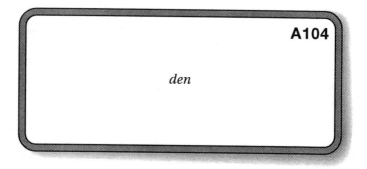

A104

den

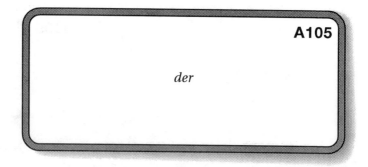

A105

der

Questions

*Your Own Answer*_____

_____

*Your Own Answer*_____

_____

*Your Own Answer*_____

_____

Correct Answers

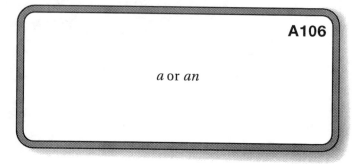

A106

a or *an*

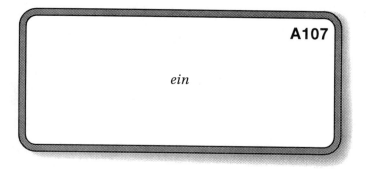

A107

ein

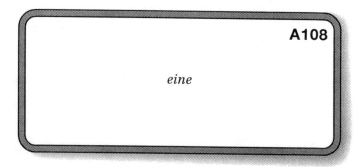

A108

eine

Questions

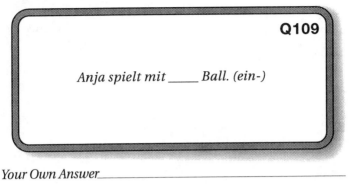

Q109

Anja spielt mit _____ Ball. (ein-)

Your Own Answer_____

_____

Q110

Wir wohnen in _____ Haus. (ein-)

Your Own Answer_____

_____

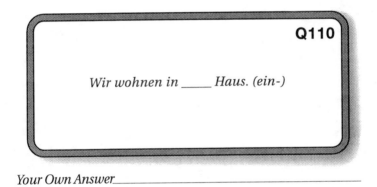

Q111

Wir brauchen _____ Lampe (ein-)

Your Own Answer_____

_____

Correct Answers

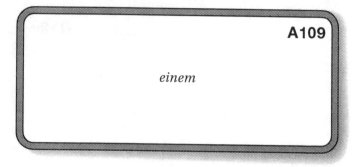

A109

einem

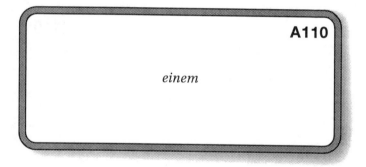

A110

einem

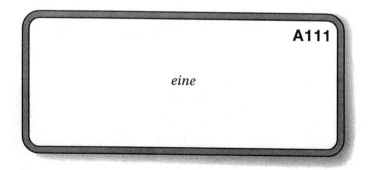

A111

eine

Questions

_____ *Film spielt in dem Kino. (ein-)*

*Your Own Answer*_____

Ich fahre mit _____ Bus in die Stadt. (ein-)

*Your Own Answer*_____

Ich spiele heute Abend mit _____ Kind. (ein-)

*Your Own Answer*_____

Correct Answers

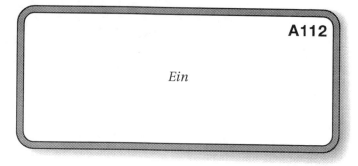

A112

Ein

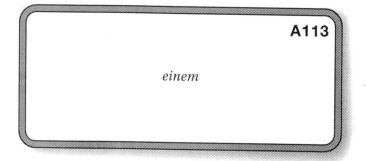

A113

einem

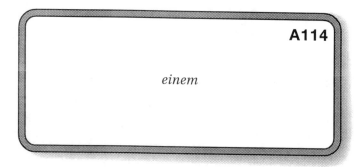

A114

einem

Questions

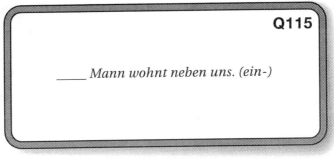

Q115

_____ *Mann wohnt neben uns. (ein-)*

*Your Own Answer*_____

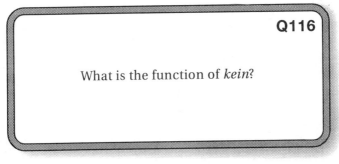

Q116

What is the function of *kein*?

*Your Own Answer*_____

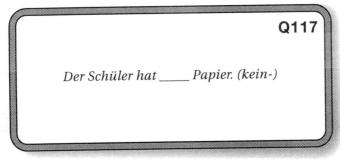

Q117

Der Schüler hat _____ Papier. (kein-)

*Your Own Answer*_____

Correct Answers

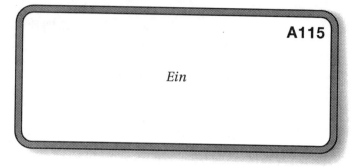

A115

Ein

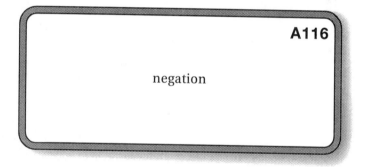

A116

negation

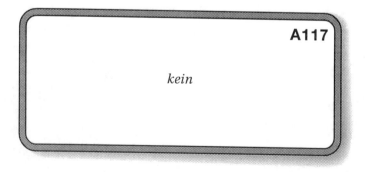

A117

kein

Questions

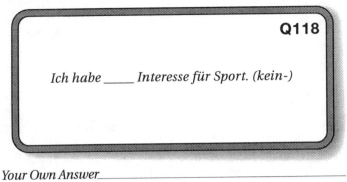

Q118

Ich habe _____ Interesse für Sport. (kein-)

Your Own Answer_____

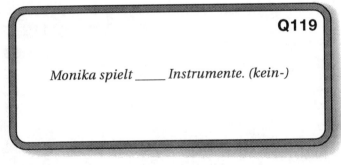

Q119

Monika spielt _____ Instrumente. (kein-)

Your Own Answer_____

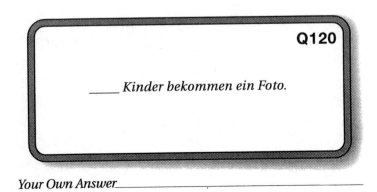

Q120

_____ Kinder bekommen ein Foto.

Your Own Answer_____

Correct Answers

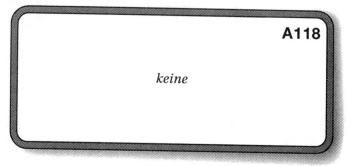

A118

keine

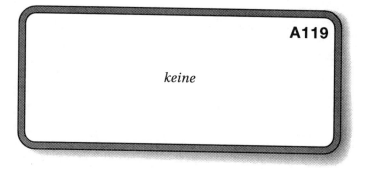

A119

keine

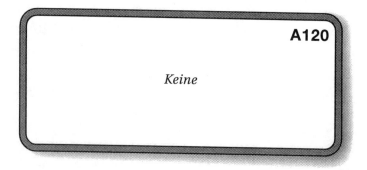

A120

Keine

Questions

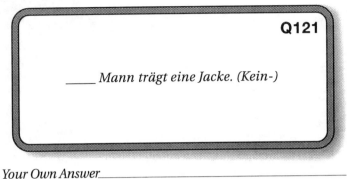

Q121

_____ Mann trägt eine Jacke. (Kein-)

*Your Own Answer*_____

Q122

Der Arbeiter bekommt _____ Geld. (kein-)

*Your Own Answer*_____

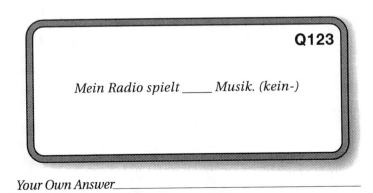

Q123

Mein Radio spielt _____ Musik. (kein-)

*Your Own Answer*_____

Correct Answers

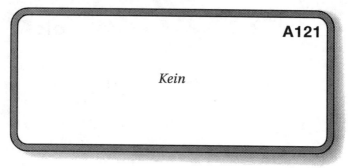

A121

Kein

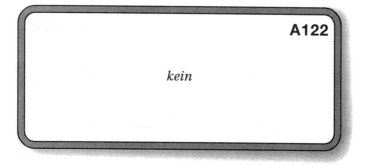

A122

kein

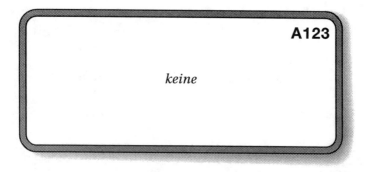

A123

keine

Questions

Q124

Das Mädchen hat _____ Spielsachen. (kein-)

*Your Own Answer*_____

Q125

Der Schüler hat _____ gute Note. (kein-)

*Your Own Answer*_____

Q126

What does the possessive adjective *mein* mean?

*Your Own Answer*_____

Correct Answers

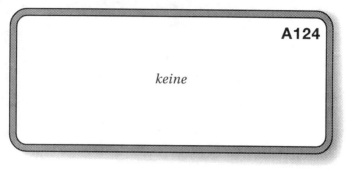

A124

keine

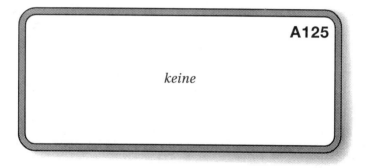

A125

keine

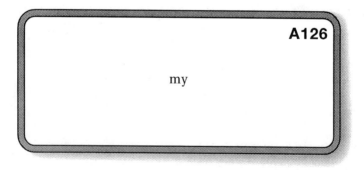

A126

my

Questions

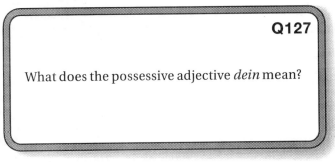

Q127

What does the possessive adjective *dein* mean?

*Your Own Answer*_____

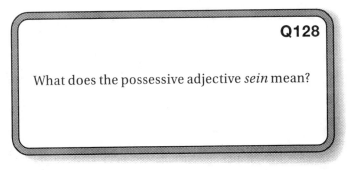

Q128

What does the possessive adjective *sein* mean?

*Your Own Answer*_____

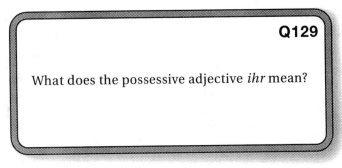

Q129

What does the possessive adjective *ihr* mean?

*Your Own Answer*_____

Correct Answers

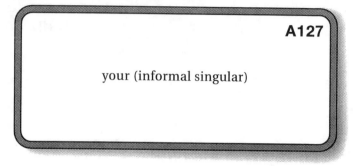

A127

your (informal singular)

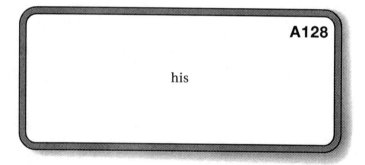

A128

his

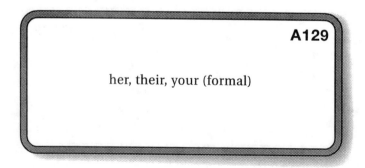

A129

her, their, your (formal)

Questions

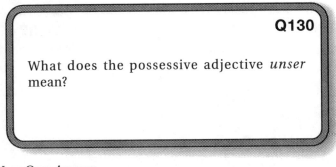

Q130

What does the possessive adjective *unser* mean?

*Your Own Answer*_____

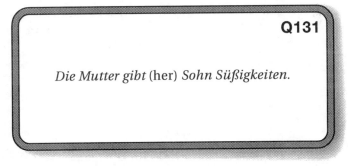

Q131

Die Mutter gibt (her) *Sohn Süßigkeiten.*

*Your Own Answer*_____

Q132

(My) *Schwester singt oft.*

*Your Own Answer*_____

Correct Answers

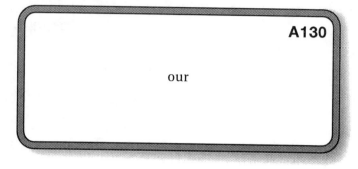

A130

our

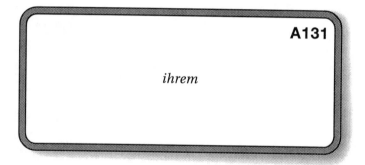

A131

ihrem

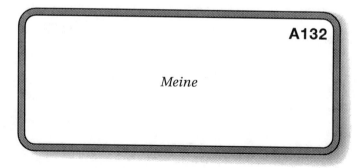

A132

Meine

Questions

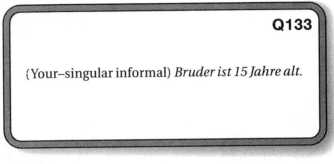

Q133

(Your–singular informal) *Bruder ist 15 Jahre alt.*

*Your Own Answer*_____

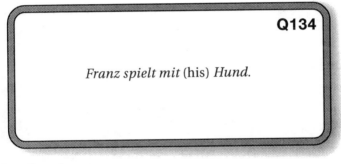

Q134

Franz spielt mit (his) *Hund.*

*Your Own Answer*_____

Q135

(Our) *Radio ist kaputt.*

*Your Own Answer*_____

Correct Answers

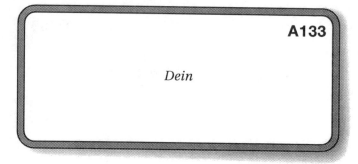

A133

Dein

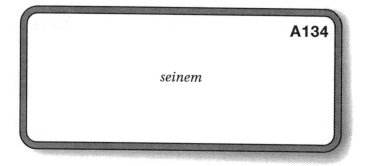

A134

seinem

A135

Unser

Questions

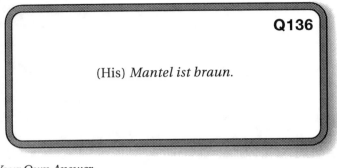

Q136

(His) *Mantel ist braun.*

*Your Own Answer*_____

Q137

Anja kauft (our) *Auto.*

*Your Own Answer*_____

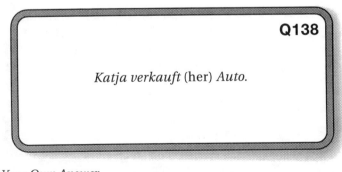

Q138

Katja verkauft (her) *Auto.*

*Your Own Answer*_____

Correct Answers

A136

Sein

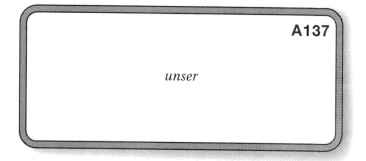

A137

unser

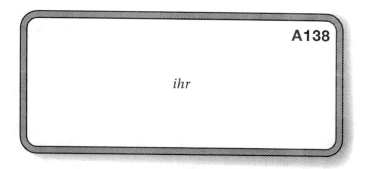

A138

ihr

Questions

Q139

Die Frau hat (her) *Mantel verloren.*

*Your Own Answer*_____

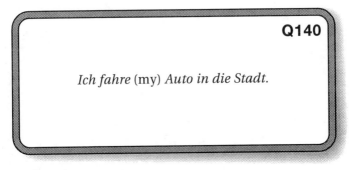

Q140

Ich fahre (my) *Auto in die Stadt.*

*Your Own Answer*_____

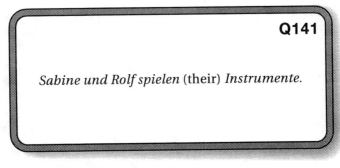

Q141

Sabine und Rolf spielen (their) *Instrumente.*

*Your Own Answer*_____

Correct Answers

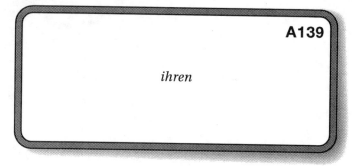

A139

ihren

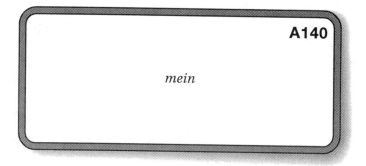

A140

mein

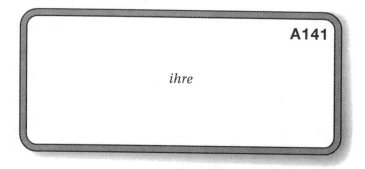

A141

ihre

Questions

Q142

Der Schüler hat (his) *Papier verloren.*

*Your Own Answer*_____

Q143

Das Kind spielt mit (his) *Ball.*

*Your Own Answer*_____

Q144

Darf ich (your) *Buch lesen?* (informal singular)

*Your Own Answer*_____

Correct Answers

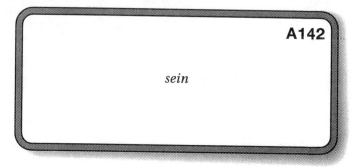

A142

sein

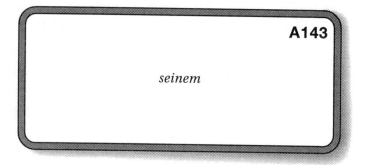

A143

seinem

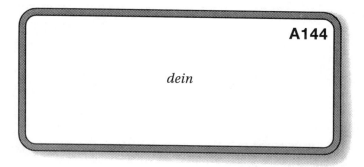

A144

dein

Questions

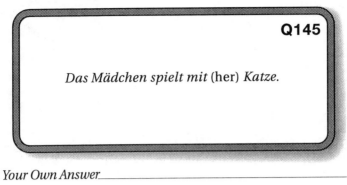

Q145

Das Mädchen spielt mit (her) *Katze.*

Your Own Answer_____

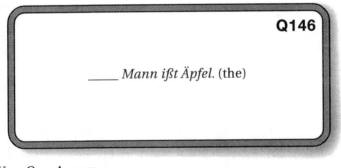

Q146

_____ *Mann ißt Äpfel.* (the)

Your Own Answer_____

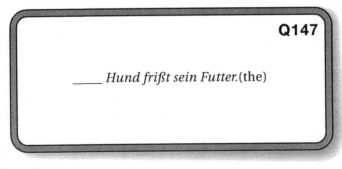

Q147

_____ *Hund frißt sein Futter.* (the)

Your Own Answer_____

Correct Answers

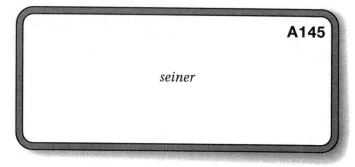

A145

seiner

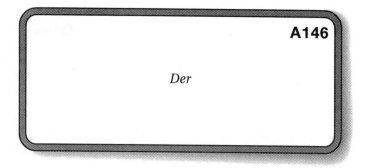

A146

Der

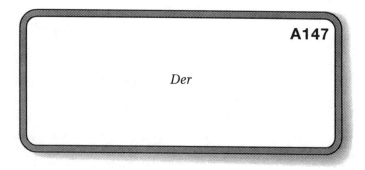

A147

Der

Questions

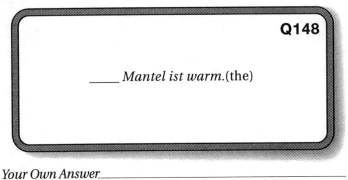

Q148

_____ Mantel ist warm.(the)

Your Own Answer_____

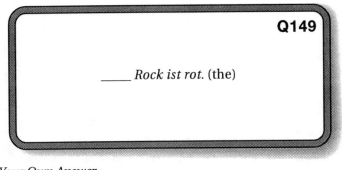

Q149

_____ Rock ist rot. (the)

Your Own Answer_____

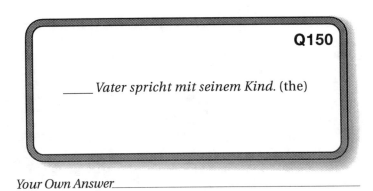

Q150

_____ Vater spricht mit seinem Kind. (the)

Your Own Answer_____

Correct Answers

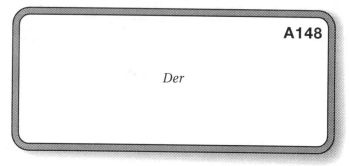

A148

Der

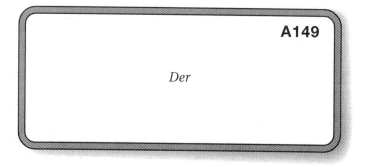

A149

Der

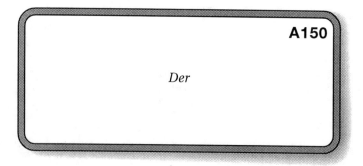

A150

Der

Questions

Q151

_____ *Mutter gibt mir Kuchen.* (the)

*Your Own Answer*_____

Q152

_____ *Blume ist rot.* (the)

*Your Own Answer*_____

Q153

_____ *Woche dauert 7 Tage.* (the)

*Your Own Answer*_____

Correct Answers

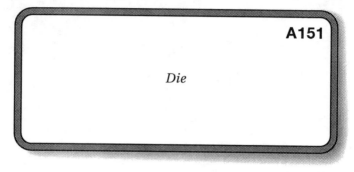

A151

Die

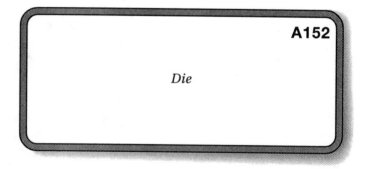

A152

Die

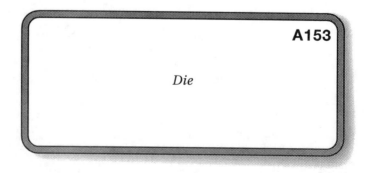

A153

Die

Questions

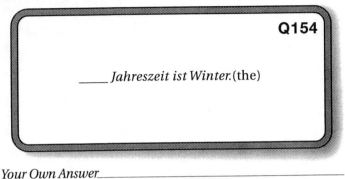

Q154

_____ *Jahreszeit ist Winter.*(the)

Your Own Answer_____

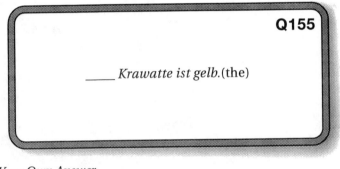

Q155

_____ *Krawatte ist gelb.*(the)

Your Own Answer_____

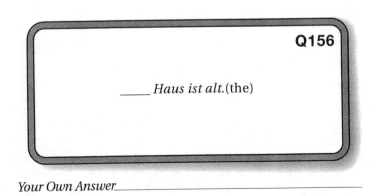

Q156

_____ *Haus ist alt.*(the)

Your Own Answer_____

Correct Answers

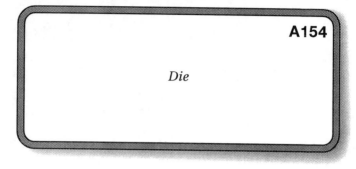

A154

Die

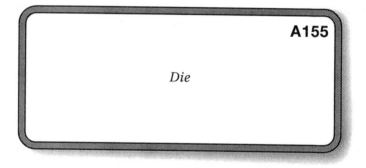

A155

Die

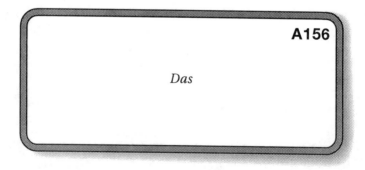

A156

Das

Questions

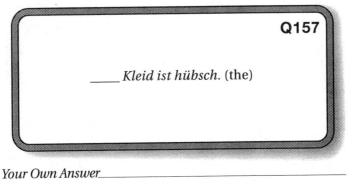

Q157

_____ *Kleid ist hübsch.* (the)

*Your Own Answer*_____

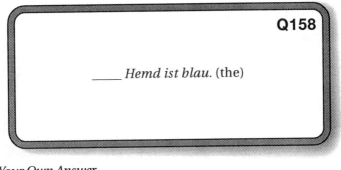

Q158

_____ *Hemd ist blau.* (the)

*Your Own Answer*_____

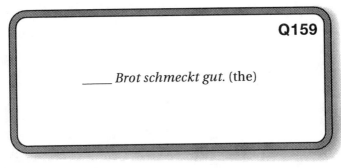

Q159

_____ *Brot schmeckt gut.* (the)

*Your Own Answer*_____

Correct Answers

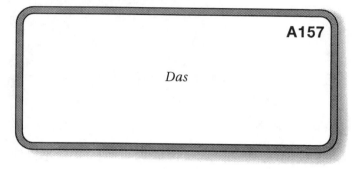

A157

Das

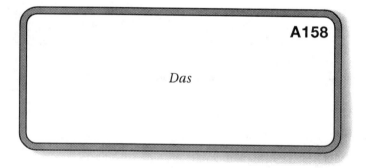

A158

Das

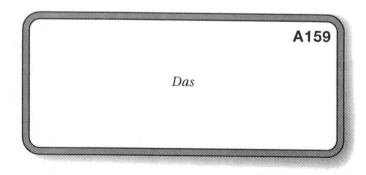

A159

Das

Questions

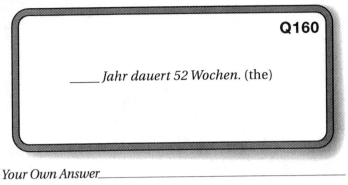

Q160

_____ *Jahr dauert 52 Wochen.* (the)

_Your Own Answer_____

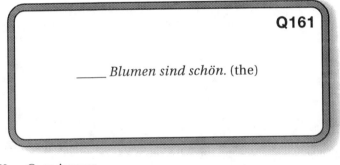

Q161

_____ *Blumen sind schön.* (the)

_Your Own Answer_____

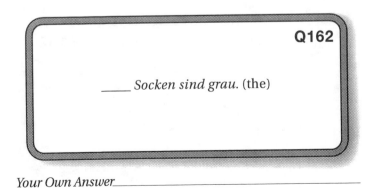

Q162

_____ *Socken sind grau.* (the)

_Your Own Answer_____

Correct Answers

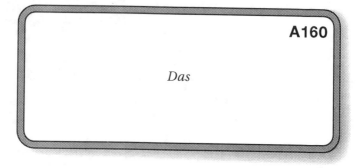

A160

Das

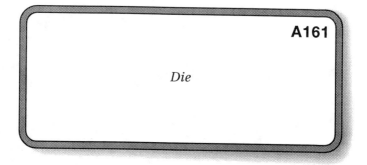

A161

Die

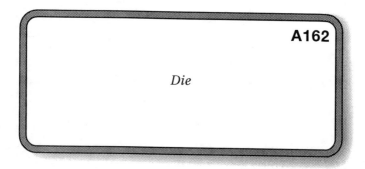

A162

Die

Questions

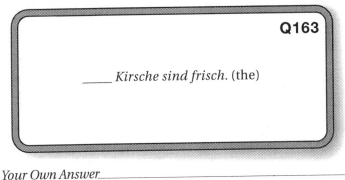

Q163

_____ Kirsche sind frisch. (the)

*Your Own Answer*_____

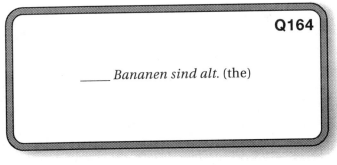

Q164

_____ Bananen sind alt. (the)

*Your Own Answer*_____

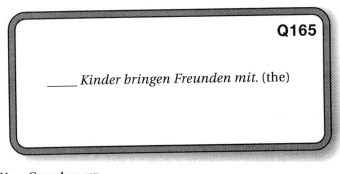

Q165

_____ Kinder bringen Freunden mit. (the)

*Your Own Answer*_____

Correct Answers

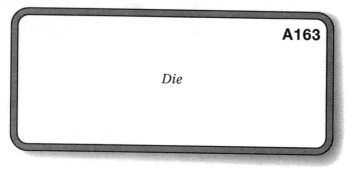

A163

Die

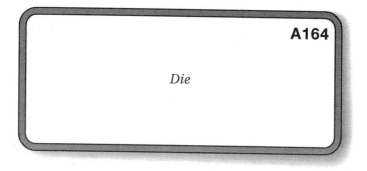

A164

Die

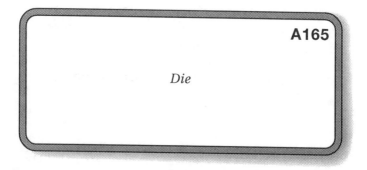

A165

Die

Questions

Q166

Er schreibt _____ Brief. (the)

*Your Own Answer*_____

Q167

Ich futtere _____ Hund. (the)

*Your Own Answer*_____

Q168

Ich trage _____ Mantel. (the)

*Your Own Answer*_____

Correct Answers

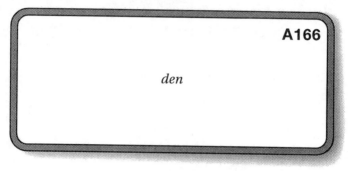

A166

den

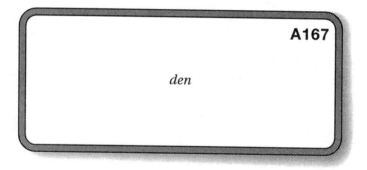

A167

den

A168

den

Questions

Q169

Frank spielt Fußball gegen _____ *Mann.* (the)

*Your Own Answer*_____

Q170

Herr Meier trägt _____ *Anzug.* (the)

*Your Own Answer*_____

Q171

Frau Schmidt trägt _____ *Rock.* (the)

*Your Own Answer*_____

Correct Answers

A169

den

A170

den

A171

den

Questions

Q172

Simon sagt, "Fassen Sie _____ Kopf an." (the)

*Your Own Answer*_____

_____

Q173

Simon sagt, "Fassen Sie _____ Fuß an." (the)

*Your Own Answer*_____

_____

Q174

Simon sagt, "Fassen Sie _____ Arm an." (the)

*Your Own Answer*_____

_____

Correct Answers

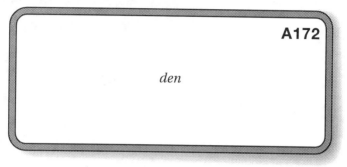

A172

den

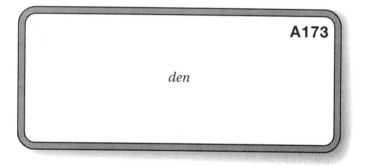

A173

den

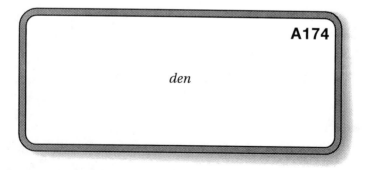

A174

den

Questions

Simon sagt, "Fassen Sie _____ Mund an." (the)

*Your Own Answer*_____

Er trägt _____ Jacke. (the)

*Your Own Answer*_____

Sie trägt _____ Bluse. (the)

*Your Own Answer*_____

Correct Answers

A175

den

A176

die

A177

die

Questions

Q178

Herr Schmidt trägt _____ Hose. (the)

*Your Own Answer*_____

Q179

Simon sagt, "Fassen Sie _____ Nase an." (the)

*Your Own Answer*_____

Q180

Simon sagt, "Fassen Sie _____ Hand an." (the)

*Your Own Answer*_____

Correct Answers

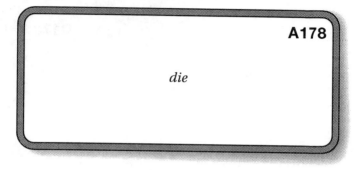

A178

die

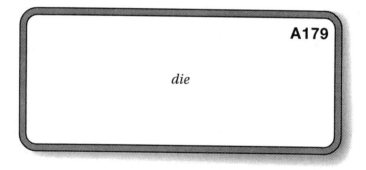

A179

die

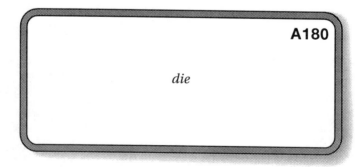

A180

die

Questions

Q181

Monika trägt _____ Kleid. (the)

*Your Own Answer*_____

Q182

Hans trägt _____ Hemd. (the)

*Your Own Answer*_____

Q183

Simon sagt, "Fassen Sie _____ Gesicht an." (the)

*Your Own Answer*_____

Correct Answers

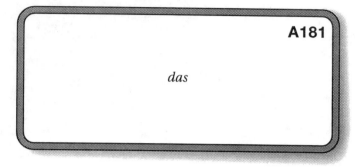

A181

das

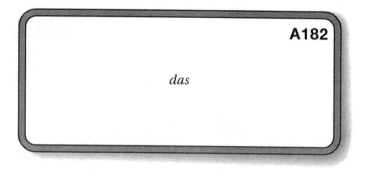

A182

das

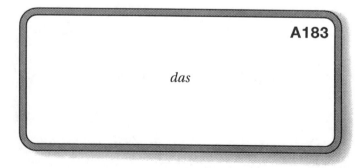

A183

das

Questions

Q184

Simon sagt, "Fassen Sie _____ Bein an." (the)

Your Own Answer _____

Q185

Mark ißt _____ Brot. (the)

Your Own Answer _____

Q186

Jens trägt _____ Socken. (the)

Your Own Answer _____

Correct Answers

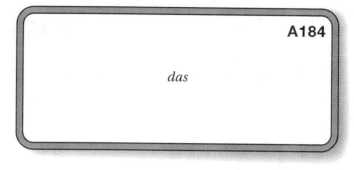

A184

das

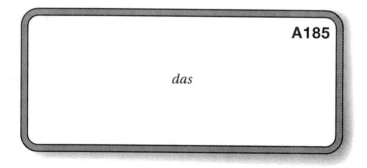

A185

das

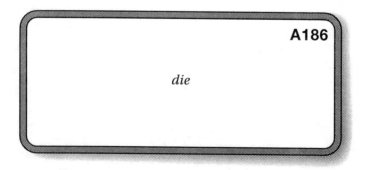

A186

die

Questions

Q187

Helmut ißt _____ Tomaten. (the)

Your Own Answer_____

_____

Q188

Wir schauen _____ Bilder an. (the)

Your Own Answer_____

_____

Q189

Wir kaufen _____ Krawatten. (the)

Your Own Answer_____

_____

Correct Answers

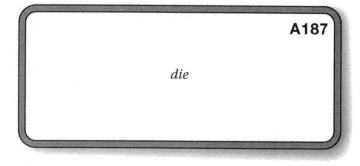

A187

die

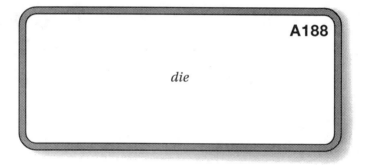

A188

die

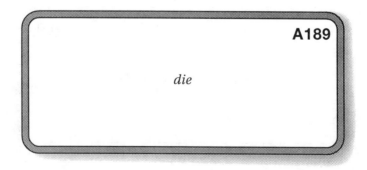

A189

die

Questions

Meine Schwester kauft _____ Kleider. (the)

*Your Own Answer*_____

Ich schreibe _____ Mann einen Buch. (the)

*Your Own Answer*_____

Ich glaube _____ nicht. (him)

*Your Own Answer*_____

Correct Answers

A190

die

A191

dem

A192

ihm

Questions

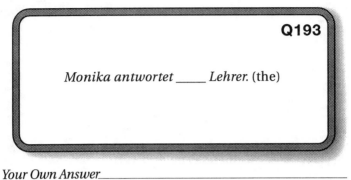

Q193

Monika antwortet _____ Lehrer. (the)

*Your Own Answer*_____

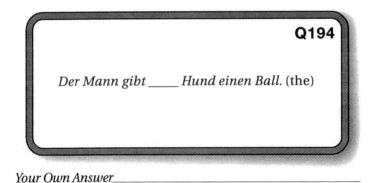

Q194

Der Mann gibt _____ Hund einen Ball. (the)

*Your Own Answer*_____

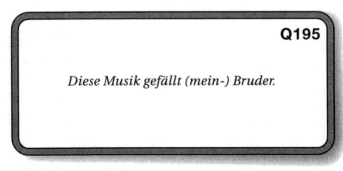

Q195

Diese Musik gefällt (mein-) Bruder.

*Your Own Answer*_____

Correct Answers

A193

dem

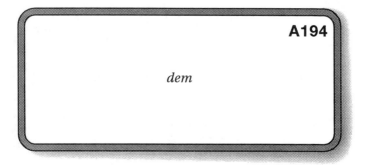

A194

dem

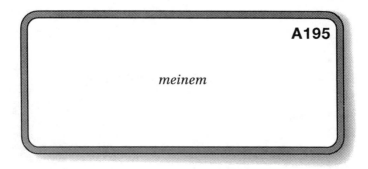

A195

meinem

Questions

Die Bücher gehören (dein-) Großvater.

*Your Own Answer*_____

Außer _____ Rock, gefällt mir nichts (the).

*Your Own Answer*_____

Ich fahre mit (mein-) Onkel in die Stadt.

*Your Own Answer*_____

Correct Answers

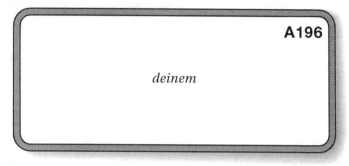

A196

deinem

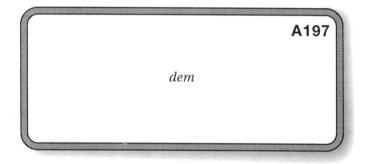

A197

dem

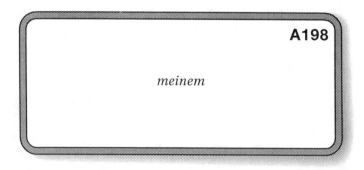

A198

meinem

Questions

Q199

Ich habe _____ Dezember Geburtstag. (in)

Your Own Answer_____

Q200

Ich gebe _____ Bekannte meine Adresse. (the)

Your Own Answer_____

Q201

Herr Meier gibt _____ Frau die Blumen. (the)

Your Own Answer_____

Correct Answers

A199

im (in + dem = im)

A200

dem or *der*

A201

der

Questions

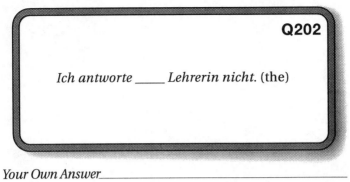

Q202

Ich antworte _____ Lehrerin nicht. (the)

*Your Own Answer*_____

Q203

Monika spielt mit _____ Katze. (the)

*Your Own Answer*_____

Q204

Diese Bluse gefällt (mein-) Schwester.

*Your Own Answer*_____

Correct Answers

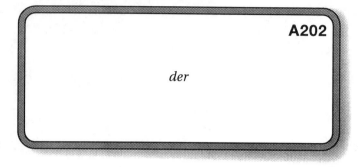

A202

der

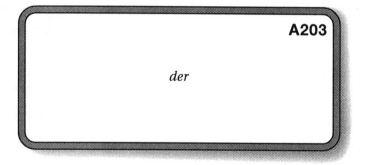

A203

der

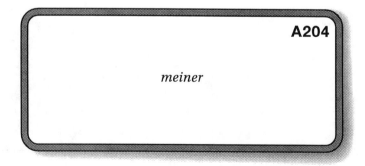

A204

meiner

Questions

Q205

Kannst du _____ Frau helfen? (the)

*Your Own Answer*_____

_____

Q206

Wir danken _____ Angestellte für ihre Hilfe. (the)

*Your Own Answer*_____

_____

Q207

Klaus singt oft in _____ Kirche. (the)

*Your Own Answer*_____

_____

Correct Answers

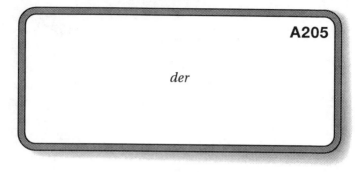

A205

der

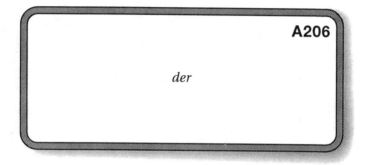

A206

der

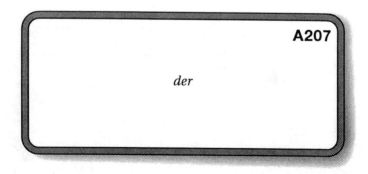

A207

der

Questions

Q208

Der Rock gehört (mein-) Schwester.

*Your Own Answer*_____

Q209

Das Rathaus ist gegenüber von _____ Post. (the)

*Your Own Answer*_____

Q210

Dieser Mantel gehört _____ Dame. (the)

*Your Own Answer*_____

Correct Answers

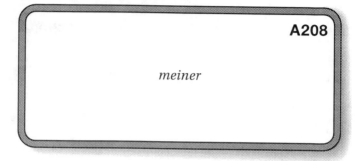

A208

meiner

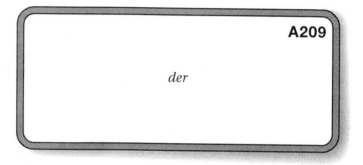

A209

der

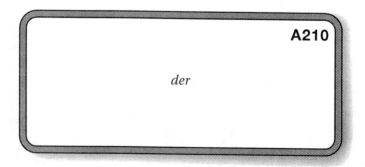

A210

der

Questions

Q211

Ich gebe _____ Kind Süßigkeiten. (the)

Your Own Answer

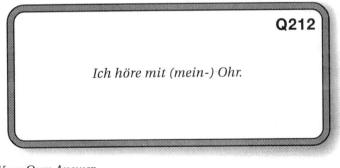

Q212

Ich höre mit (mein-) Ohr.

Your Own Answer

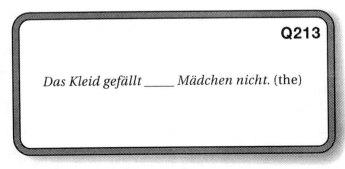

Q213

Das Kleid gefällt _____ Mädchen nicht. (the)

Your Own Answer

Correct Answers

A211

dem

A212

meinem

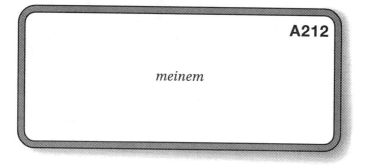

A213

dem

Questions

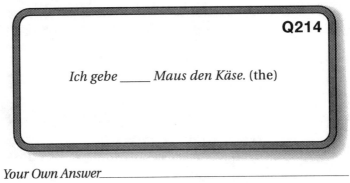

Q214

Ich gebe _____ Maus den Käse. (the)

Your Own Answer_____

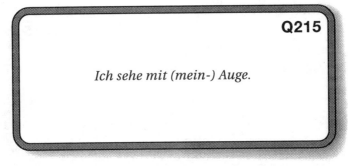

Q215

Ich sehe mit (mein-) Auge.

Your Own Answer_____

Q216

Die Mutter antwortet _____ Kind. (the)

Your Own Answer_____

Correct Answers

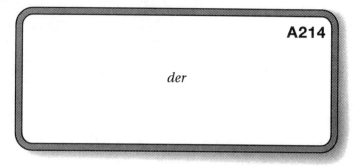

A214

der

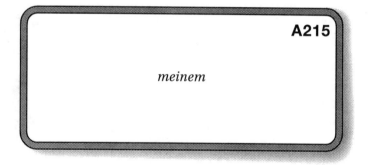

A215

meinem

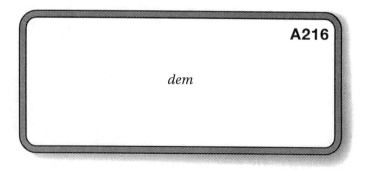

A216

dem

Questions

Außer _____ Hemd, gefällt mir alles. (the)

*Your Own Answer*_____

Thomas gibt _____ Mädchen eine Blume. (the)

*Your Own Answer*_____

Monika geht zu _____ Haus. (the)

*Your Own Answer*_____

Correct Answers

A217

dem

A218

dem

A219

dem

Questions

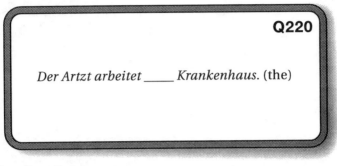

Q220

Der Artzt arbeitet _____ Krankenhaus. (the)

*Your Own Answer*_____

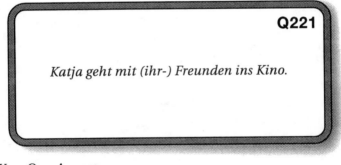

Q221

Katja geht mit (ihr-) Freunden ins Kino.

*Your Own Answer*_____

Q222

Rolf gibt _____ Katzen Milch. (the)

*Your Own Answer*_____

Correct Answers

A220

dem (in + dem = im)

A221

ihren

A222

den

Questions

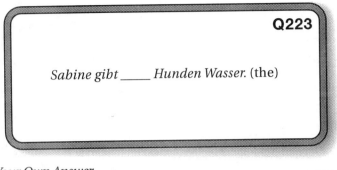

Q223

Sabine gibt _____ Hunden Wasser. (the)

Your Own Answer_____

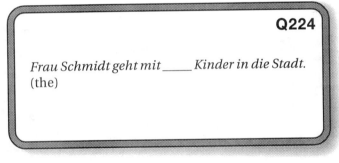

Q224

Frau Schmidt geht mit _____ Kinder in die Stadt. (the)

Your Own Answer_____

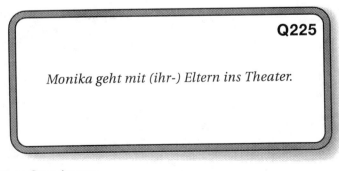

Q225

Monika geht mit (ihr-) Eltern ins Theater.

Your Own Answer_____

Correct Answers

A223

den

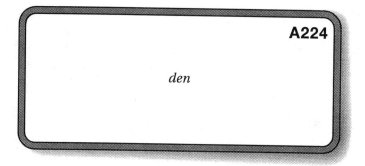

A224

den

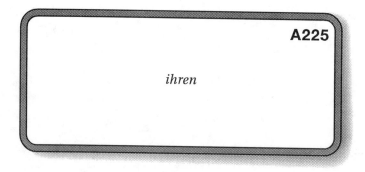

A225

ihren

Questions

Q226

Außer (sein-) Brüdern, hat Hans keine Verwandten.

Your Own Answer_____

Q227

Anja gibt (ihr-) Freunden die Fotos.

Your Own Answer_____

Q228

Wir spielen mit _____ Katzen. (the)

Your Own Answer_____

Correct Answers

A226

seinen

A227

ihren

A228

den

Questions

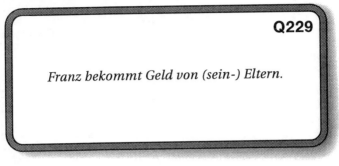

Q229

Franz bekommt Geld von (sein-) Eltern.

Your Own Answer_____

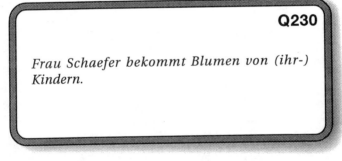

Q230

Frau Schaefer bekommt Blumen von (ihr-) Kindern.

Your Own Answer_____

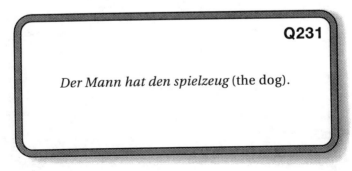

Q231

Der Mann hat den spielzeug (the dog).

Your Own Answer_____

Correct Answers

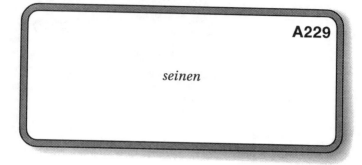

A229

seinen

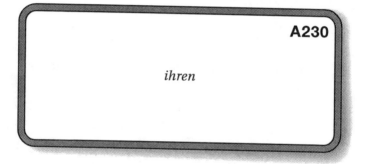

A230

ihren

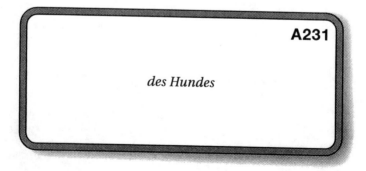

A231

des Hundes

Questions

Q232

Das ist die Adresse (the friend).

*Your Own Answer*_____

_____

Q233

Trotz _____ Regens, spielen wir heute Tennis.
(the)

*Your Own Answer*_____

_____

Q234

Das Hemd (the father) ist grün.

*Your Own Answer*_____

_____

Correct Answers

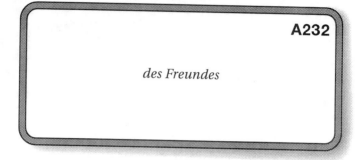

A232

des Freundes

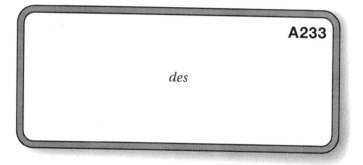

A233

des

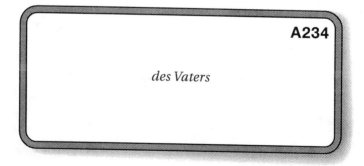

A234

des Vaters

Questions

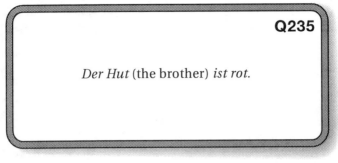

Q235

Der Hut (the brother) *ist rot.*

*Your Own Answer*_____

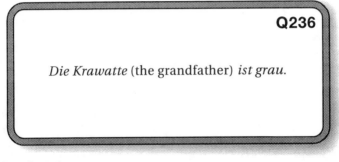

Q236

Die Krawatte (the grandfather) *ist grau.*

*Your Own Answer*_____

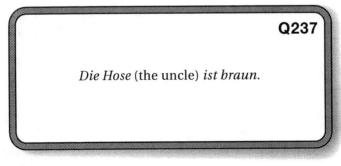

Q237

Die Hose (the uncle) *ist braun.*

*Your Own Answer*_____

Correct Answers

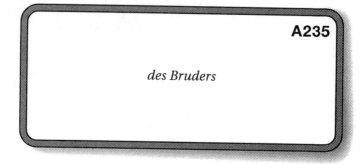

A235

des Bruders

A236

des Großvaters

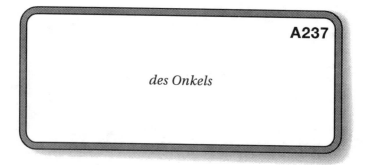

A237

des Onkels

Questions

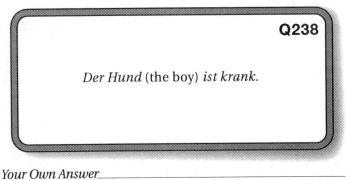

Q238

Der Hund (the boy) *ist krank.*

Your Own Answer_____

Q239

Der Anfang (the winter) *ist im Dezember.*

Your Own Answer_____

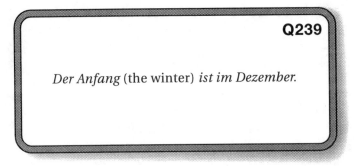

Q240

Während _____ *Regens, bleiben wir zu Hause.*
(the)

Your Own Answer_____

Correct Answers

A238

des Jungens

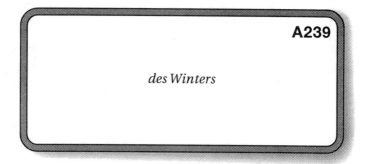

A239

des Winters

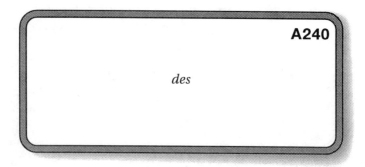

A240

des

Questions

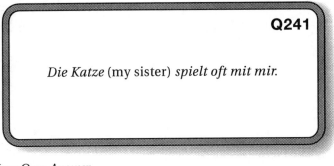

Q241

Die Katze (my sister) *spielt oft mit mir.*

*Your Own Answer*_____

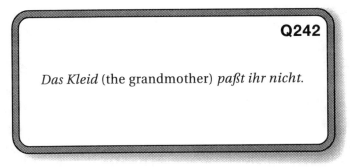

Q242

Das Kleid (the grandmother) *paßt ihr nicht.*

*Your Own Answer*_____

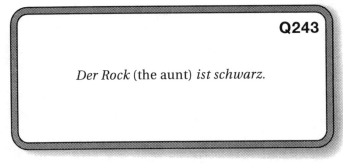

Q243

Der Rock (the aunt) *ist schwarz.*

*Your Own Answer*_____

Correct Answers

A241

meiner Schwester

A242

der Großmutter

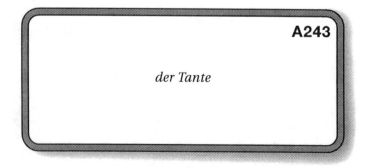

A243

der Tante

Questions

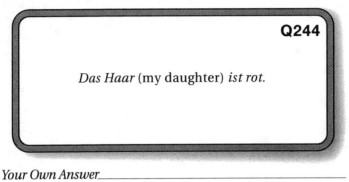

Q244

Das Haar (my daughter) *ist rot.*

Your Own Answer_____

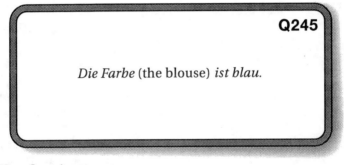

Q245

Die Farbe (the blouse) *ist blau.*

Your Own Answer_____

Q246

Die Farbe (the tie) *ist gelb.*

Your Own Answer_____

Correct Answers

A244

meiner Tochter

A245

der Bluse

A246

der Krawatte

Questions

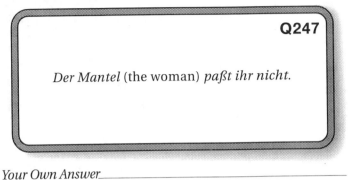

Q247

Der Mantel (the woman) *paßt ihr nicht.*

*Your Own Answer*_____

_____

Q248

Der Hund _____ *Fräuleins ist alt.* (the)

*Your Own Answer*_____

_____

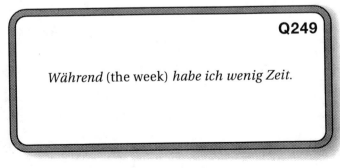

Q249

Während (the week) *habe ich wenig Zeit.*

*Your Own Answer*_____

_____

Correct Answers

A247

der Frau

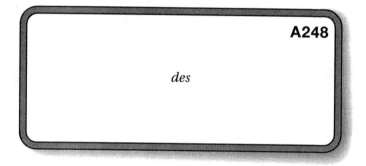

A248

des

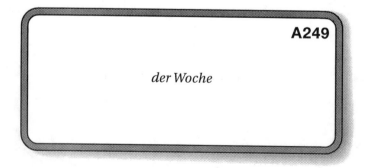

A249

der Woche

Questions

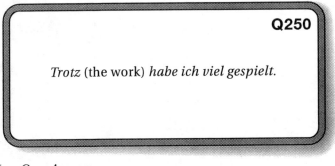

Q250

Trotz (the work) *habe ich viel gespielt.*

*Your Own Answer*_____

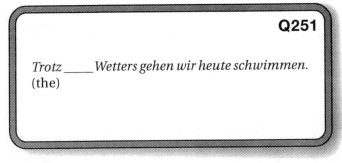

Q251

Trotz _____ *Wetters gehen wir heute schwimmen.*
(the)

*Your Own Answer*_____

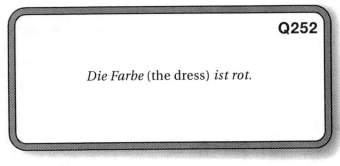

Q252

Die Farbe (the dress) *ist rot.*

*Your Own Answer*_____

Correct Answers

A250

der Arbeit

A251

des

A252

des Kleides

Questions

Q253

Der Ball (the child) *ist blau.*

*Your Own Answer*_____

Q254

Wegen _____ *Wetters spielen wir heute kein Tennis.* (the)

*Your Own Answer*_____

Q255

Das Kleid (the girl) *ist zu klein.*

*Your Own Answer*_____

Correct Answers

A253

des Kindes

A254

des

A255

des Mädchens

Questions

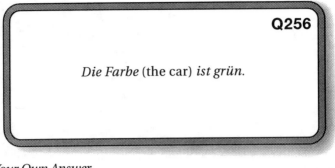

Q256

Die Farbe (the car) *ist grün.*

Your Own Answer_____

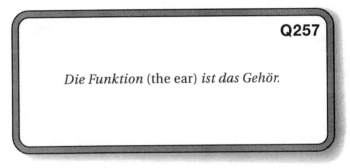

Q257

Die Funktion (the ear) *ist das Gehör.*

Your Own Answer_____

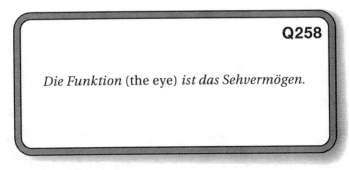

Q258

Die Funktion (the eye) *ist das Sehvermögen.*

Your Own Answer_____

Correct Answers

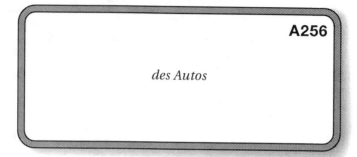

A256

des Autos

A257

des Ohres

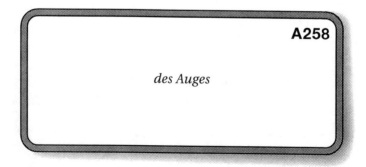

A258

des Auges

Questions

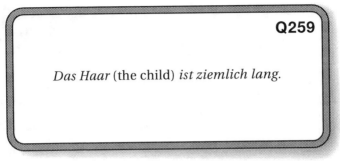

Q259

Das Haar (the child) *ist ziemlich lang.*

*Your Own Answer*_____

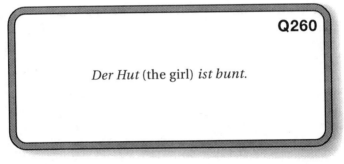

Q260

Der Hut (the girl) *ist bunt.*

*Your Own Answer*_____

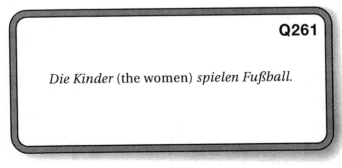

Q261

Die Kinder (the women) *spielen Fußball.*

*Your Own Answer*_____

Correct Answers

A259

des Kindes

A260

des Mädchens

A261

der Frauen

Questions

Q262

Die Kleidung _____ *Geschäfte sind oft teuer.* (the)

*Your Own Answer*_____

_____

Q263

Die Bücher _____ *Bibliotheken sind kostenlos.*
(the)

*Your Own Answer*_____

_____

Q264

Die Spielsachen (the children) *sind kaputt.*

*Your Own Answer*_____

_____

Correct Answers

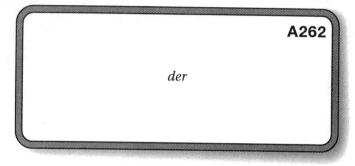

A262

der

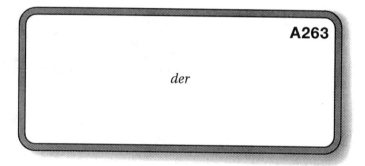

A263

der

A264

der Kinder

Questions

Q265

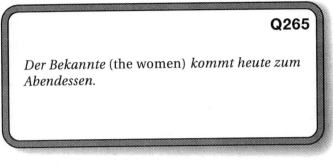

Der Bekannte (the women) *kommt heute zum Abendessen.*

*Your Own Answer*_____

Q266

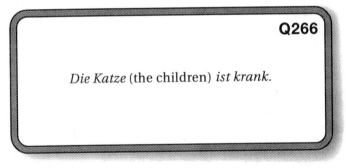

Die Katze (the children) *ist krank.*

*Your Own Answer*_____

Q267

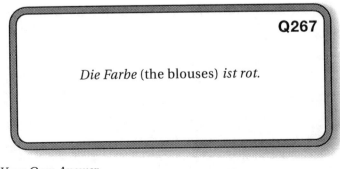

Die Farbe (the blouses) *ist rot.*

*Your Own Answer*_____

Correct Answers

A265

der Frauen

A266

der Kinder

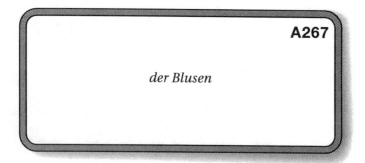

A267

der Blusen

Questions

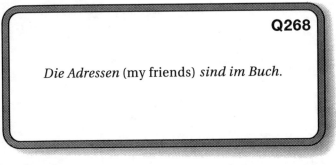

Q268

Die Adressen (my friends) *sind im Buch.*

*Your Own Answer*_____

_____

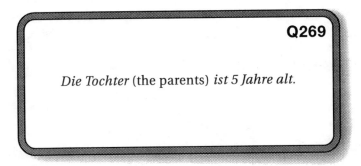

Q269

Die Tochter (the parents) *ist 5 Jahre alt.*

*Your Own Answer*_____

_____

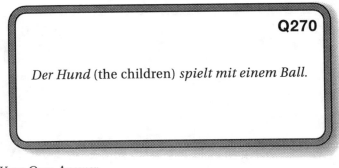

Q270

Der Hund (the children) *spielt mit einem Ball.*

*Your Own Answer*_____

_____

Correct Answers

A268

meiner Freunden

A269

der Eltern

A270

der Kinder

Questions

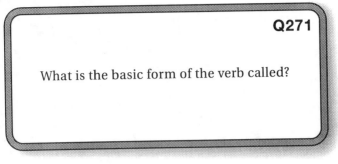

Q271

What is the basic form of the verb called?

*Your Own Answer*_____

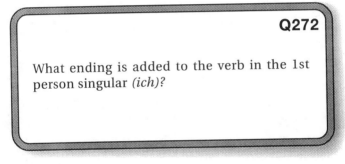

Q272

What ending is added to the verb in the 1st person singular *(ich)?*

*Your Own Answer*_____

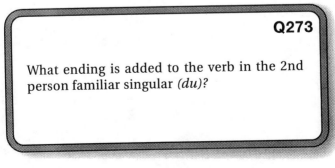

Q273

What ending is added to the verb in the 2nd person familiar singular *(du)?*

*Your Own Answer*_____

Correct Answers

A271

infinitive

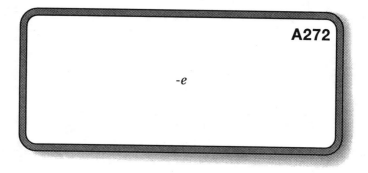

A272

-e

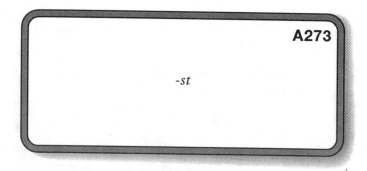

A273

-st

Questions

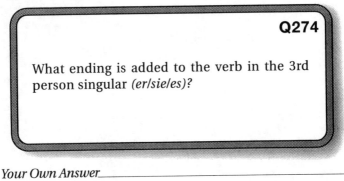

Q274

What ending is added to the verb in the 3rd person singular *(er/sie/es)?*

*Your Own Answer*_____

_____

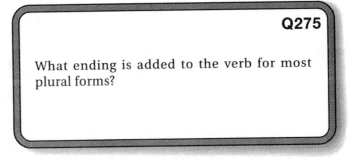

Q275

What ending is added to the verb for most plural forms?

*Your Own Answer*_____

_____

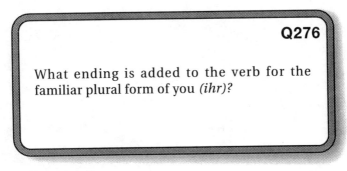

Q276

What ending is added to the verb for the familiar plural form of you *(ihr)?*

*Your Own Answer*_____

_____

Correct Answers

-*t*

-*en* (infinitive)

-*t*

Questions

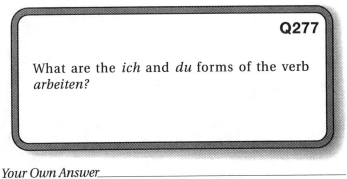

Q277

What are the *ich* and *du* forms of the verb *arbeiten?*

*Your Own Answer*_____

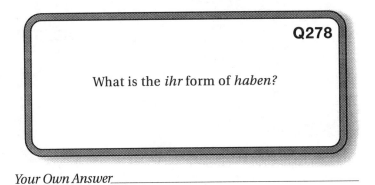

Q278

What is the *ihr* form of *haben?*

*Your Own Answer*_____

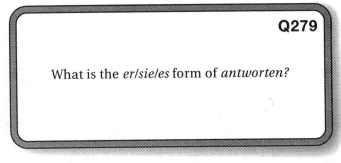

Q279

What is the *er/sie/es* form of *antworten?*

*Your Own Answer*_____

Correct Answers

A277

arbeite; arbeitest

A278

habt

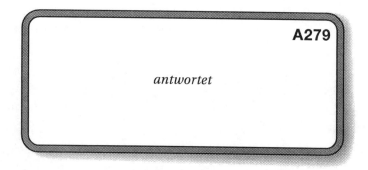

A279

antwortet

Questions

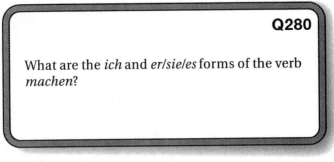

Q280

What are the *ich* and *er/sie/es* forms of the verb *machen*?

*Your Own Answer*_____

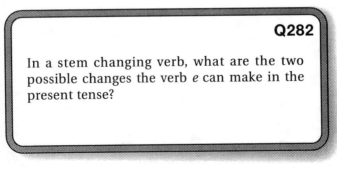

Q281

In a stem changing verb, what does the vowel *a* change to in the present tense?

*Your Own Answer*_____

Q282

In a stem changing verb, what are the two possible changes the verb *e* can make in the present tense?

*Your Own Answer*_____

Correct Answers

A280

mache; macht

A281

ä

A282

i or *ie*

Questions

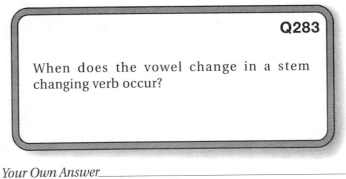

Q283

When does the vowel change in a stem changing verb occur?

*Your Own Answer*_____

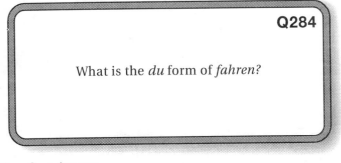

Q284

What is the *du* form of *fahren?*

*Your Own Answer*_____

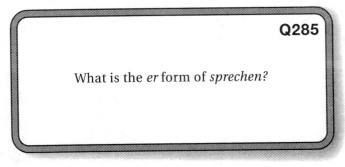

Q285

What is the *er* form of *sprechen?*

*Your Own Answer*_____

Correct Answers

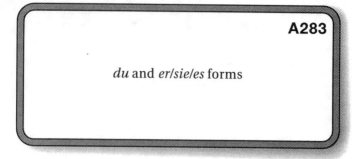

A283

du and *er/sie/es* forms

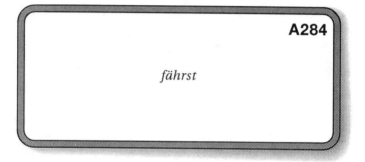

A284

fährst

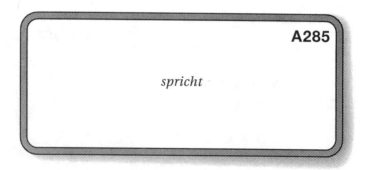

A285

spricht

Questions

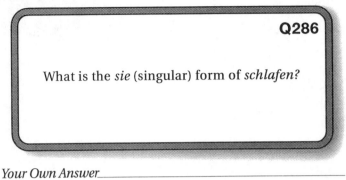

Q286

What is the *sie* (singular) form of *schlafen*?

Your Own Answer_____

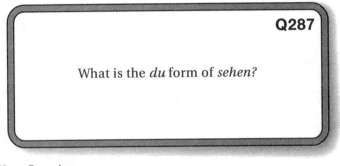

Q287

What is the *du* form of *sehen*?

Your Own Answer_____

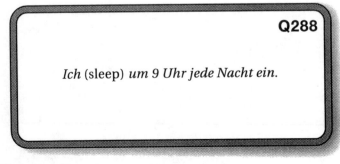

Q288

Ich (sleep) *um 9 Uhr jede Nacht ein.*

Your Own Answer_____

Correct Answers

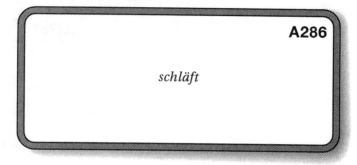

A286

schläft

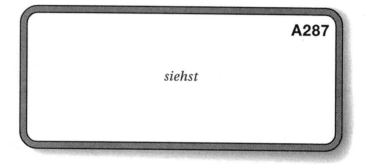

A287

siehst

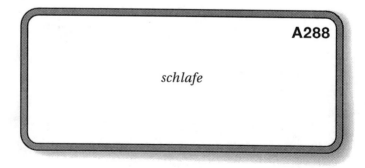

A288

schlafe

Questions

Q289

Er (see) *die Katze.*

Your Own Answer_____

_____

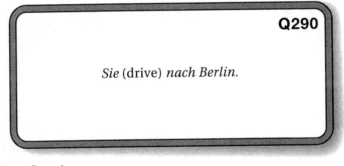

Q290

Sie (drive) *nach Berlin.*

Your Own Answer_____

_____

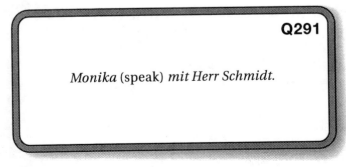

Q291

Monika (speak) *mit Herr Schmidt.*

Your Own Answer_____

_____

Correct Answers

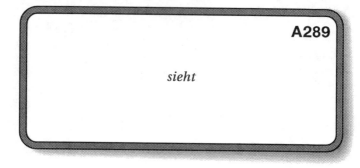

A289

sieht

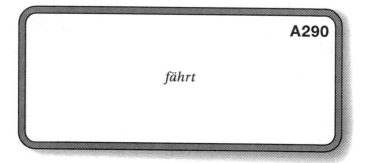

A290

fährt

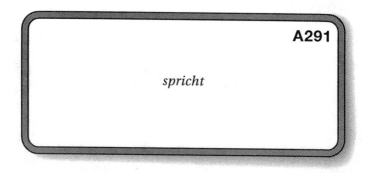

A291

spricht

Questions

Q292

(See) *du Monika da?*

*Your Own Answer*_____

_____

Q293

(Drive) *du morgen nach Köln?*

*Your Own Answer*_____

_____

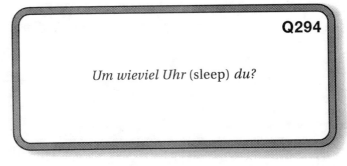

Q294

Um wieviel Uhr (sleep) *du?*

*Your Own Answer*_____

_____

Correct Answers

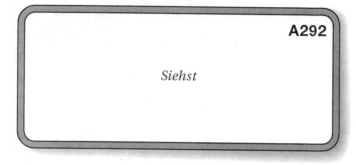

A292

Siehst

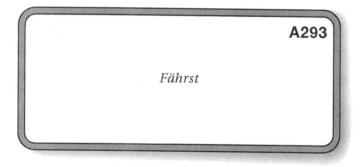

A293

Fährst

A294

schläfst

Questions

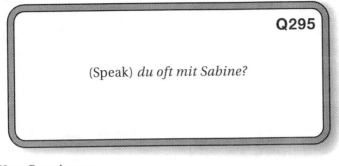

Q295

(Speak) *du oft mit Sabine?*

Your Own Answer_____

Q296

With a separable prefix verb, where does the prefix go?

Your Own Answer_____

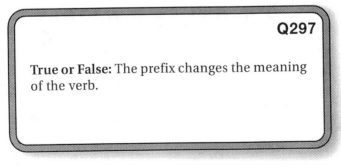

Q297

True or False: The prefix changes the meaning of the verb.

Your Own Answer_____

Correct Answers

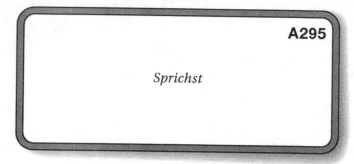

A295

Sprichst

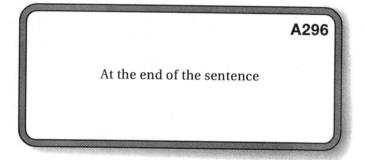

A296

At the end of the sentence

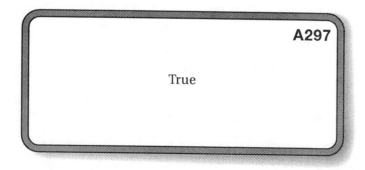

A297

True

Questions

Q298

Distinguish between the verbs *fahren* and *abfahren.*

*Your Own Answer*_____

Q299

Wir (abfahren) um halb sieben _____.

*Your Own Answer*_____

Q300

Ich (einschlafen) bald _____.

*Your Own Answer*_____

Correct Answers

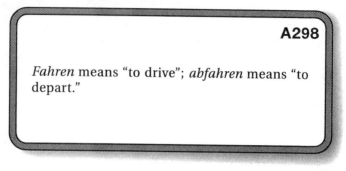

A298

Fahren means "to drive"; *abfahren* means "to depart."

A299

fahren... ab

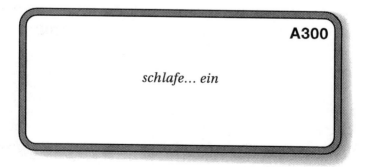

A300

schlafe... ein

Questions

Q301

Die Kinder (zuhören) gut ____.

*Your Own Answer*_____

_____

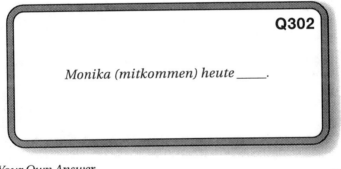

Q302

Monika (mitkommen) heute ____.

*Your Own Answer*_____

_____

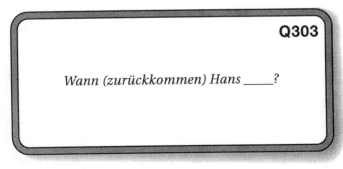

Q303

Wann (zurückkommen) Hans ____?

*Your Own Answer*_____

_____

Correct Answers

A301

hören... zu

A302

kommt... mit

A303

kommt... zurück

Questions

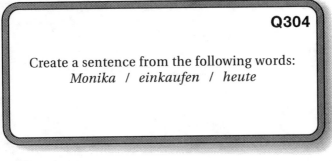

Q304

Create a sentence from the following words:
Monika / einkaufen / heute

*Your Own Answer*_____

Q305

Create a sentence from the following words:
vorbeikommen / heute / Abend du ?

*Your Own Answer*_____

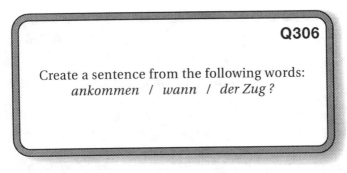

Q306

Create a sentence from the following words:
ankommen / wann / der Zug ?

*Your Own Answer*_____

Correct Answers

A304

Monika kauft heute ein.

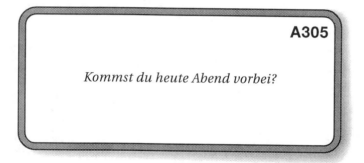

A305

Kommst du heute Abend vorbei?

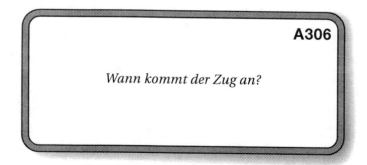

A306

Wann kommt der Zug an?

Questions

Q307

Create a sentence from the following words:
mitmachen / heute Nachmittag / Franz

*Your Own Answer*_____

Q308

Create a sentence from the following words:
abfahren / wann / wir?

*Your Own Answer*_____

Q309

Create a sentence from the following words:
Das Kind / einschlafen

*Your Own Answer*_____

Correct Answers

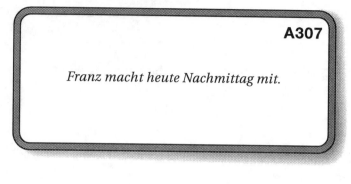

A307

Franz macht heute Nachmittag mit.

A308

Wann fahren wir ab?

A309

Das Kind schläft ein.

Questions

Create a sentence from the following words:
zuhören / bitte / Sie!

*Your Own Answer*_____

Create a sentence from the following words:
aufmachen / das Licht / Katja

*Your Own Answer*_____

Create a sentence from the following words:
die Tür / er / zumachen

*Your Own Answer*_____

Correct Answers

A310

Hören Sie bitte zu!

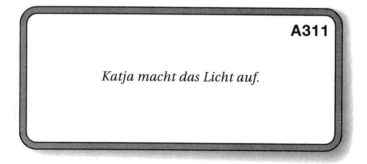

A311

Katja macht das Licht auf.

A312

Er macht die Tür zu.

Questions

Q313

Create a sentence from the following words:
aufmachen / das Fenster / Thomas

*Your Own Answer*_____

_____

Q314

Create a sentence from the following words:
das Radio / anmachen / Anja

*Your Own Answer*_____

_____

Q315

Distinguish between the verbs *kommen* and *mitkommen*.

*Your Own Answer*_____

_____

Correct Answers

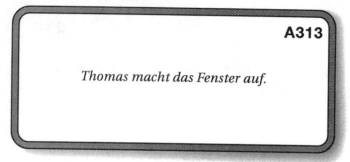

A313

Thomas macht das Fenster auf.

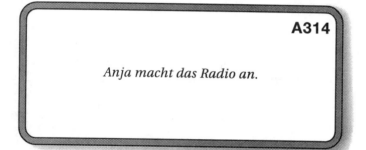

A314

Anja macht das Radio an.

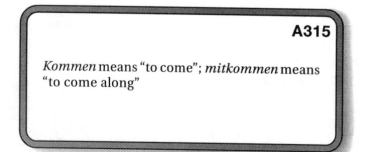

A315

Kommen means "to come"; *mitkommen* means "to come along"

Questions

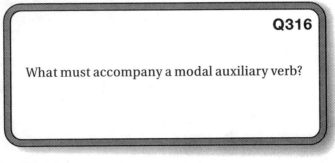

Q316

What must accompany a modal auxiliary verb?

*Your Own Answer*_____

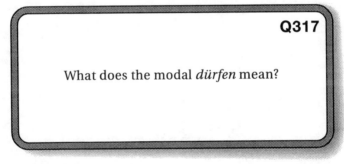

Q317

What does the modal *dürfen* mean?

*Your Own Answer*_____

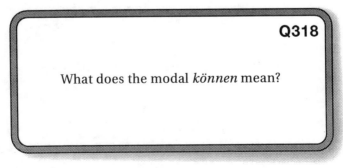

Q318

What does the modal *können* mean?

*Your Own Answer*_____

Correct Answers

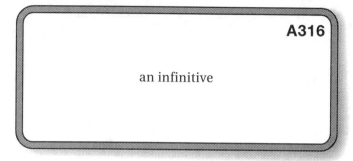

A316

an infinitive

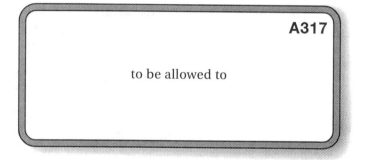

A317

to be allowed to

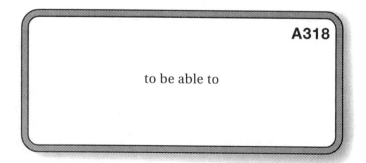

A318

to be able to

Questions

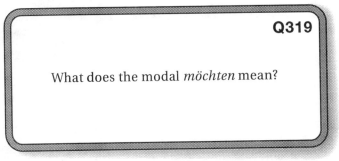

Q319

What does the modal *möchten* mean?

*Your Own Answer*_____

_____

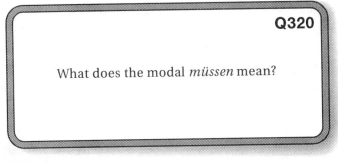

Q320

What does the modal *müssen* mean?

*Your Own Answer*_____

_____

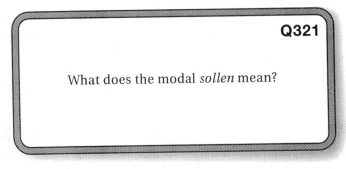

Q321

What does the modal *sollen* mean?

*Your Own Answer*_____

_____

Correct Answers

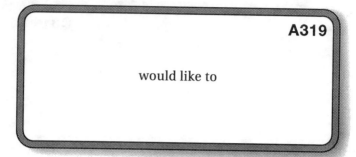

A319

would like to

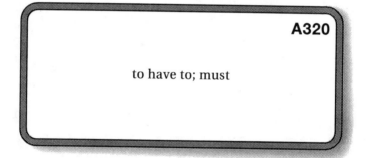

A320

to have to; must

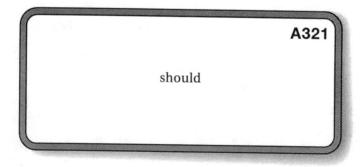

A321

should

Questions

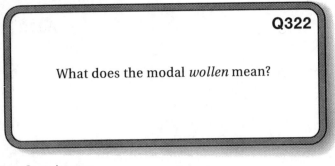

Q322

What does the modal *wollen* mean?

*Your Own Answer*_____

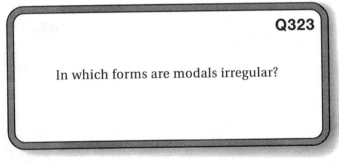

Q323

In which forms are modals irregular?

*Your Own Answer*_____

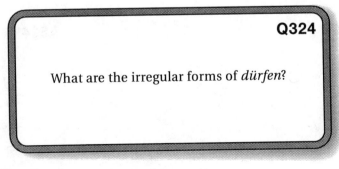

Q324

What are the irregular forms of *dürfen*?

*Your Own Answer*_____

Correct Answers

A322

to want to

A323

ich, du, er/sie/es forms

A324

darf, darfst, darf

Questions

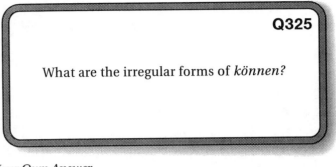

Q325

What are the irregular forms of *können?*

*Your Own Answer*_____

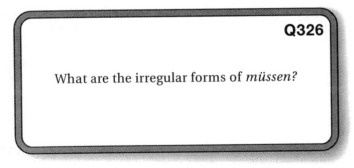

Q326

What are the irregular forms of *müssen?*

*Your Own Answer*_____

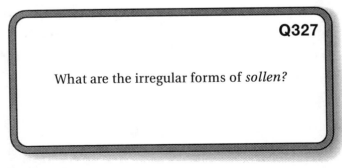

Q327

What are the irregular forms of *sollen?*

*Your Own Answer*_____

Correct Answers

A325

kann, kannst, kann

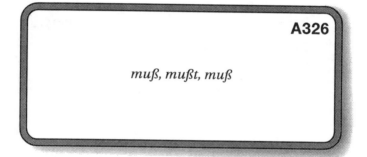

A326

muß, mußt, muß

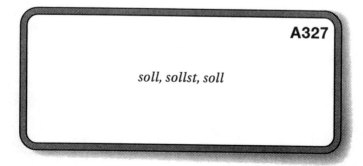

A327

soll, sollst, soll

Questions

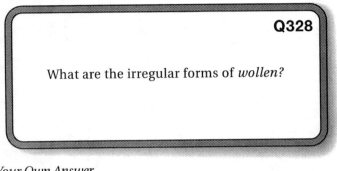

Q328

What are the irregular forms of *wollen?*

*Your Own Answer*_____

Q329

Ich (can) *gut singen.*

*Your Own Answer*_____

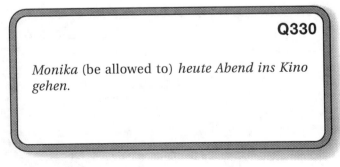

Q330

Monika (be allowed to) *heute Abend ins Kino gehen.*

*Your Own Answer*_____

Correct Answers

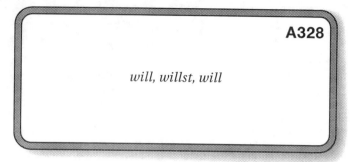

A328

will, willst, will

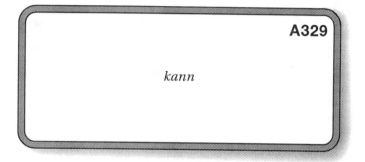

A329

kann

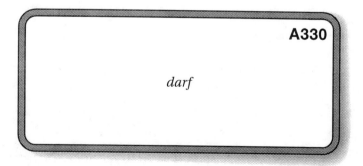

A330

darf

Questions

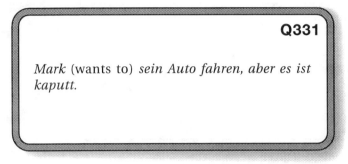

Q331

Mark (wants to) *sein Auto fahren, aber es ist kaputt.*

*Your Own Answer*_____

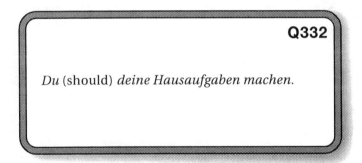

Q332

Du (should) *deine Hausaufgaben machen.*

*Your Own Answer*_____

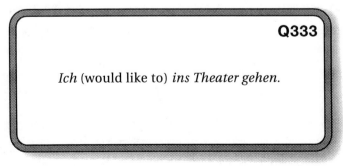

Q333

Ich (would like to) *ins Theater gehen.*

*Your Own Answer*_____

Correct Answers

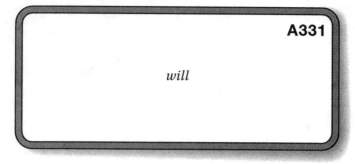

A331

will

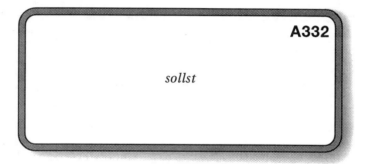

A332

sollst

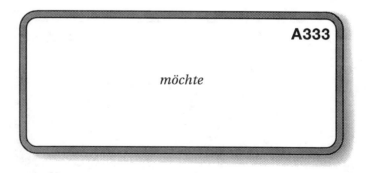

A333

möchte

Questions

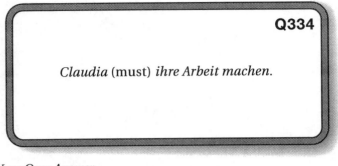

Q334

Claudia (must) *ihre Arbeit machen.*

Your Own Answer_____

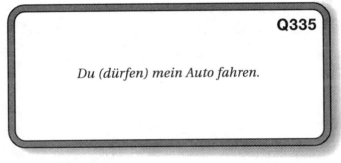

Q335

Du (dürfen) mein Auto fahren.

Your Own Answer_____

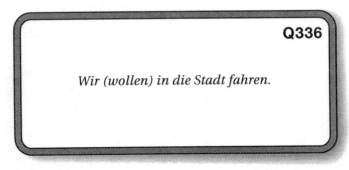

Q336

Wir (wollen) in die Stadt fahren.

Your Own Answer_____

Correct Answers

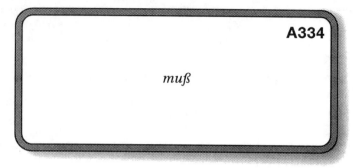

A334

muß

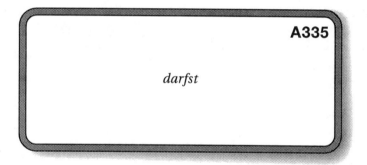

A335

darfst

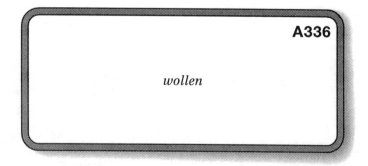

A336

wollen

Questions

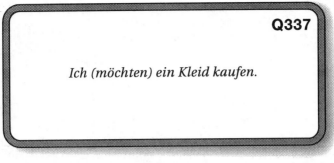

Q337

Ich (möchten) ein Kleid kaufen.

Your Own Answer_____

_____

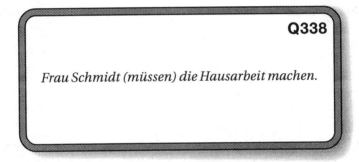

Q338

Frau Schmidt (müssen) die Hausarbeit machen.

Your Own Answer_____

_____

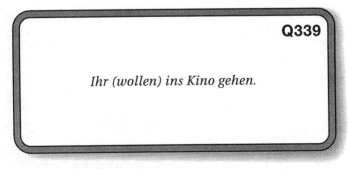

Q339

Ihr (wollen) ins Kino gehen.

Your Own Answer_____

_____

Correct Answers

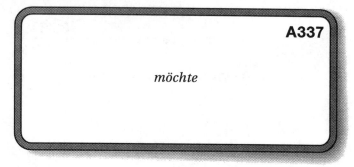

A337

möchte

A338

muß

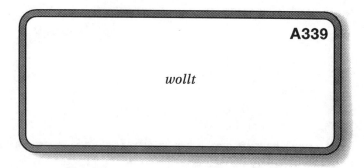

A339

wollt

Questions

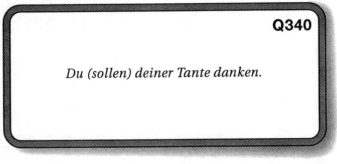

Q340

Du (sollen) deiner Tante danken.

Your Own Answer_____

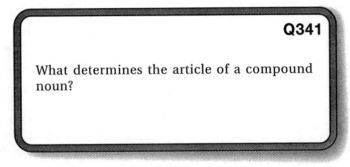

Q341

What determines the article of a compound noun?

Your Own Answer_____

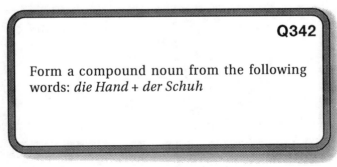

Q342

Form a compound noun from the following words: *die Hand + der Schuh*

Your Own Answer_____

Correct Answers

A340

sollst

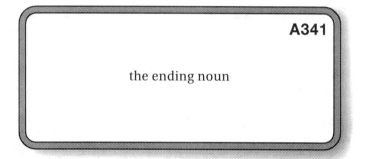

A341

the ending noun

A342

der Handschuh

Questions

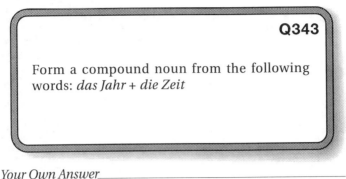

Q343

Form a compound noun from the following words: *das Jahr + die Zeit*

Your Own Answer_____

Q344

Form a compound noun from the following words: *schreiben + die Maschine*

Your Own Answer_____

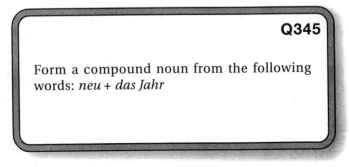

Q345

Form a compound noun from the following words: *neu + das Jahr*

Your Own Answer_____

Correct Answers

A343

die Jahreszeit

A344

die Schreibmaschine

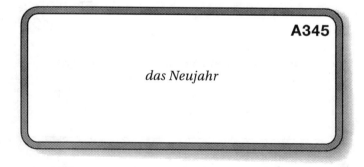

A345

das Neujahr

Questions

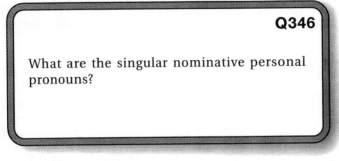

Q346

What are the singular nominative personal pronouns?

*Your Own Answer*_____

_____

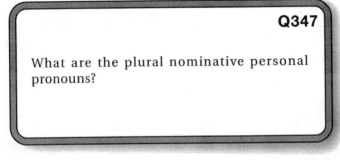

Q347

What are the plural nominative personal pronouns?

*Your Own Answer*_____

_____

Q348

Wie findest du die Farbe? _____ *ist schön.*

*Your Own Answer*_____

_____

Correct Answers

ich, du, er, sie, es

wir, ihr, sie, Sie

Sie

Questions

Q349

Der Dom ist schön. ____ ist herrlich.

Your Own Answer_____

Q350

Wie ist das Buch? ____ ist interessant.

Your Own Answer_____

Q351

Fährst du das Auto? ____ ist toll.

Your Own Answer_____

Correct Answers

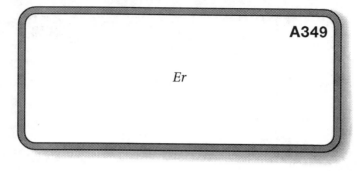

A349

Er

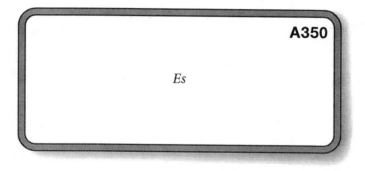

A350

Es

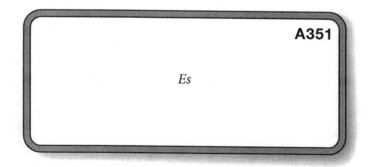

A351

Es

Questions

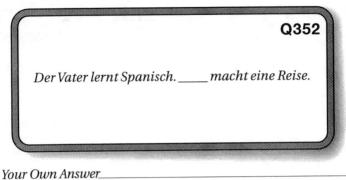

Q352

Der Vater lernt Spanisch. _____ macht eine Reise.

*Your Own Answer*_____

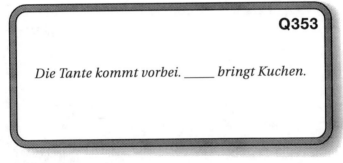

Q353

Die Tante kommt vorbei. _____ bringt Kuchen.

*Your Own Answer*_____

Q354

Das Essen ist bereit. _____ schmeckt gut.

*Your Own Answer*_____

Correct Answers

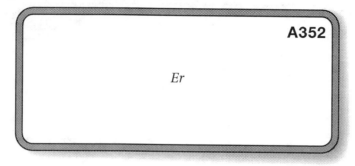

A352

Er

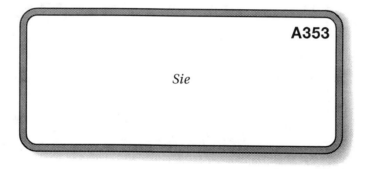

A353

Sie

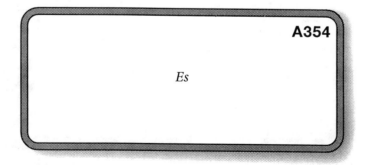

A354

Es

Questions

Q355

Der Mann fährt schnell. ____ ist spät.

Your Own Answer_____

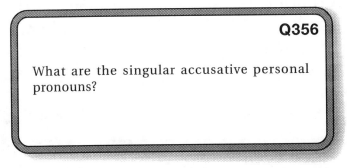

Q356

What are the singular accusative personal pronouns?

Your Own Answer_____

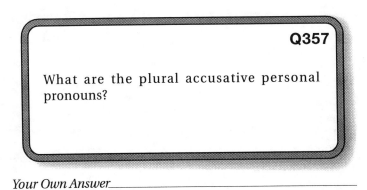

Q357

What are the plural accusative personal pronouns?

Your Own Answer_____

Correct Answers

A355

Er

A356

mich, dich, ihn, sie, es, Sie

A357

uns, euch, sie, Sie

Questions

Ich habe etwas für (you singular).

*Your Own Answer*_____

Was hat er gegen (me)?

*Your Own Answer*_____

Rolf geht nicht ohne (her).

*Your Own Answer*_____

Correct Answers

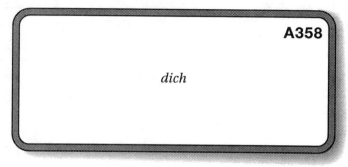

A358

dich

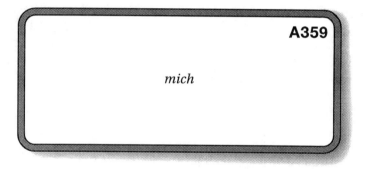

A359

mich

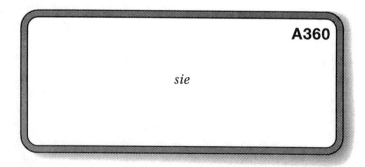

A360

sie

Questions

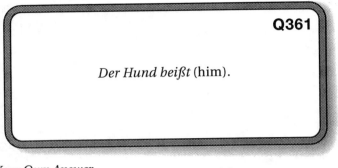

Q361

Der Hund beißt (him).

Your Own Answer_____

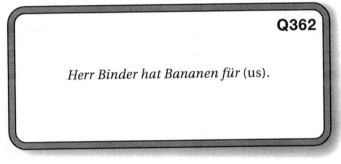

Q362

Herr Binder hat Bananen für (us).

Your Own Answer_____

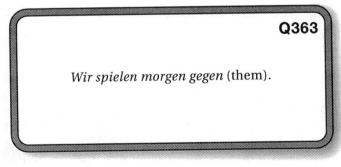

Q363

Wir spielen morgen gegen (them).

Your Own Answer_____

Correct Answers

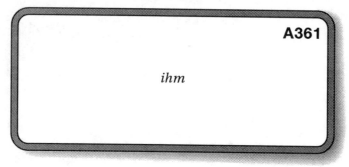

A361

ihm

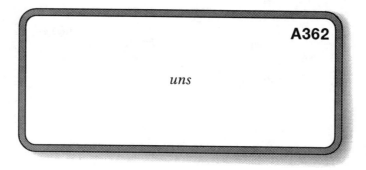

A362

uns

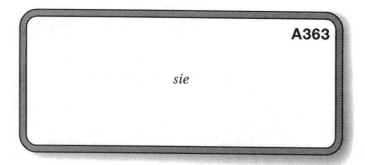

A363

sie

Questions

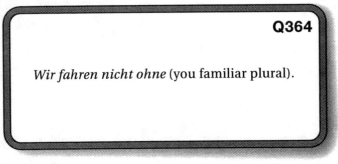

Q364

Wir fahren nicht ohne (you familiar plural).

Your Own Answer_____

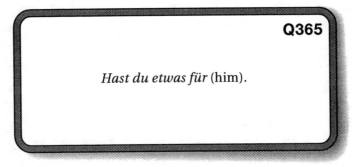

Q365

Hast du etwas für (him).

Your Own Answer_____

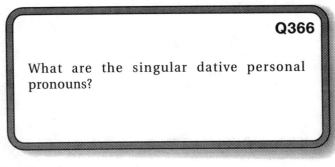

Q366

What are the singular dative personal pronouns?

Your Own Answer_____

Correct Answers

A364

euch

A365

ihn

A366

mir, dir, ihm, ihr, ihm, Ihnen

Questions

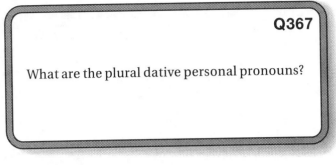

Q367

What are the plural dative personal pronouns?

*Your Own Answer*_____

_____

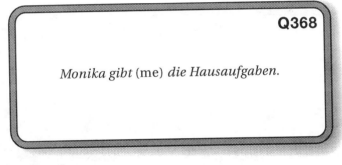

Q368

Monika gibt (me) *die Hausaufgaben.*

*Your Own Answer*_____

_____

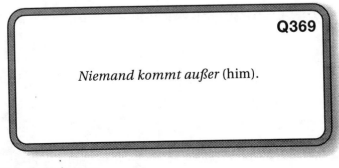

Q369

Niemand kommt außer (him).

*Your Own Answer*_____

_____

Correct Answers

A367

uns, euch, ihnen, Ihnen

A368

mir

A369

ihm

Questions

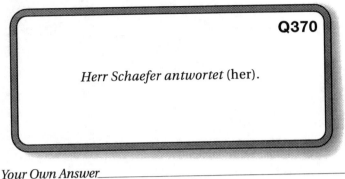

Q370

Herr Schaefer antwortet (her).

Your Own Answer_____

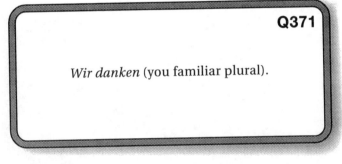

Q371

Wir danken (you familiar plural).

Your Own Answer_____

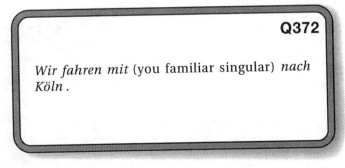

Q372

Wir fahren mit (you familiar singular) *nach Köln* .

Your Own Answer_____

Correct Answers

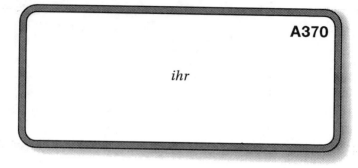

A370

ihr

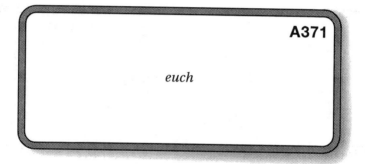

A371

euch

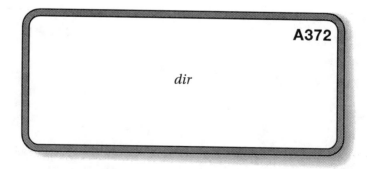

A372

dir

Questions

Q373

Thomas wohnt bei (us).

Your Own Answer_____

Q374

Können Sie (me) *helfen?*

Your Own Answer_____

Q375

Die Musik gefällt (them).

Your Own Answer_____

Correct Answers

A373

uns

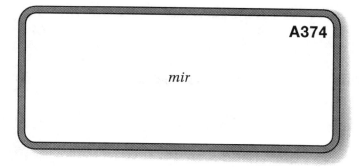

A374

mir

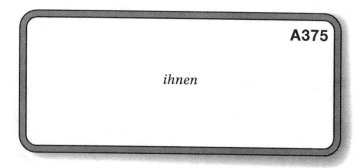

A375

ihnen

Questions

Q376

What are the genitive personal pronouns?

*Your Own Answer*_____

_____

Q377

When is the familiar form of *you* used?

*Your Own Answer*_____

_____

Q378

How is the formal form of *you* distinguishable in written form?

*Your Own Answer*_____

_____

Correct Answers

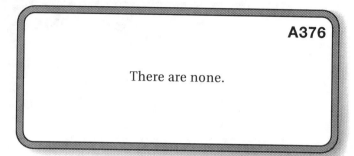

A376

There are none.

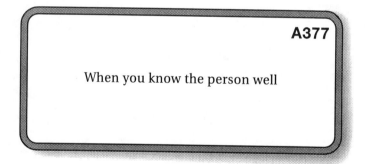

A377

When you know the person well

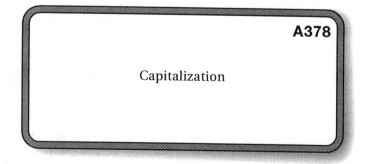

A378

Capitalization

Questions

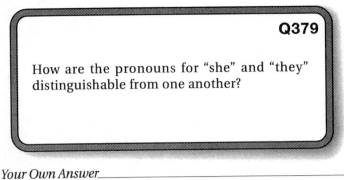

Q379

How are the pronouns for "she" and "they" distinguishable from one another?

*Your Own Answer*_____

_____

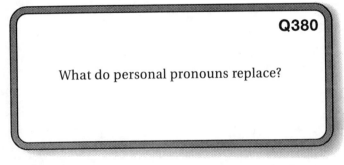

Q380

What do personal pronouns replace?

*Your Own Answer*_____

_____

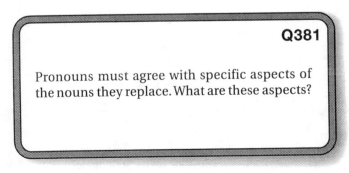

Q381

Pronouns must agree with specific aspects of the nouns they replace. What are these aspects?

*Your Own Answer*_____

_____

Correct Answers

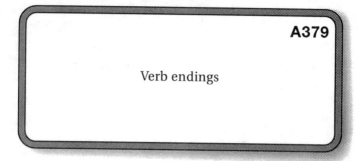

A379

Verb endings

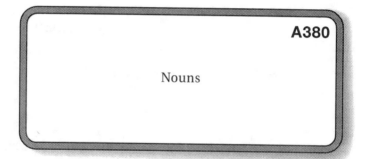

A380

Nouns

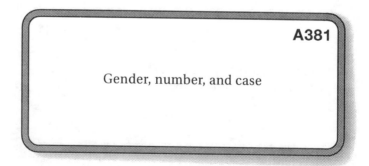

A381

Gender, number, and case

Questions

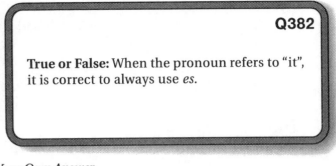

Q382

True or False: When the pronoun refers to "it", it is correct to always use *es*.

*Your Own Answer*_____

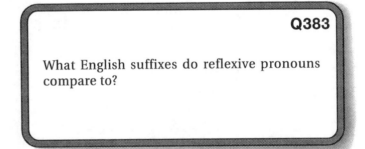

Q383

What English suffixes do reflexive pronouns compare to?

*Your Own Answer*_____

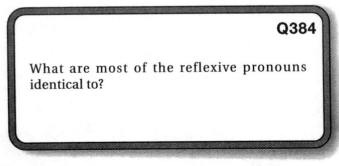

Q384

What are most of the reflexive pronouns identical to?

*Your Own Answer*_____

Correct Answers

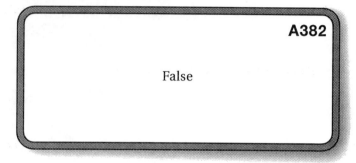

A382

False

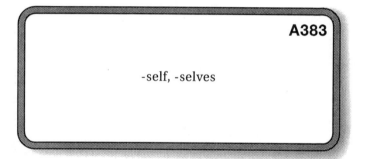

A383

-self, -selves

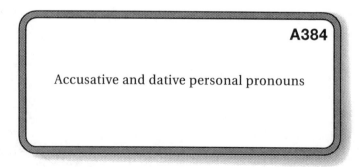

A384

Accusative and dative personal pronouns

Questions

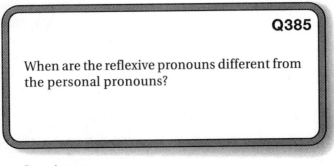

Q385

When are the reflexive pronouns different from the personal pronouns?

*Your Own Answer*_____

_____

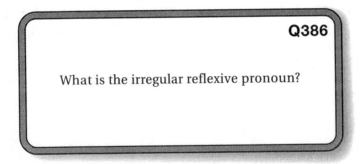

Q386

What is the irregular reflexive pronoun?

*Your Own Answer*_____

_____

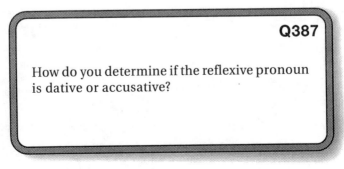

Q387

How do you determine if the reflexive pronoun is dative or accusative?

*Your Own Answer*_____

_____

Correct Answers

A385

3rd person singular and plural forms; *you* formal

A386

sich

A387

If there is another direct object in the sentence, the pronoun is dative.

Questions

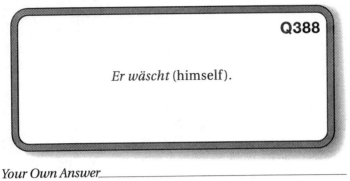

Q388

Er wäscht (himself).

Your Own Answer_____

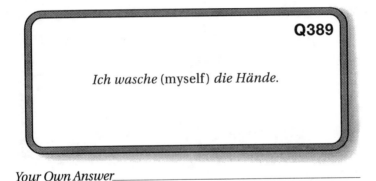

Q389

Ich wasche (myself) *die Hände.*

Your Own Answer_____

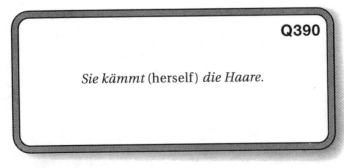

Q390

Sie kämmt (herself) *die Haare.*

Your Own Answer_____

Correct Answers

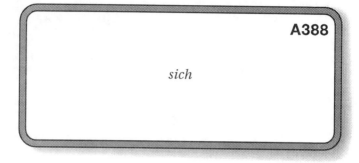

A388

sich

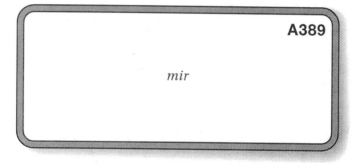

A389

mir

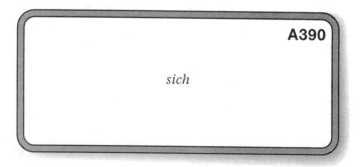

A390

sich

Questions

Du duscht (yourself).

*Your Own Answer*_____

Sie waschen (themselves).

*Your Own Answer*_____

Ich putze _____ *die Zähne.*

*Your Own Answer*_____

Correct Answers

A391

dich

A392

sich

A393

mir

Questions

Er wäscht _____ die Arme.

*Your Own Answer*_____

Wir putzen _____ die Zähne.

*Your Own Answer*_____

Ihr duscht _____.

*Your Own Answer*_____

Correct Answers

A394

sich

A395

uns

A396

euch

Questions

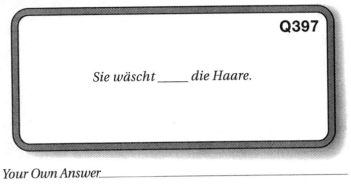

Q397

Sie wäscht _____ die Haare.

Your Own Answer_____

Q398

Ich wasche _____ das Gesicht.

Your Own Answer_____

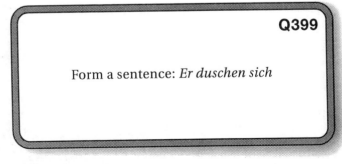

Q399

Form a sentence: *Er duschen sich*

Your Own Answer_____

Correct Answers

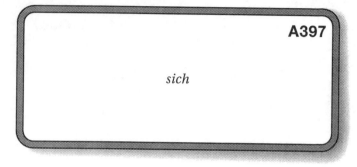

A397

sich

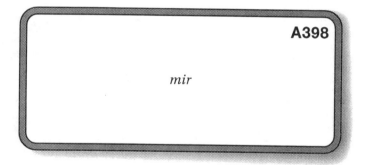

A398

mir

A399

Er duscht sich.

Questions

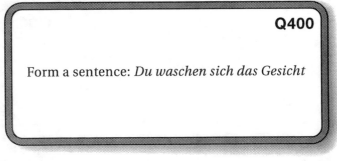

Q400

Form a sentence: *Du waschen sich das Gesicht*

*Your Own Answer*_____

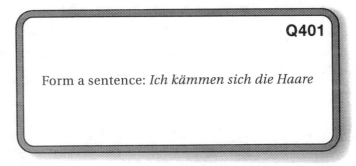

Q401

Form a sentence: *Ich kämmen sich die Haare*

*Your Own Answer*_____

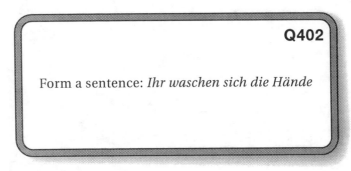

Q402

Form a sentence: *Ihr waschen sich die Hände*

*Your Own Answer*_____

Correct Answers

A400

Du wäschst dir das Gesicht.

A401

Ich kämme mir die Haare.

A402

Ihr wascht euch die Hände.

Questions

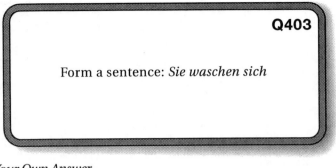

Q403

Form a sentence: *Sie waschen sich*

*Your Own Answer*_____

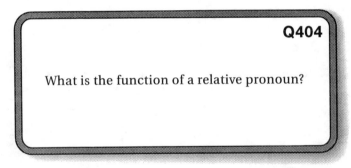

Q404

What is the function of a relative pronoun?

*Your Own Answer*_____

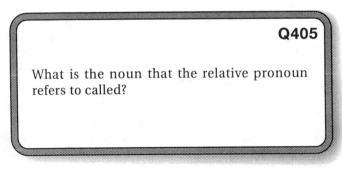

Q405

What is the noun that the relative pronoun refers to called?

*Your Own Answer*_____

Correct Answers

A403

Sie waschen sich.

A404

To relate a subordinate clause to a main clause by referring to a noun in the main clause

A405

It is called the antecedent

Questions

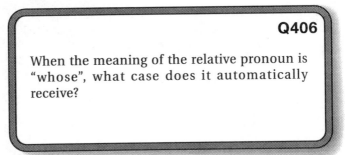

Q406

When the meaning of the relative pronoun is "whose", what case does it automatically receive?

*Your Own Answer*_____

_____

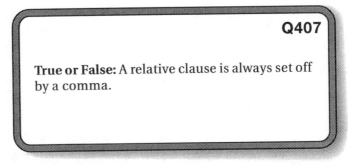

Q407

True or False: A relative clause is always set off by a comma.

*Your Own Answer*_____

_____

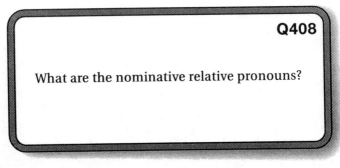

Q408

What are the nominative relative pronouns?

*Your Own Answer*_____

_____

Correct Answers

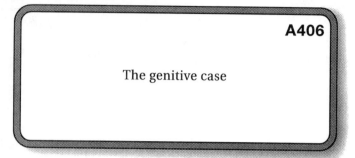

A406

The genitive case

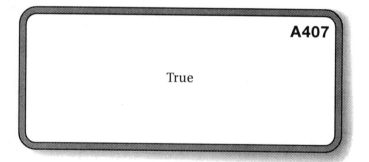

A407

True

A408

der, die, das, die

Questions

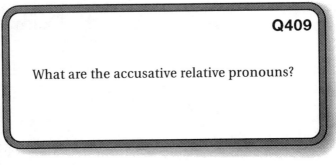

Q409

What are the accusative relative pronouns?

*Your Own Answer*_____

_____

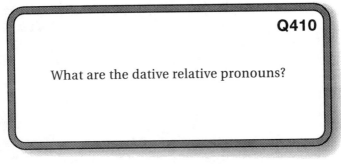

Q410

What are the dative relative pronouns?

*Your Own Answer*_____

_____

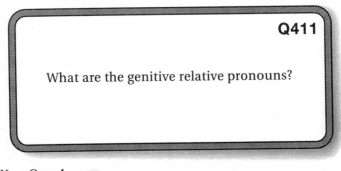

Q411

What are the genitive relative pronouns?

*Your Own Answer*_____

_____

Correct Answers

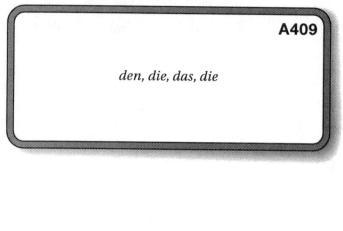

A409

den, die, das, die

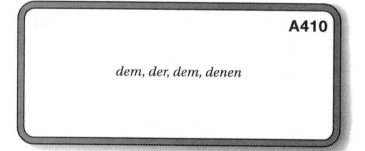

A410

dem, der, dem, denen

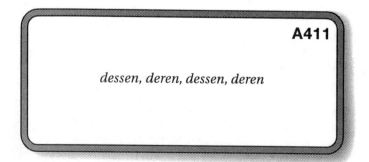

A411

dessen, deren, dessen, deren

Questions

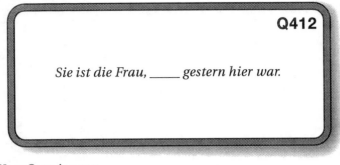

Q412

Sie ist die Frau, _____ gestern hier war.

Your Own Answer_____

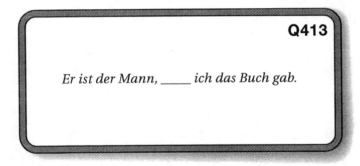

Q413

Er ist der Mann, _____ ich das Buch gab.

Your Own Answer_____

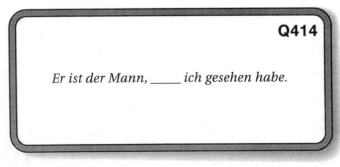

Q414

Er ist der Mann, _____ ich gesehen habe.

Your Own Answer_____

Correct Answers

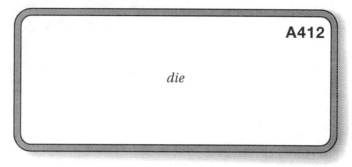

A412

die

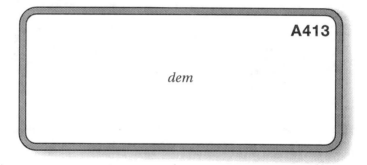

A413

dem

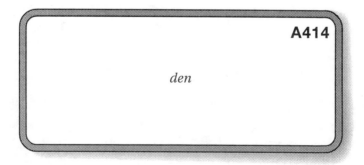

A414

den

Questions

Q415

Sie ist die Frau, in _____ Haus ich wohne.

*Your Own Answer*_____

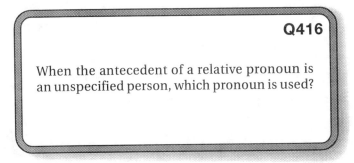

Q416

When the antecedent of a relative pronoun is an unspecified person, which pronoun is used?

*Your Own Answer*_____

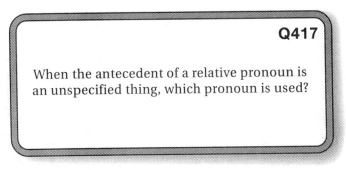

Q417

When the antecedent of a relative pronoun is an unspecified thing, which pronoun is used?

*Your Own Answer*_____

Correct Answers

A415

deren

A416

form of *wer* (depends on case)

A417

was

Questions

Q418

When the antecedent of a relative pronoun is an entire main clause, which pronoun is used?

*Your Own Answer*_____

Q419

When the antecedent of a relative pronoun is an indefinite pronoun (i.e., *alles, vieles,* etc.), which pronoun is used?

*Your Own Answer*_____

Q420

Ich weiß nicht, _____ kommt. (unspecified person)

*Your Own Answer*_____

Correct Answers

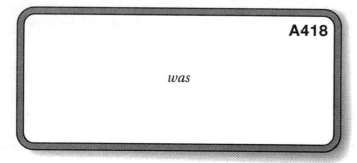

A418

was

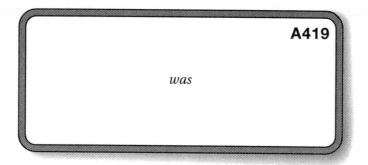

A419

was

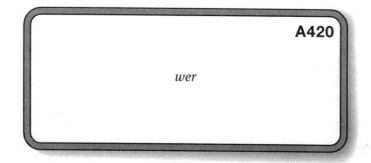

A420

wer

Questions

Q421

Sie meint, er kann nicht kommen, _____ ich nicht glaube.

Your Own Answer_____

Q422

Ich weiß nicht, _____ er das Buch gab.

Your Own Answer_____

Q423

Nicht alles, _____ er sagt, ist interessant.

Your Own Answer_____

Correct Answers

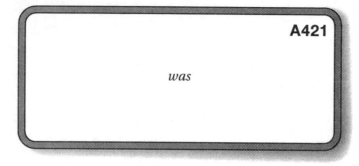

A421

was

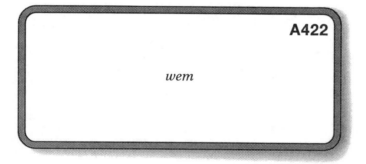

A422

wem

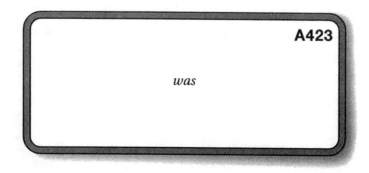

A423

was

Questions

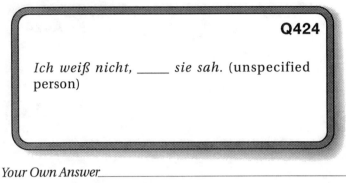

Ich weiß nicht, _____ sie sah. (unspecified person)

*Your Own Answer*_____

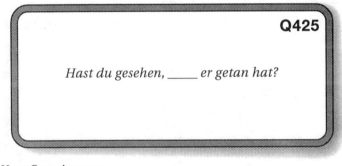

Q425

Hast du gesehen, _____ er getan hat?

*Your Own Answer*_____

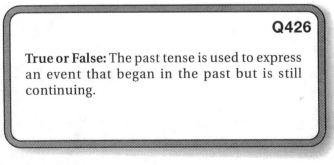

Q426

True or False: The past tense is used to express an event that began in the past but is still continuing.

*Your Own Answer*_____

Correct Answers

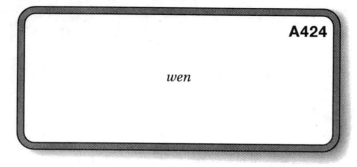

A424

wen

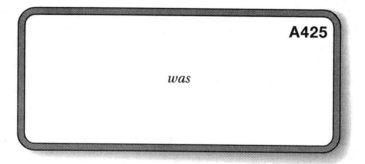

A425

was

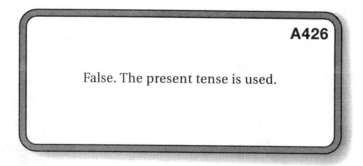

A426

False. The present tense is used.

Questions

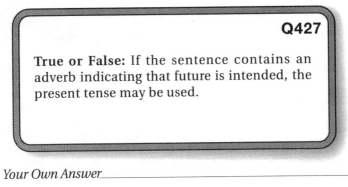

Q427

True or False: If the sentence contains an adverb indicating that future is intended, the present tense may be used.

*Your Own Answer*_____

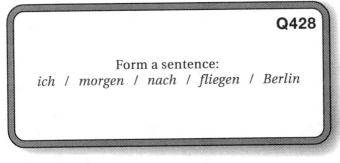

Q428

Form a sentence:
ich / morgen / nach / fliegen / Berlin

*Your Own Answer*_____

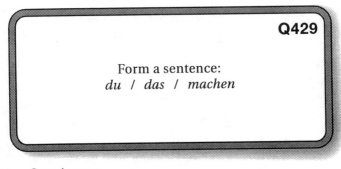

Q429

Form a sentence:
du / das / machen

*Your Own Answer*_____

Correct Answers

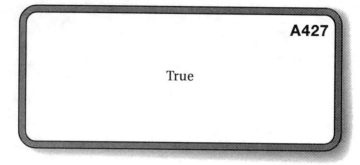

A427

True

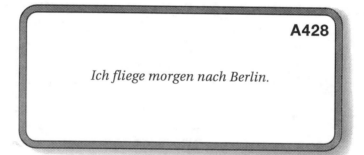

A428

Ich fliege morgen nach Berlin.

A429

Du machst das.

Questions

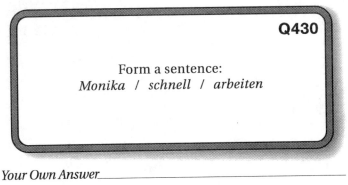

Q430

Form a sentence:
Monika / schnell / arbeiten

*Your Own Answer*_____

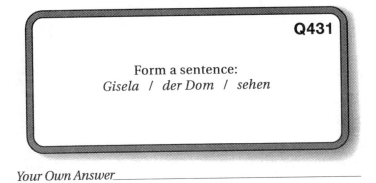

Q431

Form a sentence:
Gisela / der Dom / sehen

*Your Own Answer*_____

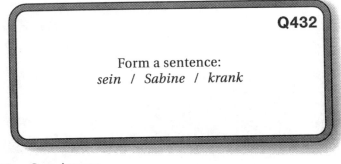

Q432

Form a sentence:
sein / Sabine / krank

*Your Own Answer*_____

Correct Answers

A430

Monika arbeitet schnell.

A431

Gisela sieht den Dom.

A432

Sabine ist krank.

Questions

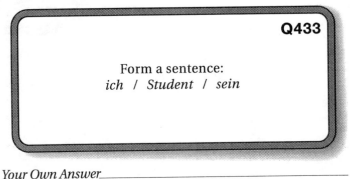

Q433

Form a sentence:
ich / Student / sein

*Your Own Answer*_____

_____

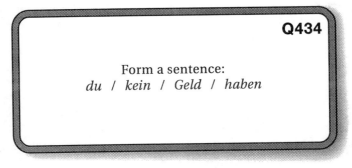

Q434

Form a sentence:
du / kein / Geld / haben

*Your Own Answer*_____

_____

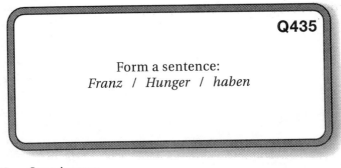

Q435

Form a sentence:
Franz / Hunger / haben

*Your Own Answer*_____

_____

Correct Answers

A433

Ich bin Student.

A434

Du hast kein Geld.

A435

Franz hat Hunger.

Questions

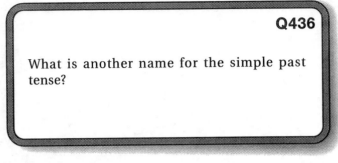

Q436

What is another name for the simple past tense?

*Your Own Answer*_____

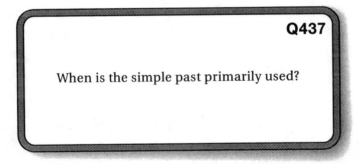

Q437

When is the simple past primarily used?

*Your Own Answer*_____

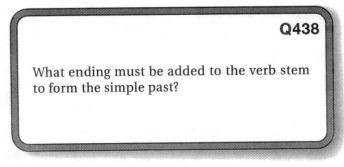

Q438

What ending must be added to the verb stem to form the simple past?

*Your Own Answer*_____

Correct Answers

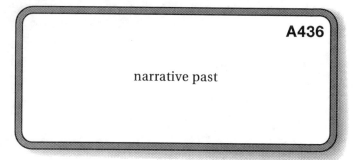

A436

narrative past

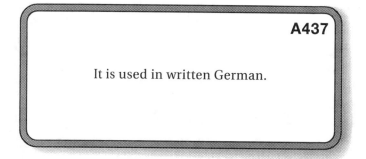

A437

It is used in written German.

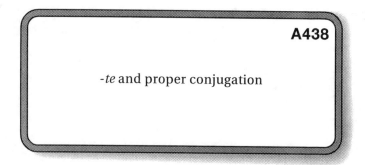

A438

-te and proper conjugation

Questions

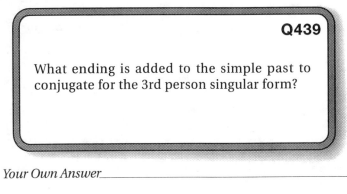

Q439

What ending is added to the simple past to conjugate for the 3rd person singular form?

*Your Own Answer*_____

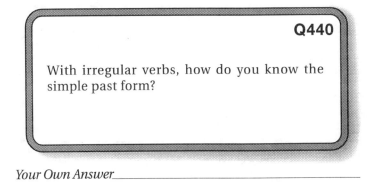

Q440

With irregular verbs, how do you know the simple past form?

*Your Own Answer*_____

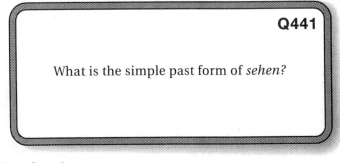

Q441

What is the simple past form of *sehen?*

*Your Own Answer*_____

Correct Answers

It must be memorized.

sah

Questions

Q442

Ich (machen) meine Hausaufgaben. (simple past)

*Your Own Answer*_____

Q443

Frank (spielen) Fußball. (simple past)

*Your Own Answer*_____

Q444

Wir (singen) das Lied. (simple past)

*Your Own Answer*_____

Correct Answers

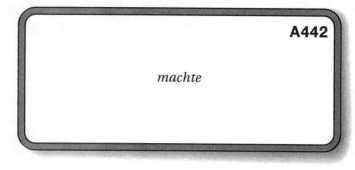

A442

machte

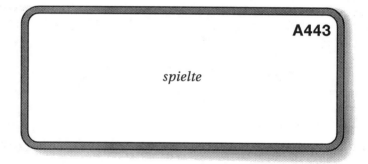

A443

spielte

A444

sangen

Questions

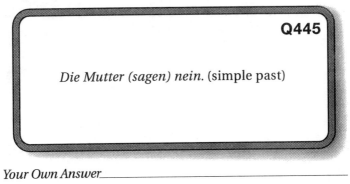

Q445

Die Mutter (sagen) nein. (simple past)

Your Own Answer_____

Q446

Sie (wissen) die Antwort. (simple past)

Your Own Answer_____

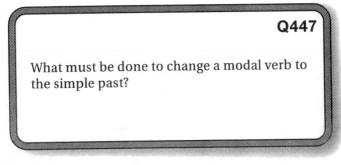

Q447

What must be done to change a modal verb to
the simple past?

Your Own Answer_____

Correct Answers

sagte

wußte

drop any umlauts; add -*te*; conjugate

Questions

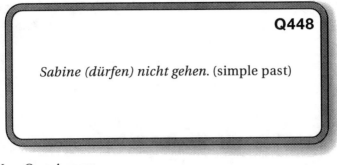

Q448

Sabine (dürfen) nicht gehen. (simple past)

Your Own Answer _____

_____

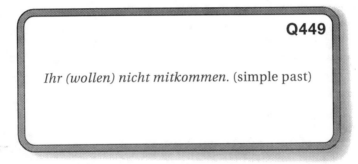

Q449

Ihr (wollen) nicht mitkommen. (simple past)

Your Own Answer _____

_____

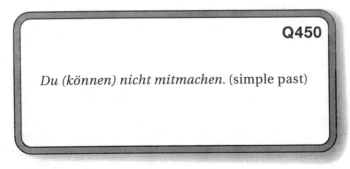

Q450

Du (können) nicht mitmachen. (simple past)

Your Own Answer _____

_____

Correct Answers

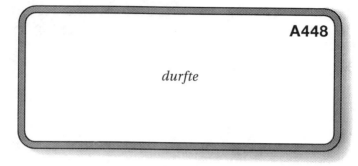

A448

durfte

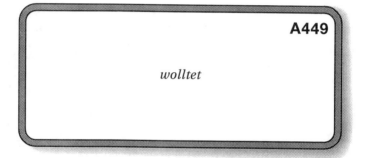

A449

wolltet

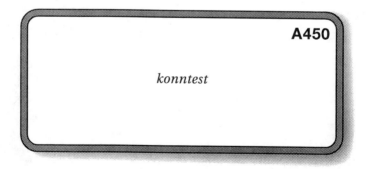

A450

konntest

Questions

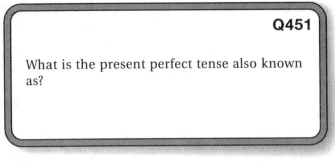

Q451

What is the present perfect tense also known as?

*Your Own Answer*_____

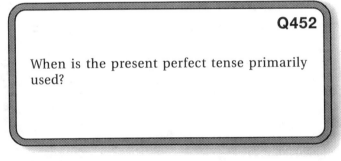

Q452

When is the present perfect tense primarily used?

*Your Own Answer*_____

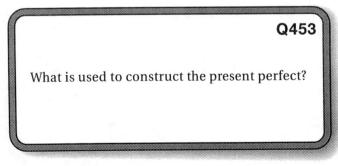

Q453

What is used to construct the present perfect?

*Your Own Answer*_____

Correct Answers

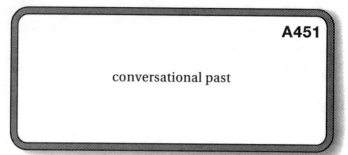

A451

conversational past

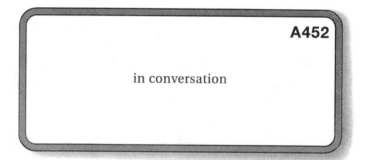

A452

in conversation

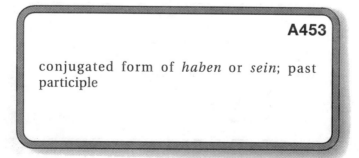

A453

conjugated form of *haben* or *sein*; past participle

Questions

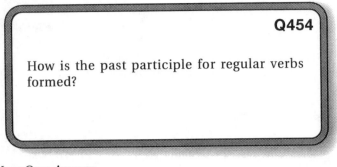

Q454

How is the past participle for regular verbs formed?

*Your Own Answer*_____

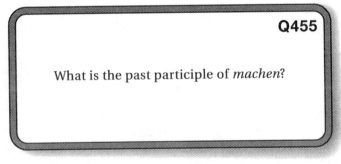

Q455

What is the past participle of *machen*?

*Your Own Answer*_____

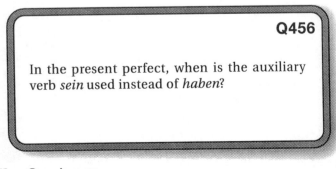

Q456

In the present perfect, when is the auxiliary verb *sein* used instead of *haben*?

*Your Own Answer*_____

Correct Answers

A454

add *ge-* prefix to 3rd person singular form

A455

gemacht

A456

When a change of location or condition is indicated

Questions

Q457

Where does the past participle go in the sentence?

*Your Own Answer*_____

Q458

True or False: Forming the past participle with a separable prefix verb, the prefix comes after the *ge-* prefix.

*Your Own Answer*_____

Q459

Ich _____ das _____. (machen) (present perfect)

*Your Own Answer*_____

Correct Answers

A457

at the end

A458

False. It comes before the *ge-* prefix

A459

habe… gemacht

Questions

Er _____ *lang* _____. *(arbeiten)* (present perfect)

*Your Own Answer*_____

Katja _____ *nach New York* _____. *(fahren)* (present perfect)

*Your Own Answer*_____

Ich _____ *sein Auto* _____. *(fahren)* (present perfect)

*Your Own Answer*_____

Correct Answers

A460

hat... gearbeitet

A461

ist... gefahren

A462

habe... gefahren

Questions

Rolf_____ Wasser _____. (trinken) (present perfect)

*Your Own Answer*_____

Thomas _____ seine Tante _____ (sehen) (present perfect)

*Your Own Answer*_____

Franz _____ das Fenster _____. (aufmachen) (present perfect)

*Your Own Answer*_____

Correct Answers

A463

hat... getrunken

A464

hat... gesehen

A465

hat... aufgemacht

Questions

Q466

What is the function of the past perfect tense?

*Your Own Answer*_____

Q467

What is used to construct the past perfect?

*Your Own Answer*_____

Q468

Conjugate the simple past of *haben.*

*Your Own Answer*_____

Correct Answers

A466

To express a time farther in the past than the simple past or present perfect

A467

The conjugated form of the simple past of *haben* or *sein* + past participle

A468

hatte; hattest; hatte; hatten; hattet; hatten

Questions

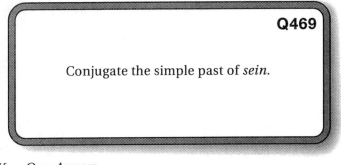

Q469

Conjugate the simple past of *sein*.

*Your Own Answer*_____

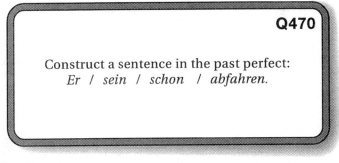

Q470

Construct a sentence in the past perfect:
Er / sein / schon / abfahren.

*Your Own Answer*_____

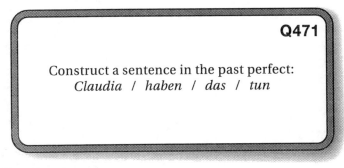

Q471

Construct a sentence in the past perfect:
Claudia / haben / das / tun

*Your Own Answer*_____

Correct Answers

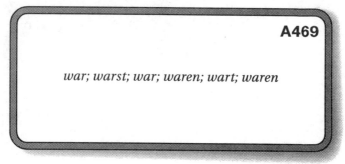

A469

war; warst; war; waren; wart; waren

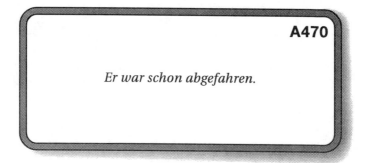

A470

Er war schon abgefahren.

A471

Claudia hatte das getan.

Questions

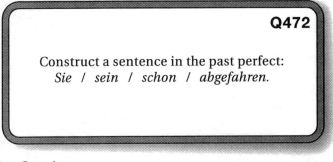

Q472

Construct a sentence in the past perfect:
Sie / sein / schon / abgefahren.

*Your Own Answer*_____

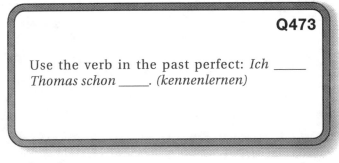

Q473

Use the verb in the past perfect: *Ich* _____
Thomas schon _____. *(kennenlernen)*

*Your Own Answer*_____

Q474

Bis dahin, _____ *ich nie ein Auto* _____. *(fahren)*
(past perfect)

*Your Own Answer*_____

Correct Answers

A472

Sie waren schon abgefahren.

A473

hatte... kennengelernt.

A474

hatte... gefahren

Questions

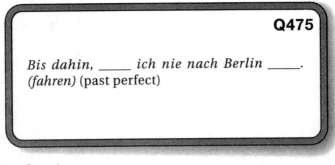

Q475

Bis dahin, _____ ich nie nach Berlin _____.
(fahren) (past perfect)

Your Own Answer_____

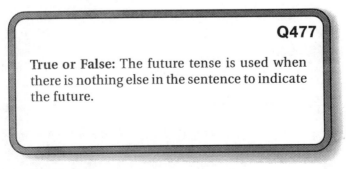

Q476

True or False: If the sentence contains an adverb indicating that the future is intended, the future tense is used.

Your Own Answer_____

Q477

True or False: The future tense is used when there is nothing else in the sentence to indicate the future.

Your Own Answer_____

Correct Answers

A475

war... gefahren

A476

False. Present tense

A477

True

Questions

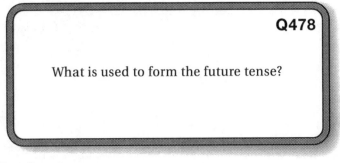

Q478

What is used to form the future tense?

*Your Own Answer*_____

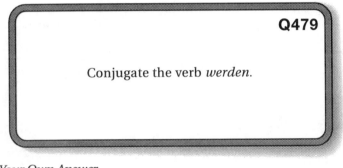

Q479

Conjugate the verb *werden*.

*Your Own Answer*_____

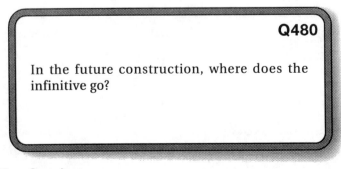

Q480

In the future construction, where does the infinitive go?

*Your Own Answer*_____

Correct Answers

A478

the correct conjugation of *werden* + infinitive

A479

werde; wirst; wird; werden; werdet; werden

A480

At the end of the sentence.

Questions

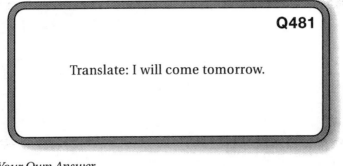

Q481

Translate: I will come tomorrow.

*Your Own Answer*_____

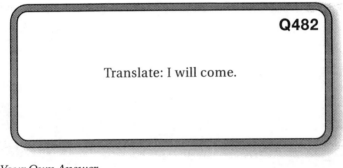

Q482

Translate: I will come.

*Your Own Answer*_____

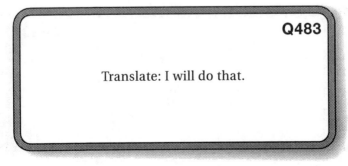

Q483

Translate: I will do that.

*Your Own Answer*_____

Correct Answers

A481

Ich komme morgen.

A482

Ich werde kommen.

A483

Ich werde das machen.

Questions

Translate: I will do that tomorrow.

*Your Own Answer*_____

Translate: I will work next week.

*Your Own Answer*_____

Translate: I will work.

*Your Own Answer*_____

Correct Answers

A484

Ich mache das morgen.

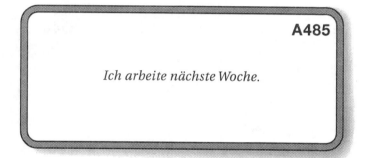

A485

Ich arbeite nächste Woche.

A486

Ich werde arbeiten.

Questions

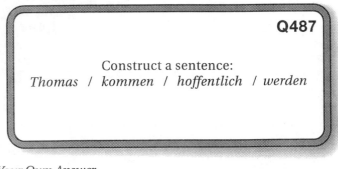

Q487

Construct a sentence:
Thomas / kommen / hoffentlich / werden

Your Own Answer_____

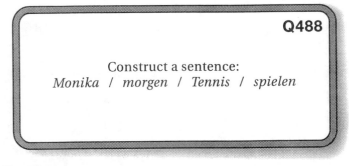

Q488

Construct a sentence:
Monika / morgen / Tennis / spielen

Your Own Answer_____

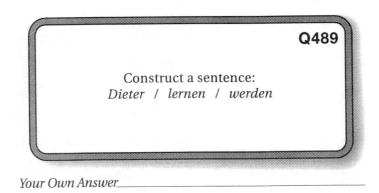

Q489

Construct a sentence:
Dieter / lernen / werden

Your Own Answer_____

Correct Answers

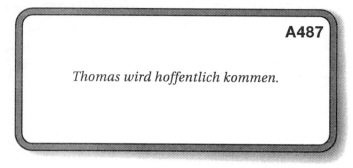

A487

Thomas wird hoffentlich kommen.

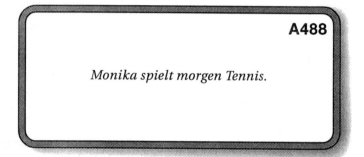

A488

Monika spielt morgen Tennis.

A489

Dieter wird lernen.

Questions

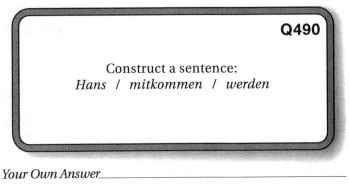

Q490

Construct a sentence:
Hans / mitkommen / werden

*Your Own Answer*_____

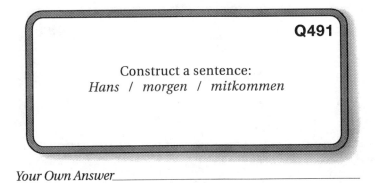

Q491

Construct a sentence:
Hans / morgen / mitkommen

*Your Own Answer*_____

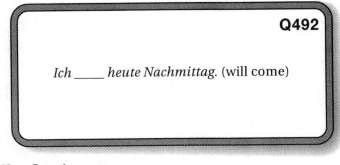

Q492

Ich _____ heute Nachmittag. (will come)

*Your Own Answer*_____

Correct Answers

A490

Hans wird mitkommen.

A491

Hans kommt morgen mit.

A492

komme

Questions

Ich _____ das Spiel _____. (will play)

*Your Own Answer*_____

_____

Ihr _____ nicht _____. (will sing)

*Your Own Answer*_____

_____

Du ___ deine Arbeit _____. (will do)

*Your Own Answer*_____

_____

Correct Answers

A493

werde... spielen

A494

werdet... singen

A495

wirst... machen

Questions

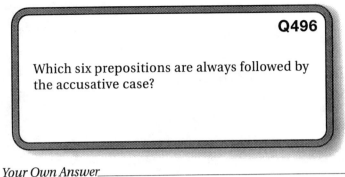

Q496

Which six prepositions are always followed by the accusative case?

*Your Own Answer*_____

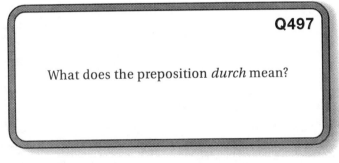

Q497

What does the preposition *durch* mean?

*Your Own Answer*_____

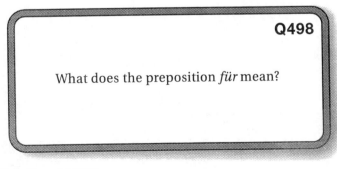

Q498

What does the preposition *für* mean?

*Your Own Answer*_____

Correct Answers

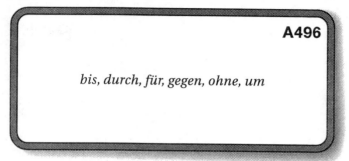

A496

bis, durch, für, gegen, ohne, um

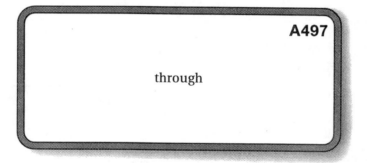

A497

through

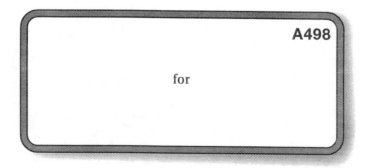

A498

for

Questions

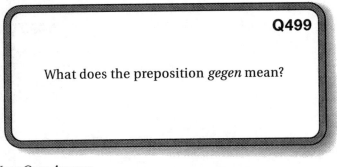

Q499

What does the preposition *gegen* mean?

*Your Own Answer*_____

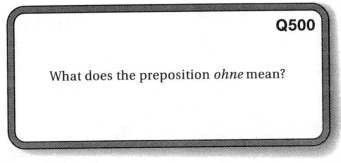

Q500

What does the preposition *ohne* mean?

*Your Own Answer*_____

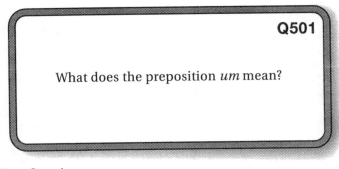

Q501

What does the preposition *um* mean?

*Your Own Answer*_____

Correct Answers

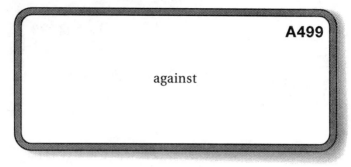

A499

against

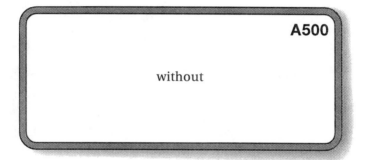

A500

without

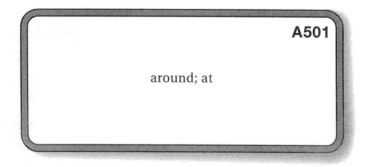

A501

around; at

Questions

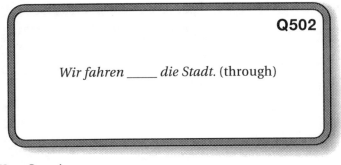

Q502

Wir fahren _____ die Stadt. (through)

Your Own Answer_____

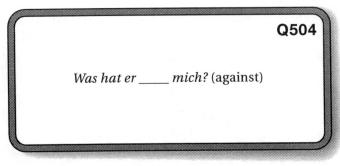

Q503

Ich habe etwas _____ dich. (for)

Your Own Answer_____

Q504

Was hat er _____ mich? (against)

Your Own Answer_____

Correct Answers

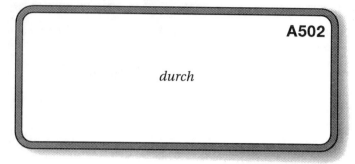

A502

durch

A503

für

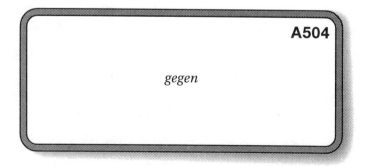

A504

gegen

Questions

Q505

Sie kommen _____ die Kinder. (without)

Your Own Answer_____

Q506

Der Hund läuft _____ den Wagen. (around)

Your Own Answer_____

Q507

_____ wieviel Uhr fahren wir los? (at)

Your Own Answer_____

Correct Answers

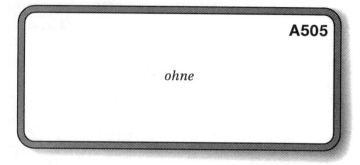

A505

ohne

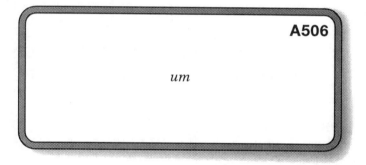

A506

um

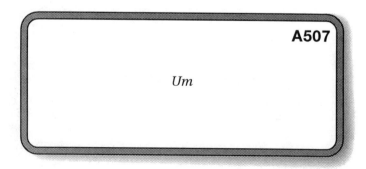

A507

Um

Questions

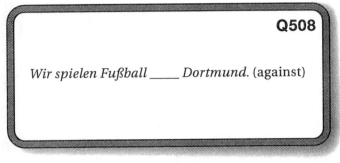

Q508

Wir spielen Fußball _____ Dortmund. (against)

Your Own Answer_____

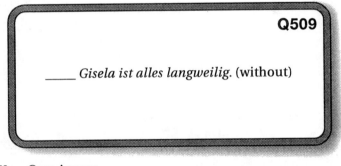

Q509

_____ Gisela ist alles langweilig. (without)

Your Own Answer_____

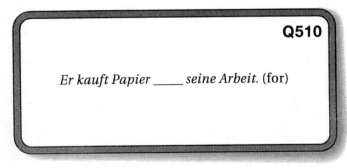

Q510

Er kauft Papier _____ seine Arbeit. (for)

Your Own Answer_____

Correct Answers

A508

gegen

A509

Ohne

A510

für

Questions

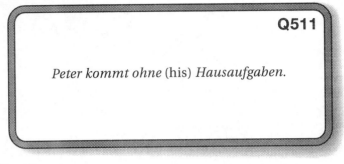

Q511

Peter kommt ohne (his) Hausaufgaben.

Your Own Answer_____

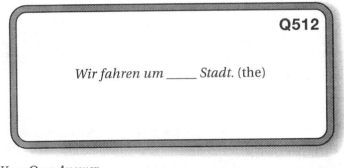

Q512

Wir fahren um _____ Stadt. (the)

Your Own Answer_____

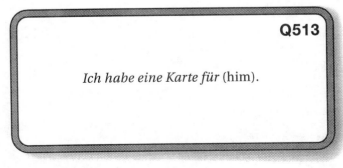

Q513

Ich habe eine Karte für (him).

Your Own Answer_____

Correct Answers

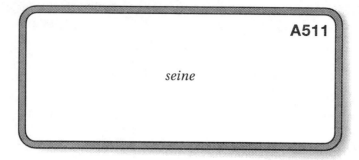

A511

seine

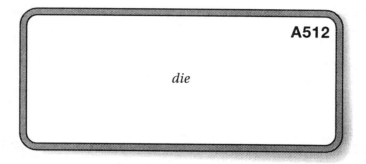

A512

die

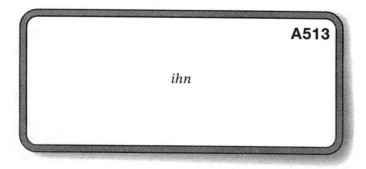

A513

ihn

Questions

Q514

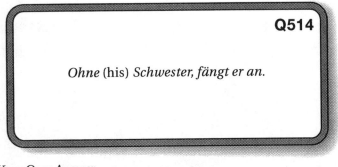

Ohne (his) *Schwester, fängt er an.*

Your Own Answer_____

Q515

Die Kinder laufen durch _____ Straßen. (the)

Your Own Answer_____

Q516

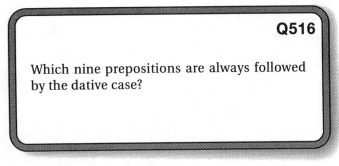

Which nine prepositions are always followed by the dative case?

Your Own Answer_____

Correct Answers

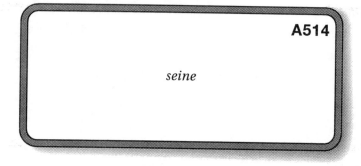

A514

seine

A515

die

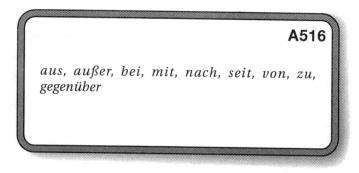

A516

aus, außer, bei, mit, nach, seit, von, zu, gegenüber

Questions

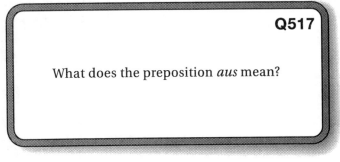

Q517

What does the preposition *aus* mean?

*Your Own Answer*_____

_____

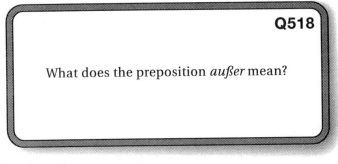

Q518

What does the preposition *außer* mean?

*Your Own Answer*_____

_____

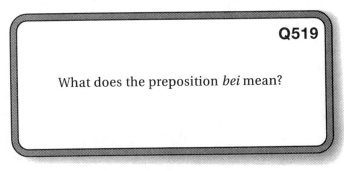

Q519

What does the preposition *bei* mean?

*Your Own Answer*_____

_____

Correct Answers

Questions

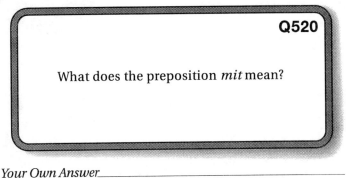

Q520

What does the preposition *mit* mean?

*Your Own Answer*_____

_____

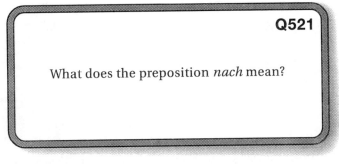

Q521

What does the preposition *nach* mean?

*Your Own Answer*_____

_____

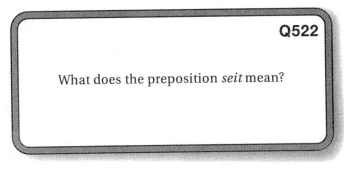

Q522

What does the preposition *seit* mean?

*Your Own Answer*_____

_____

Correct Answers

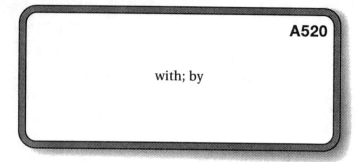

A520

with; by

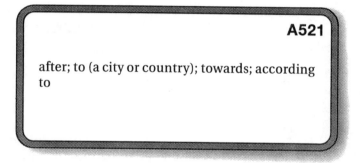

A521

after; to (a city or country); towards; according to

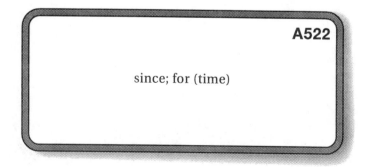

A522

since; for (time)

Questions

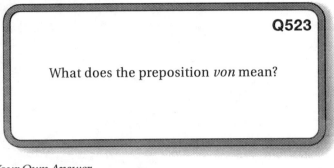

Q523

What does the preposition *von* mean?

*Your Own Answer*_____

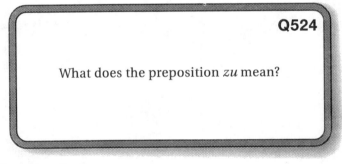

Q524

What does the preposition *zu* mean?

*Your Own Answer*_____

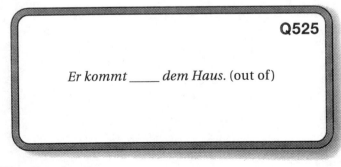

Q525

Er kommt _____ dem Haus. (out of)

*Your Own Answer*_____

Correct Answers

of; from; by

to; for (purpose)

aus

Questions

Q526

_____ *mir, war niemand dort.* (besides)

*Your Own Answer*_____

Q527

Sie wohnt _____ uns. (near)

*Your Own Answer*_____

Q528

Kommst du _____ uns? (with)

*Your Own Answer*_____

Correct Answers

A526

Außer

A527

bei

A528

mit

Questions

Q529

Er fährt_____ dem Zug. (with)

Your Own Answer_____

Q530

Was machst du _____ der Arbeit? (after)

Your Own Answer_____

Q531

Wir fliegen _____ Berlin. (to)

Your Own Answer_____

Correct Answers

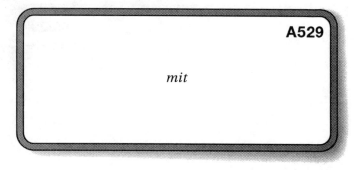

A529

mit

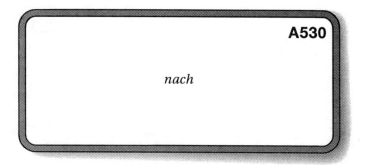

A530

nach

A531

nach

Questions

Q532

Wir arbeiten _____ Januar hier. (since)

Your Own Answer_____

Q533

Ist Sabine eine Freundin _____ dir? (of)

Your Own Answer_____

Q534

Er arbeitete _____ Januar bis Mai dort. (from)

Your Own Answer_____

Correct Answers

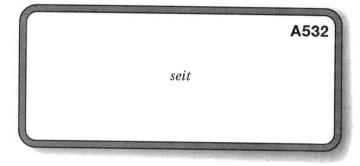

A532

seit

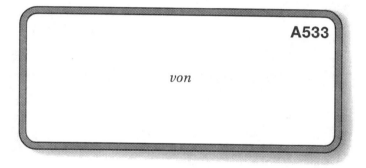

A533

von

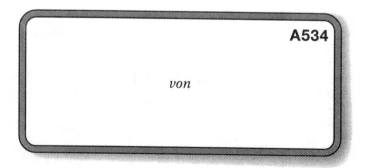

A534

von

Questions

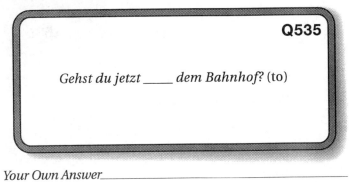

Q535

Gehst du jetzt _____ dem Bahnhof? (to)

Your Own Answer_____

_____

Q536

Er kommt aus _____ Kirche. (the)

Your Own Answer_____

_____

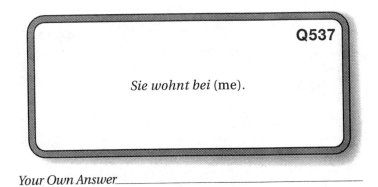

Q537

Sie wohnt bei (me).

Your Own Answer_____

_____

Correct Answers

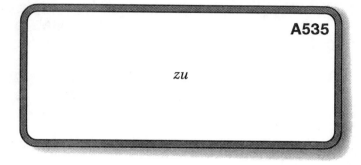

A535

zu

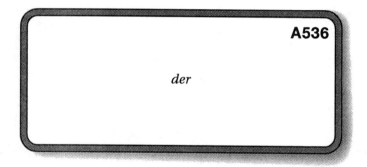

A536

der

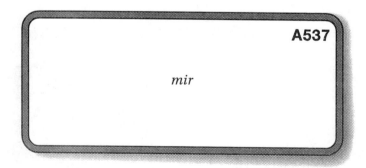

A537

mir

Questions

Kommst du mit (him)?

Your Own Answer_____

Er fährt mit_____ Bus. (the)

Your Own Answer_____

Was machst du nach _____ Film? (the)

Your Own Answer_____

Correct Answers

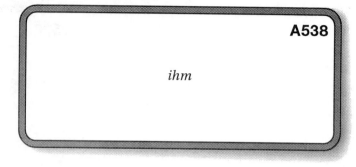

A538

ihm

A539

dem

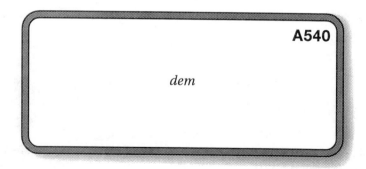

A540

dem

Questions

Q541

Ist Sabine eine Freundin von (her)?

*Your Own Answer*_____

_____

Q542

Was machst du nach _____ Schüle? (the)

*Your Own Answer*_____

_____

Q543

Gehst du zu _____ Universität? (the)

*Your Own Answer*_____

_____

Correct Answers

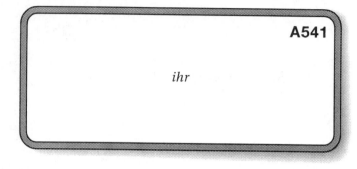

A541

ihr

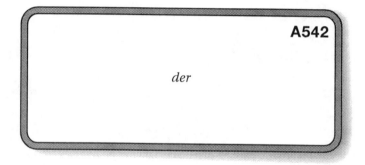

A542

der

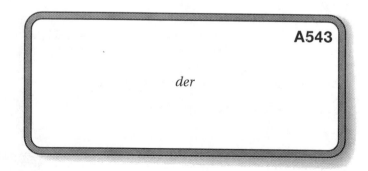

A543

der

Questions

Monika geht (from) *der Kirche* (to) *dem Bahnhof.*

*Your Own Answer*_____

Katja fährt (from) *Berlin* (to) *Köln.*

*Your Own Answer*_____

Which four prepositions take the genitive case?

*Your Own Answer*_____

Correct Answers

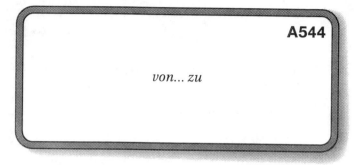

A544

von... zu

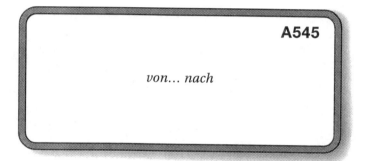

A545

von... nach

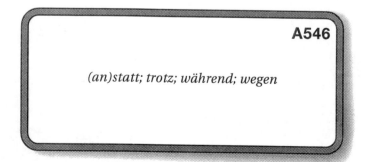

A546

(an)statt; trotz; während; wegen

Questions

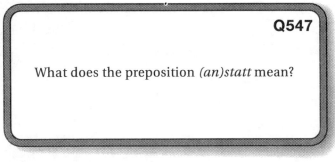

Q547

What does the preposition *(an)statt* mean?

*Your Own Answer*_____

_____

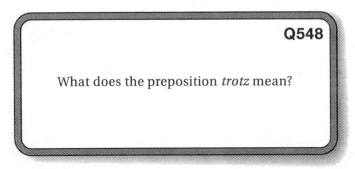

Q548

What does the preposition *trotz* mean?

*Your Own Answer*_____

_____

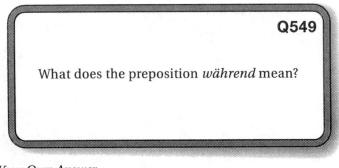

Q549

What does the preposition *während* mean?

*Your Own Answer*_____

_____

Correct Answers

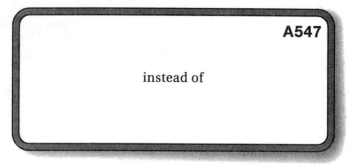

A547

instead of

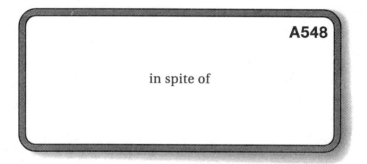

A548

in spite of

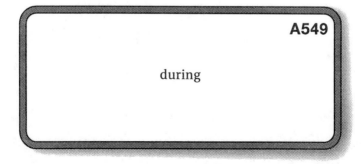

A549

during

Questions

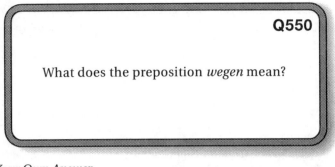

Q550

What does the preposition *wegen* mean?

*Your Own Answer*_____

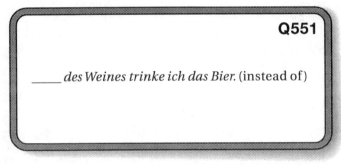

Q551

_____ *des Weines trinke ich das Bier.* (instead of)

*Your Own Answer*_____

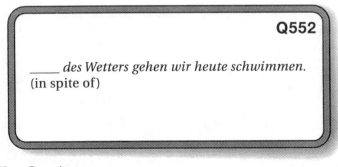

Q552

_____ *des Wetters gehen wir heute schwimmen.*
(in spite of)

*Your Own Answer*_____

Correct Answers

because of

(An)statt

Trotz

Questions

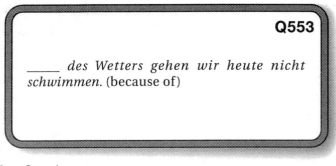

Q553

_____ des Wetters gehen wir heute nicht schwimmen. (because of)

_Your Own Answer_____

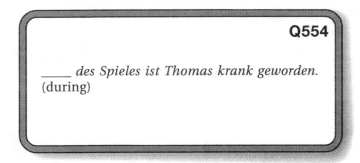

Q554

_____ des Spieles ist Thomas krank geworden. (during)

_Your Own Answer_____

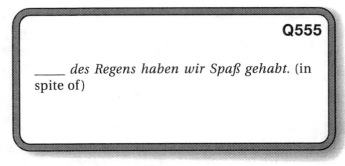

Q555

_____ des Regens haben wir Spaß gehabt. (in spite of)

_Your Own Answer_____

Correct Answers

A553

Wegen

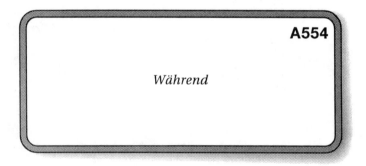

A554

Während

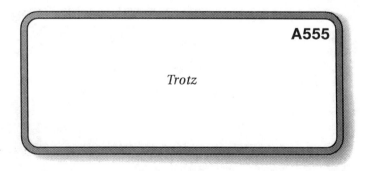

A555

Trotz

Questions

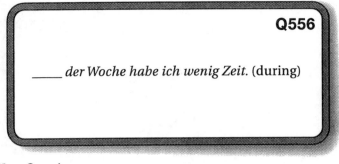

Q556

_____ der Woche habe ich wenig Zeit. (during)

Your Own Answer_____

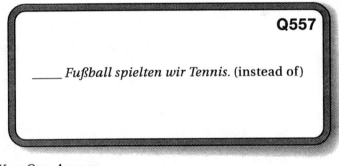

Q557

_____ Fußball spielten wir Tennis. (instead of)

Your Own Answer_____

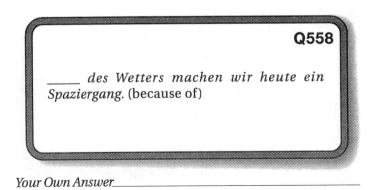

Q558

_____ des Wetters machen wir heute ein Spaziergang. (because of)

Your Own Answer_____

Correct Answers

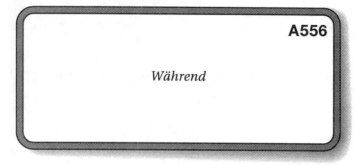

A556

Während

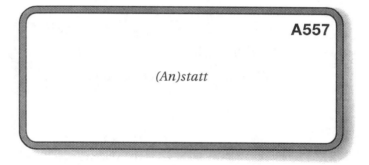

A557

(An)statt

A558

Wegen

Questions

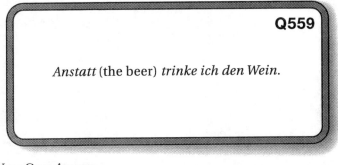

Q559

Anstatt (the beer) *trinke ich den Wein.*

*Your Own Answer*_____

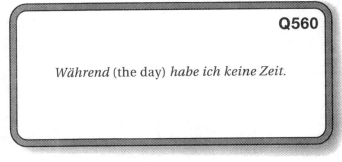

Q560

Während (the day) *habe ich keine Zeit.*

*Your Own Answer*_____

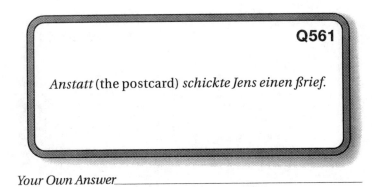

Q561

Anstatt (the postcard) *schickte Jens einen ßrief.*

*Your Own Answer*_____

Correct Answers

des Bieres

des Tages

der Postkarte

Questions

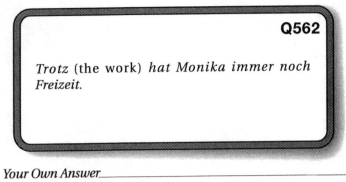

Q562

Trotz (the work) *hat Monika immer noch Freizeit.*

*Your Own Answer*_____

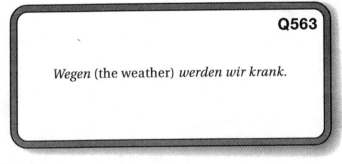

Q563

Wegen (the weather) *werden wir krank.*

*Your Own Answer*_____

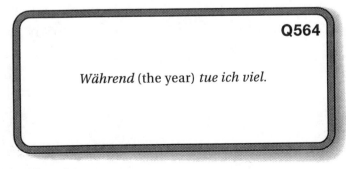

Q564

Während (the year) *tue ich viel.*

*Your Own Answer*_____

Correct Answers

der Arbeit

des Wetters

des Jahres

Questions

Trotz (the rain) *ist alles immer noch trocknet.*

Your Own Answer

Which prepositions can be used as either dative or accusative?

Your Own Answer

What does the preposition *an* mean?

Your Own Answer

Correct Answers

des Regens

an, auf, hinter, in, neben, über, unter, vor, zwischen

on; at; by; on the side of

Questions

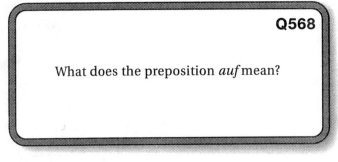

Q568

What does the preposition *auf* mean?

*Your Own Answer*_____

_____

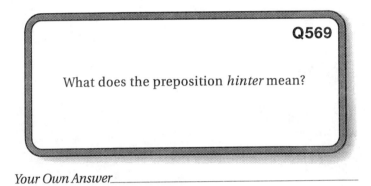

Q569

What does the preposition *hinter* mean?

*Your Own Answer*_____

_____

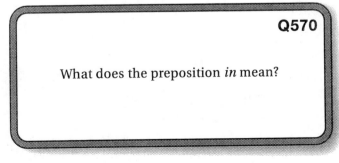

Q570

What does the preposition *in* mean?

*Your Own Answer*_____

_____

Correct Answers

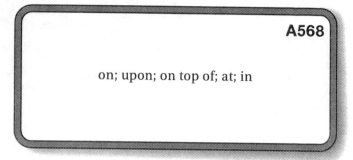

A568

on; upon; on top of; at; in

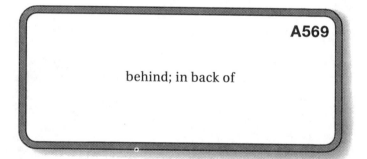

A569

behind; in back of

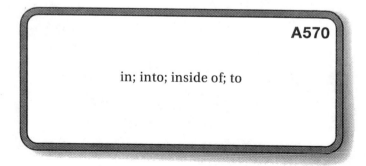

A570

in; into; inside of; to

Questions

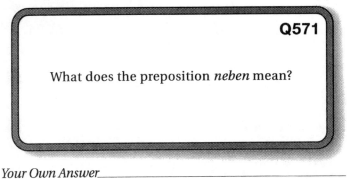

Q571

What does the preposition *neben* mean?

*Your Own Answer*_____

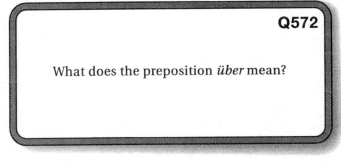

Q572

What does the preposition *über* mean?

*Your Own Answer*_____

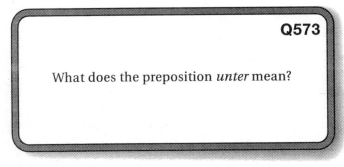

Q573

What does the preposition *unter* mean?

*Your Own Answer*_____

Correct Answers

A571

next to; beside

A572

over; above; across; beyond; via; about;
concerning

A573

under; among; below

Questions

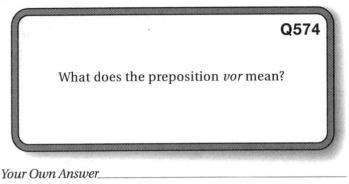

Q574

What does the preposition *vor* mean?

*Your Own Answer*_____

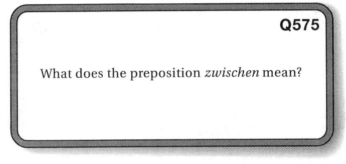

Q575

What does the preposition *zwischen* mean?

*Your Own Answer*_____

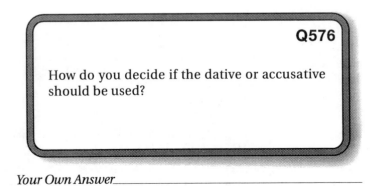

Q576

How do you decide if the dative or accusative should be used?

*Your Own Answer*_____

Correct Answers

A574

in front of; ago

A575

between

A576

If it answers the question *wo?* (where), dative is used. If it answers the question *wohin?* (where to), accusative is used.

Questions

Q577

Das Buch liegt (on) _____ *Tisch.*

.

Your Own Answer_____

Q578

Er legt das Buch (on) _____ *Tisch.*

Your Own Answer_____

Q579

Das Bild hängt (on) _____ *Wand.*

Your Own Answer_____

Correct Answers

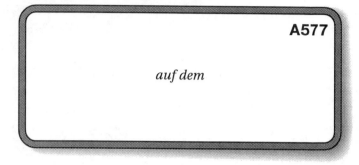

A577

auf dem

A578

auf den

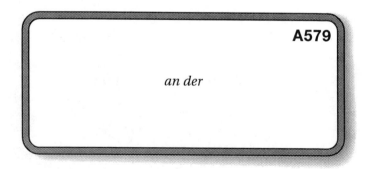

A579

an der

Questions

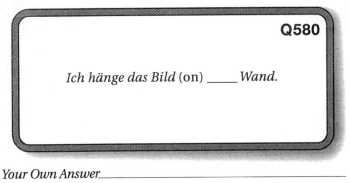

Q580

Ich hänge das Bild (on) _____ *Wand.*

*Your Own Answer*_____

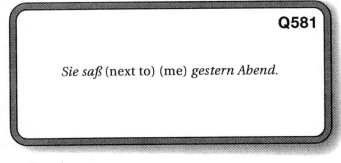

Q581

Sie saß (next to) (me) *gestern Abend.*

*Your Own Answer*_____

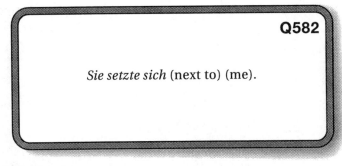

Q582

Sie setzte sich (next to) (me).

*Your Own Answer*_____

Correct Answers

A580

an die

A581

neben mir

A582

neben mich

Questions

Q583

Der Hund liegt (under) _____ *Tisch.*

*Your Own Answer*_____

Q584

Der Ball rollt (under) _____ *Tisch.*

*Your Own Answer*_____

Q585

Das Auto steht (in front of) _____ *Haus.*

*Your Own Answer*_____

Correct Answers

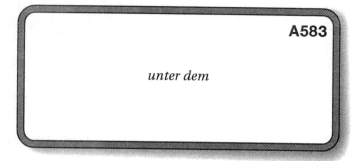

A583

unter dem

A584

unter den

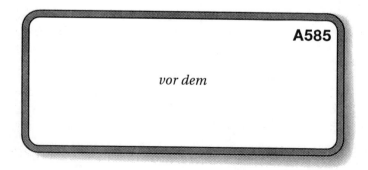

A585

vor dem

Questions

Er fährt das Auto (in front of) *Haus.*

Your Own Answer_____

Wir arbeiten (behind) _____ *Haus.*

Your Own Answer_____

Wir gehen (behind) _____ *Haus.*

Your Own Answer_____

Correct Answers

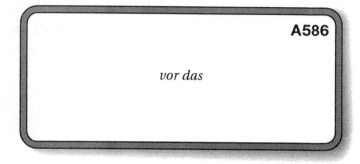

A586

vor das

A587

hinter dem

A588

hinter das

Questions

Q589

Ich gehe gern (in) (this) *Restaurant.*

*Your Own Answer*_____

Q590

Ich esse gern (in) (this) *Restaurant.*

*Your Own Answer*_____

Q591

Sie hängt die Lampe (over) _____ *Tisch.*

*Your Own Answer*_____

Correct Answers

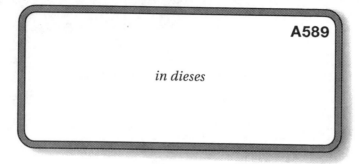

A589

in dieses

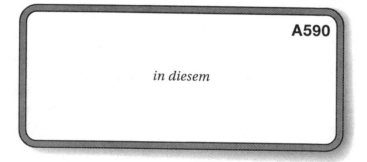

A590

in diesem

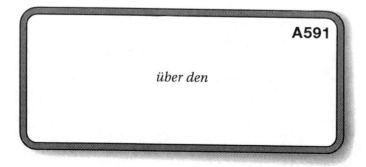

A591

über den

Questions

Q592

Die Lampe hängt (over) _____ *Tisch.*

*Your Own Answer*_____

Q593

Wir gehen (across) _____ *Straße.*

*Your Own Answer*_____

Q594

Mein Wagen steht (between) (the green) *und*
_____ (the blue) *Auto.*

*Your Own Answer*_____

Correct Answers

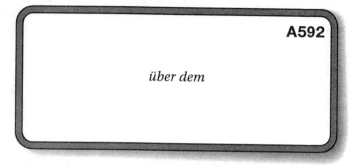

A592

über dem

A593

über die

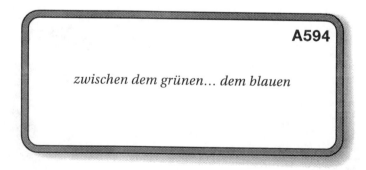

A594

zwischen dem grünen... dem blauen

Questions

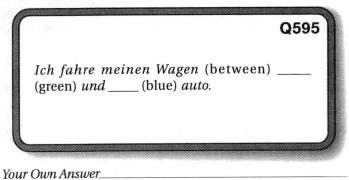

Q595

Ich fahre meinen Wagen (between) _____
(green) *und* _____ (blue) *auto.*

Your Own Answer _____

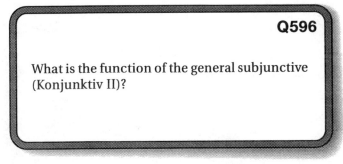

Q596

What is the function of the general subjunctive
(Konjunktiv II)?

Your Own Answer _____

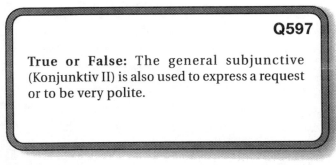

Q597

True or False: The general subjunctive
(Konjunktiv II) is also used to express a request
or to be very polite.

Your Own Answer _____

Correct Answers

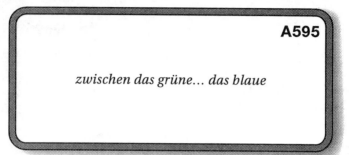

A595

zwischen das grüne... das blaue

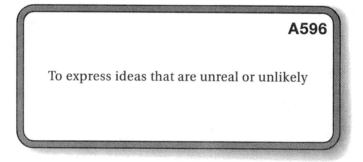

A596

To express ideas that are unreal or unlikely

A597

True

Questions

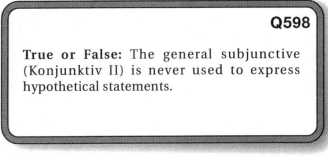

Q598

True or False: The general subjunctive (Konjunktiv II) is never used to express hypothetical statements.

*Your Own Answer*_____

Q599

True or False: The general subjunctive (Konjunktiv II) can be used to express a wish.

*Your Own Answer*_____

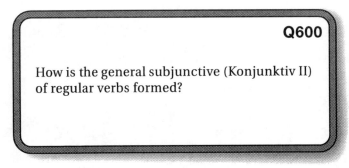

Q600

How is the general subjunctive (Konjunktiv II) of regular verbs formed?

*Your Own Answer*_____

Correct Answers

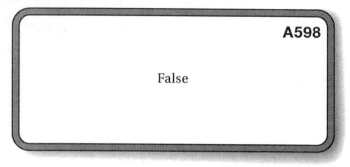

A598

False

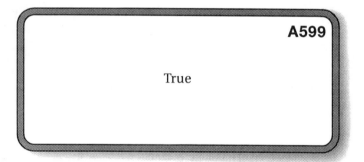

A599

True

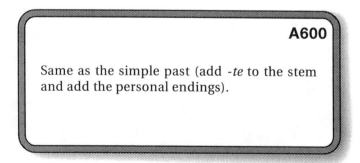

A600

Same as the simple past (add *-te* to the stem and add the personal endings).

Questions

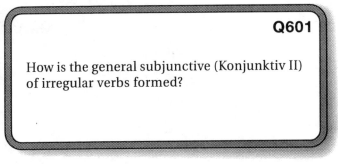

Q601

How is the general subjunctive (Konjunktiv II) of irregular verbs formed?

*Your Own Answer*_____

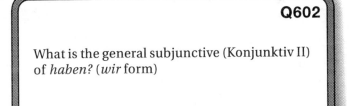

Q602

What is the general subjunctive (Konjunktiv II) of *haben?* (*wir* form)

*Your Own Answer*_____

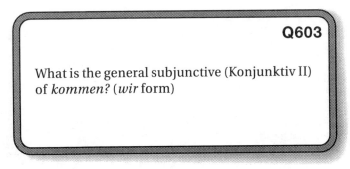

Q603

What is the general subjunctive (Konjunktiv II) of *kommen?* (*wir* form)

*Your Own Answer*_____

Correct Answers

A601

Only the personal endings are added to the stem of the simple past form. Third person singular takes an (*–e*) ending; *du* takes (*–est*) and *ihr* takes (*–et*). Vowels *a, o, u* add umlauts.

A602

hätten

A603

kämen

Questions

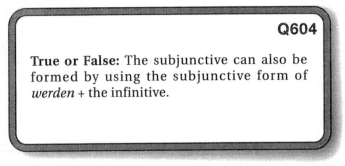

Q604

True or False: The subjunctive can also be formed by using the subjunctive form of *werden* + the infinitive.

*Your Own Answer*_____

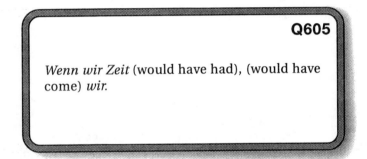

Q605

Wenn wir Zeit (would have had), (would have come) *wir.*

*Your Own Answer*_____

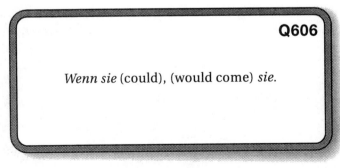

Q606

Wenn sie (could), (would come) *sie.*

*Your Own Answer*_____

Correct Answers

A604

True

A605

hätten... kämen

A606

könnte... käme

Questions

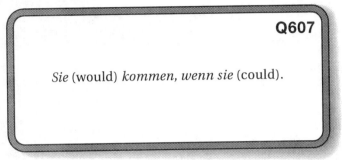

Q607

Sie (would) *kommen, wenn sie* (could).

*Your Own Answer*_____

_____

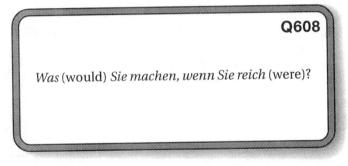

Q608

Was (would) *Sie machen, wenn Sie reich* (were)?

*Your Own Answer*_____

_____

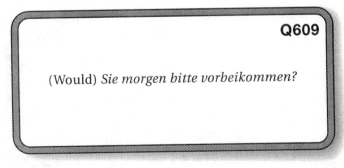

Q609

(Would) *Sie morgen bitte vorbeikommen?*

*Your Own Answer*_____

_____

Correct Answers

A607

würde... könnte

A608

würden... wären

A609

Würden

Questions

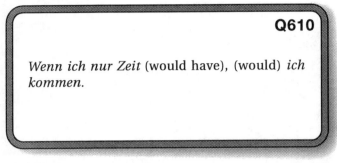

Q610

Wenn ich nur Zeit (would have), (would) *ich kommen.*

Your Own Answer_____

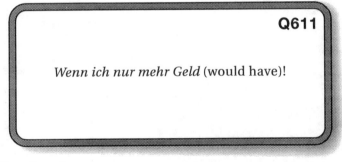

Q611

Wenn ich nur mehr Geld (would have)!

Your Own Answer_____

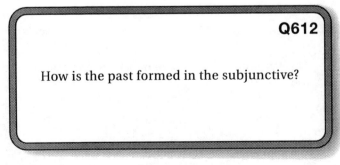

Q612

How is the past formed in the subjunctive?

Your Own Answer_____

Correct Answers

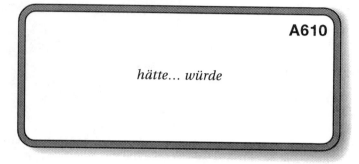

A610

hätte... würde

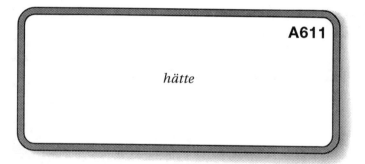

A611

hätte

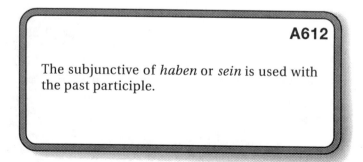

A612

The subjunctive of *haben* or *sein* is used with the past participle.

Questions

Q613

Wir (would have) *das* (done).

Your Own Answer_____

Q614

Er (would have come).

Your Own Answer_____

Q615

Sie (would have) *die Arbeit* (done).

Your Own Answer_____

Correct Answers

A613

hätten... getan

A614

wäre... gekommen

A615

hätte... gemacht

Questions

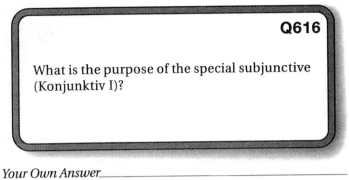

Q616

What is the purpose of the special subjunctive (Konjunktiv I)?

*Your Own Answer*_____

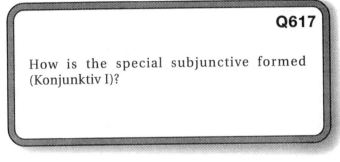

Q617

How is the special subjunctive formed (Konjunktiv I)?

*Your Own Answer*_____

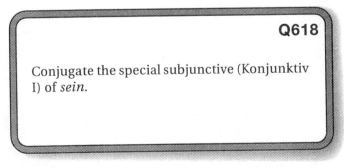

Q618

Conjugate the special subjunctive (Konjunktiv I) of *sein*.

*Your Own Answer*_____

Correct Answers

To convey thoughts and opinions of someone else in indirect discourse

The present tense of the verb is used, with the personal endings added to the stem; third person singular takes an (*–e*) ending; *du* takes (*–est*) and *ihr* takes (*–et*).

sei, sei(e)st, sei, seien, seiet, seien

Questions

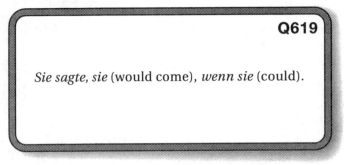

Q619

Sie sagte, sie (would come), *wenn sie* (could).

*Your Own Answer*_____

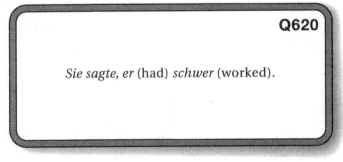

Q620

Sie sagte, er (had) *schwer* (worked).

*Your Own Answer*_____

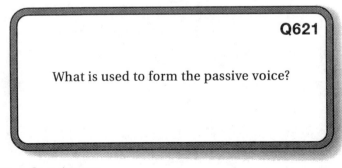

Q621

What is used to form the passive voice?

*Your Own Answer*_____

Correct Answers

A619

werde kommen... könne

A620

habe... gearbeitet

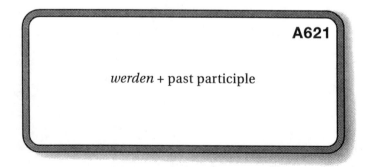

A621

werden + past participle

Questions

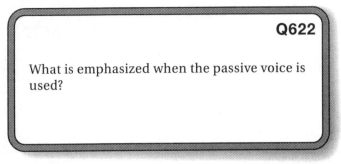

Q622

What is emphasized when the passive voice is used?

*Your Own Answer*_____

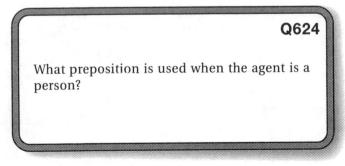

Q623

True or False: In a passive sentence, the agent, or person or thing performing the action, is often omitted.

*Your Own Answer*_____

Q624

What preposition is used when the agent is a person?

*Your Own Answer*_____

Correct Answers

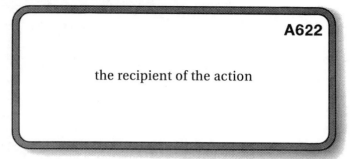

A622

the recipient of the action

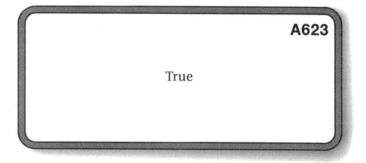

A623

True

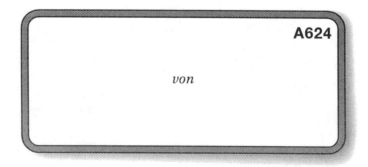

A624

von

Questions

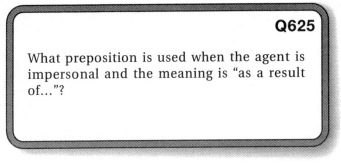

Q625

What preposition is used when the agent is impersonal and the meaning is "as a result of..."?

*Your Own Answer*_____

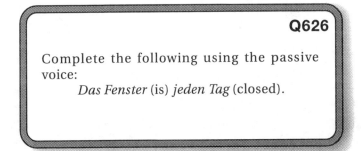

Q626

Complete the following using the passive voice:

> *Das Fenster* (is) *jeden Tag* (closed).

*Your Own Answer*_____

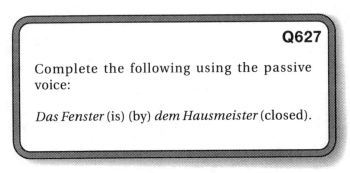

Q627

Complete the following using the passive voice:

Das Fenster (is) (by) *dem Hausmeister* (closed).

*Your Own Answer*_____

Correct Answers

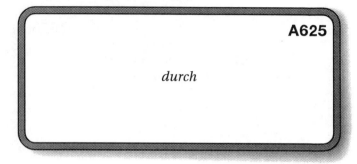

A625

durch

A626

wird... geschlossen

A627

wird von... geschlossen

Questions

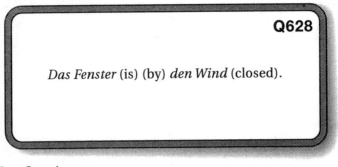

Q628

Das Fenster (is) (by) *den Wind* (closed).

*Your Own Answer*_____

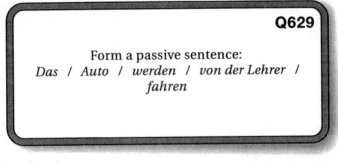

Q629

Form a passive sentence:
Das / Auto / werden / von der Lehrer / fahren

*Your Own Answer*_____

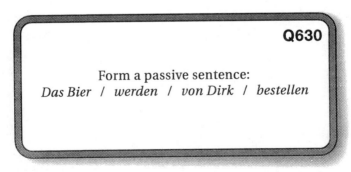

Q630

Form a passive sentence:
Das Bier / werden / von Dirk / bestellen

*Your Own Answer*_____

Correct Answers

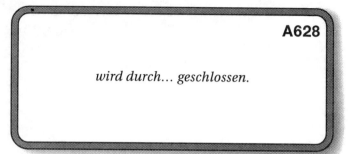

A628

wird durch... geschlossen.

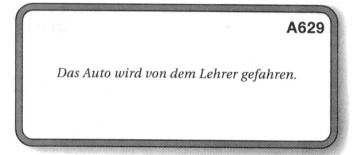

A629

Das Auto wird von dem Lehrer gefahren.

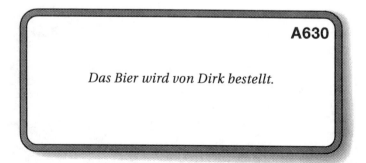

A630

Das Bier wird von Dirk bestellt.

Questions

How is the simple past tense of the passive voice formed?

*Your Own Answer*_____

What is the simple past form of *werden*? (*wir* form)

*Your Own Answer*_____

How is the present perfect tense of the passive voice formed?

*Your Own Answer*_____

Correct Answers

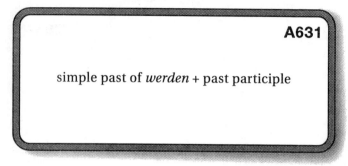

A631

simple past of *werden* + past participle

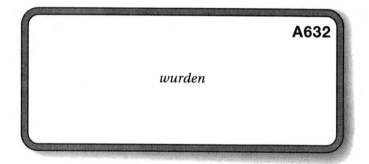

A632

wurden

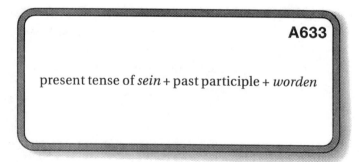

A633

present tense of *sein* + past participle + *worden*

Questions

Q634

True or False: The auxiliary verb *haben* is sometimes used with the present perfect of the passive voice

*Your Own Answer*_____

Q635

How is the past perfect tense formed in the passive voice?

*Your Own Answer*_____

Q636

True or False: *Worden* is a form that only appears in the perfect tenses of the passive voice.

*Your Own Answer*_____

Correct Answers

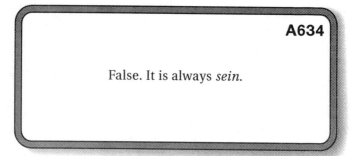

A634

False. It is always *sein*.

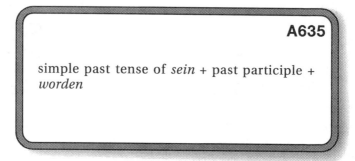

A635

simple past tense of *sein* + past participle + *worden*

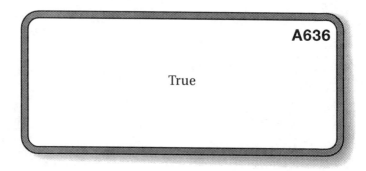

A636

True

Questions

Complete the following using the passive voice:
Das Fenster _____ vom Hausmeister (closed). (simple past)

*Your Own Answer*_____

Complete the following using the passive voice:
Das Fenster _____ vom Hausmeister (closed). (present perfect)

*Your Own Answer*_____

Complete the following using the passive voice:
Das Fenster _____ vom Hausmeister (closed). (past perfect)

*Your Own Answer*_____

Correct Answers

A637

wurde geschlossen

A638

ist... geschlossen worden

A639

war... geschlossen worden

Questions

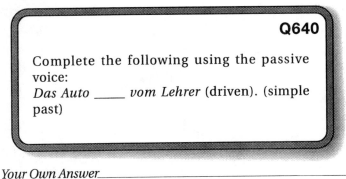

Q640

Complete the following using the passive voice:
Das Auto ____ *vom Lehrer* (driven). (simple past)

*Your Own Answer*_____

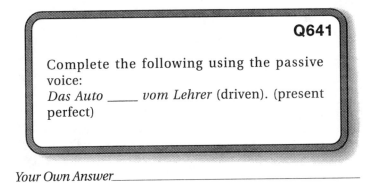

Q641

Complete the following using the passive voice:
Das Auto ____ *vom Lehrer* (driven). (present perfect)

*Your Own Answer*_____

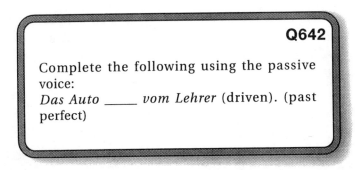

Q642

Complete the following using the passive voice:
Das Auto ____ *vom Lehrer* (driven). (past perfect)

*Your Own Answer*_____

Correct Answers

wurde... gefahren

ist... gefahren worden

war... gefahren worden

Questions

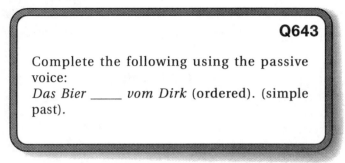

Q643

Complete the following using the passive voice:
Das Bier _____ vom Dirk (ordered). (simple past).

Your Own Answer_____

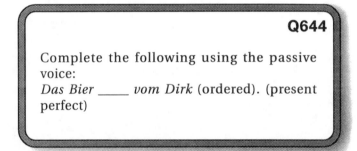

Q644

Complete the following using the passive voice:
Das Bier _____ vom Dirk (ordered). (present perfect)

Your Own Answer_____

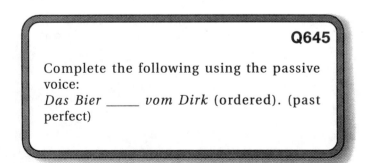

Q645

Complete the following using the passive voice:
Das Bier _____ vom Dirk (ordered). (past perfect)

Your Own Answer_____

Correct Answers

A643

wurde... bestellt

A644

ist... bestellt worden

A645

war... bestellt worden

Questions

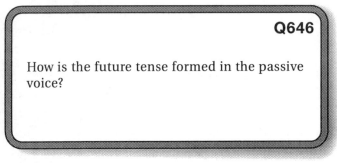

Q646

How is the future tense formed in the passive voice?

*Your Own Answer*_____

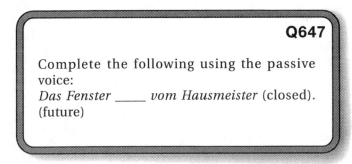

Q647

Complete the following using the passive voice:
Das Fenster _____ vom Hausmeister (closed). (future)

*Your Own Answer*_____

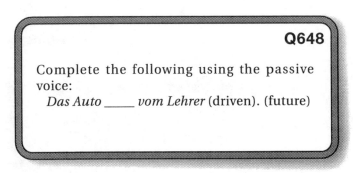

Q648

Complete the following using the passive voice:
Das Auto _____ vom Lehrer (driven). (future)

*Your Own Answer*_____

Correct Answers

A646

werden + past participle + werden

A647

wird... geschlossen werden

A648

wird... gefahren werden

Questions

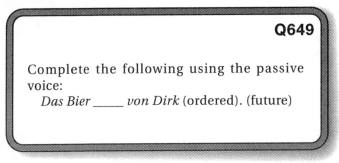

Q649

Complete the following using the passive voice:

Das Bier _____ von Dirk (ordered). (future)

*Your Own Answer*_____

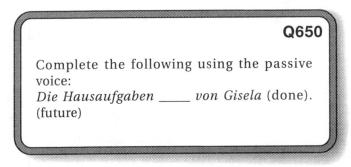

Q650

Complete the following using the passive voice:

Die Hausaufgaben _____ von Gisela (done). (future)

*Your Own Answer*_____

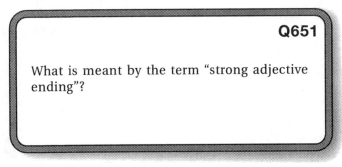

Q651

What is meant by the term "strong adjective ending"?

*Your Own Answer*_____

Correct Answers

A649

wird... bestellt werden

A650

werden... gemacht werden

A651

The adjective is not preceded by a definite or indefinite article.

Questions

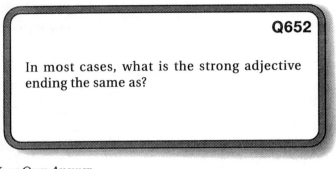

Q652

In most cases, what is the strong adjective ending the same as?

*Your Own Answer*_____

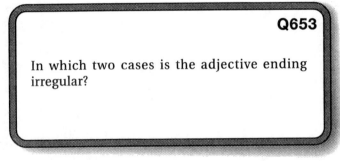

Q653

In which two cases is the adjective ending irregular?

*Your Own Answer*_____

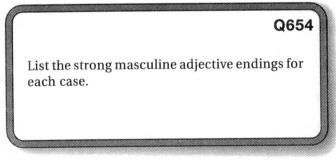

Q654

List the strong masculine adjective endings for each case.

*Your Own Answer*_____

Correct Answers

A652

ending of the definite article

A653

masculine and neuter in the genitive case

A654

Nominative: (*-er*); Accusative: (*-en*); Dative: (*-em*); Genitive: (*-en*)

Questions

List the strong femine adjective endings for each case.

*Your Own Answer*_____

List the strong neuter adjective endings for each case.

*Your Own Answer*_____

List the strong plural adjective endings for each case.

*Your Own Answer*_____

Correct Answers

A655

Nominative: (*-e*); Accusative: (*-e*); Dative: (*-er*);
Genitive: (*-er*)

A656

Nominative: (*-es*); Accusative: (*-es*); Dative:
(*-em*); Genitive: (*-en*)

A657

Nominative: (*-e*); Accusative: (*-e*); Dative: (*-en*);
Genitive: (*-er*)

Questions

Q658

(Gut-) Wein ist teuer.

Your Own Answer

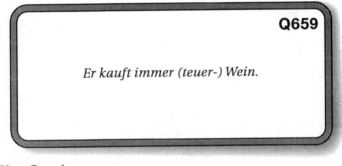

Q659

Er kauft immer (teuer-) Wein.

Your Own Answer

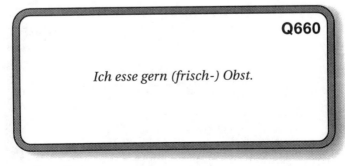

Q660

Ich esse gern (frisch-) Obst.

Your Own Answer

Correct Answers

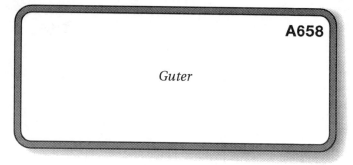

A658

Guter

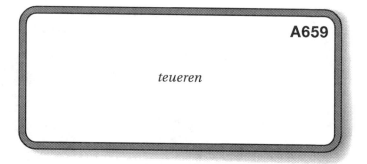

A659

teueren

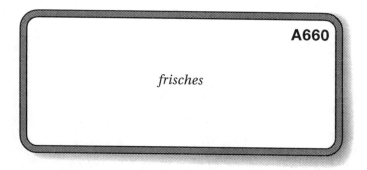

A660

frisches

Questions

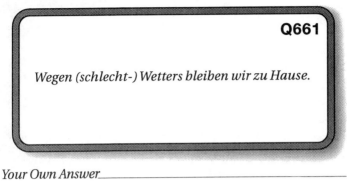

Q661

Wegen (schlecht-) Wetters bleiben wir zu Hause.

*Your Own Answer*_____

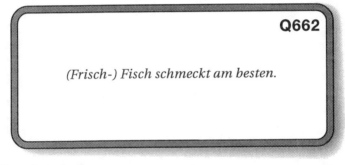

Q662

(Frisch-) Fisch schmeckt am besten.

*Your Own Answer*_____

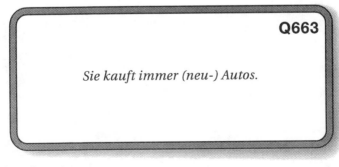

Q663

Sie kauft immer (neu-) Autos.

*Your Own Answer*_____

Correct Answers

A661

schlechten

A662

Frischer

A663

neue

Questions

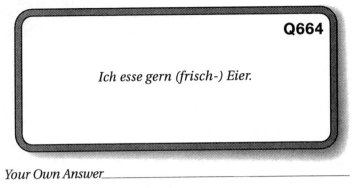

Q664

Ich esse gern (frisch-) Eier.

*Your Own Answer*_____

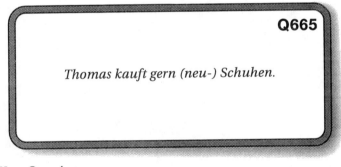

Q665

Thomas kauft gern (neu-) Schuhen.

*Your Own Answer*_____

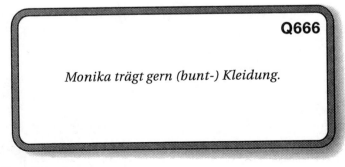

Q666

Monika trägt gern (bunt-) Kleidung.

*Your Own Answer*_____

Correct Answers

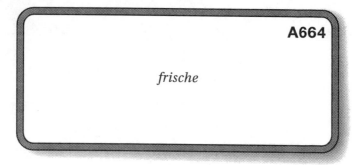

A664

frische

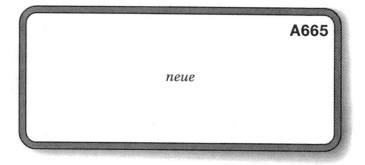

A665

neue

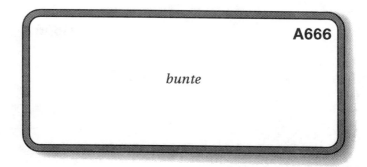

A666

bunte

Questions

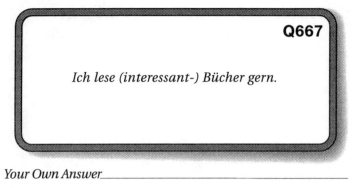

Q667

Ich lese (interessant-) Bücher gern.

*Your Own Answer*_____

_____

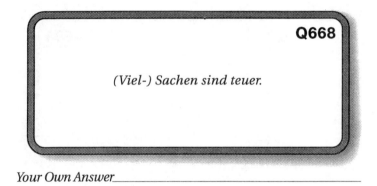

Q668

(Viel-) Sachen sind teuer.

*Your Own Answer*_____

_____

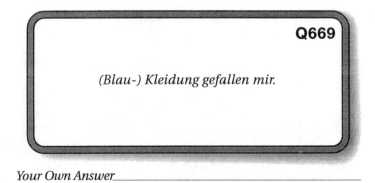

Q669

(Blau-) Kleidung gefallen mir.

*Your Own Answer*_____

_____

Correct Answers

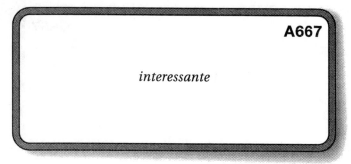

A667

interessante

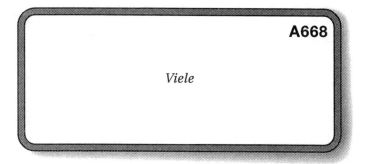

A668

Viele

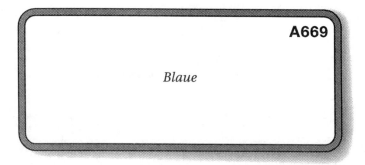

A669

Blaue

Questions

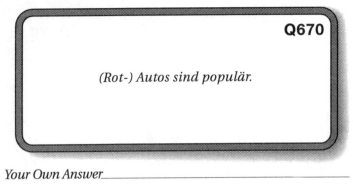

Q670

(Rot-) Autos sind populär.

*Your Own Answer*_____

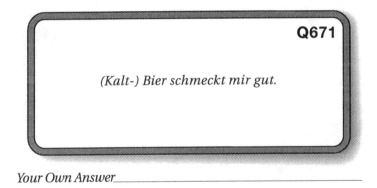

Q671

(Kalt-) Bier schmeckt mir gut.

*Your Own Answer*_____

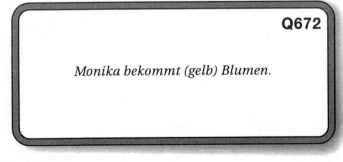

Q672

Monika bekommt (gelb) Blumen.

*Your Own Answer*_____

Correct Answers

A670

Rote

A671

Kaltes

A672

gelbe

Questions

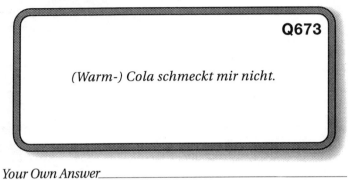

Q673

(Warm-) Cola schmeckt mir nicht.

Your Own Answer_____

Q674

(Freundlich-) Angestellte sind oft hilfsbereit.

Your Own Answer_____

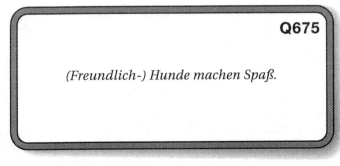

Q675

(Freundlich-) Hunde machen Spaß.

Your Own Answer_____

Correct Answers

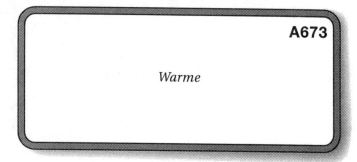

A673

Warme

A674

Freundliche

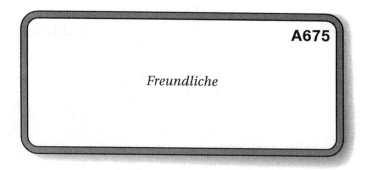

A675

Freundliche

Questions

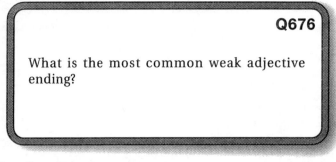

Q676

What is the most common weak adjective ending?

*Your Own Answer*_____

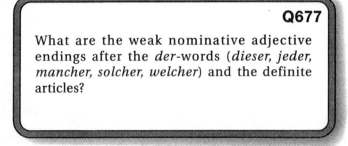

Q677

What are the weak nominative adjective endings after the *der*-words (*dieser, jeder, mancher, solcher, welcher*) and the definite articles?

*Your Own Answer*_____

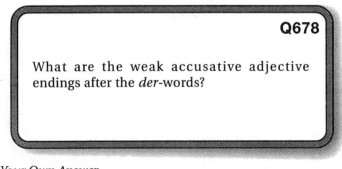

Q678

What are the weak accusative adjective endings after the *der*-words?

*Your Own Answer*_____

Correct Answers

(-en)

masculine: *(-e)*; feminine: *(-e)*; neuter: *(-e)*;
plural: *(-en)*

masculine: *(-en)*; feminine: *(-e)*; neuter: *(-e)*;
plural: *(-en)*

Questions

Q679

What are the weak dative adjective endings after the *der*-words?

*Your Own Answer*_____

Q680

What are the weak genitive adjective endings after the *der*-words?

*Your Own Answer*_____

Q681

Der (dick-) Mann ißt Schinken.

*Your Own Answer*_____

Correct Answers

A679

masculine: *(-en)*; feminine: *(-en)*; neuter: *(-en)*;
plural: *(-en)*

A680

masculine: *(-en)*; feminine: *(-en)*; neuter: *(-en)*;
plural: *(-en)*

A681

dicke

Questions

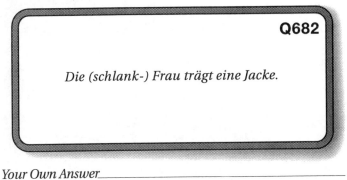

Q682

Die (schlank-) Frau trägt eine Jacke.

*Your Own Answer*_____

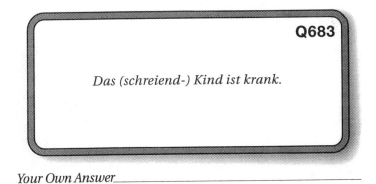

Q683

Das (schreiend-) Kind ist krank.

*Your Own Answer*_____

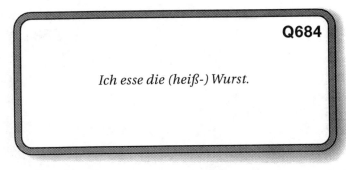

Q684

Ich esse die (heiß-) Wurst.

*Your Own Answer*_____

Correct Answers

A682

schlanke

A683

schreiende

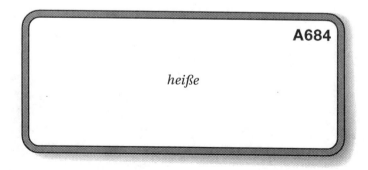

A684

heiße

Questions

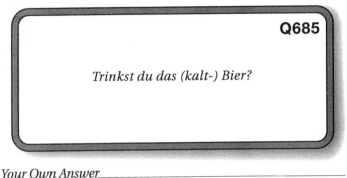

Q685

Trinkst du das (kalt-) Bier?

Your Own Answer_____

Q686

Which cases and genders are exceptions to the general rule that the weak adjectives end in *(-en)?*

Your Own Answer_____

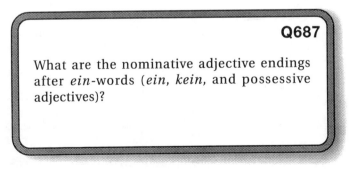

Q687

What are the nominative adjective endings after *ein*-words (*ein, kein,* and possessive adjectives)?

Your Own Answer_____

Correct Answers

kalte

all singular genders of the nominative case and feminine and neuter in the accusative case

masculine: (*-er*); feminine: (*-e*); neuter: (*-es*); plural: (*-en*)

Questions

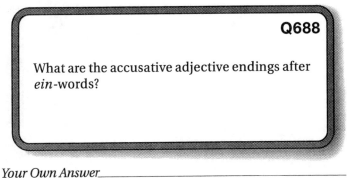

Q688

What are the accusative adjective endings after *ein*-words?

*Your Own Answer*_____

_____

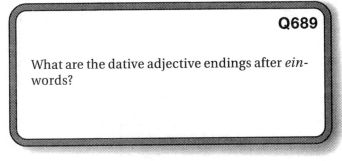

Q689

What are the dative adjective endings after *ein*-words?

*Your Own Answer*_____

_____

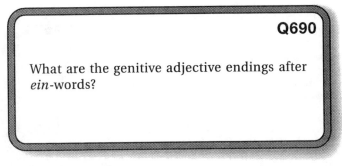

Q690

What are the genitive adjective endings after *ein*-words?

*Your Own Answer*_____

_____

Correct Answers

A688

masculine: (*-en*); feminine: (*-e*); neuter: (*-es*); plural: (*-en*)

A689

masculine: *(-en)*; feminine: (*-en*); neuter: (*-en*); plural: (*-en*)

A690

masculine: *(-en)*; feminine: (*-en*); neuter: (*-en*); plural: (*-en*)

Questions

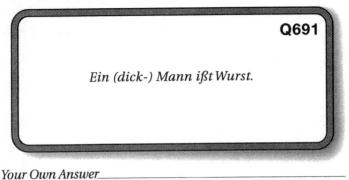

Q691

Ein (dick-) Mann ißt Wurst.

Your Own Answer_____

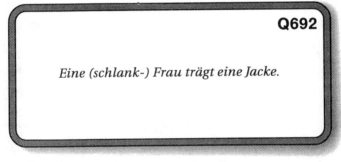

Q692

Eine (schlank-) Frau trägt eine Jacke.

Your Own Answer_____

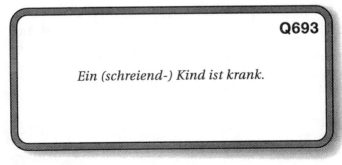

Q693

Ein (schreiend-) Kind ist krank.

Your Own Answer_____

Correct Answers

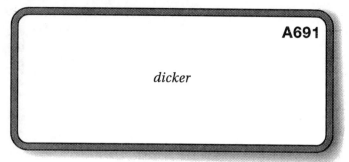

A691

dicker

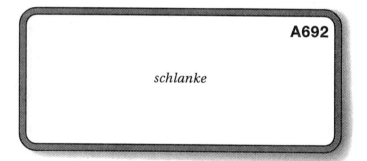

A692

schlanke

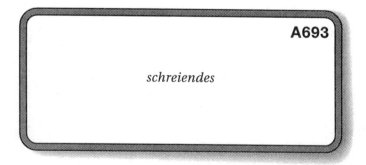

A693

schreiendes

Questions

Q694

Ich esse eine (heiß-) Wurst.

*Your Own Answer*_____

Q695

Trinkst du ein (kalt-) Bier?

*Your Own Answer*_____

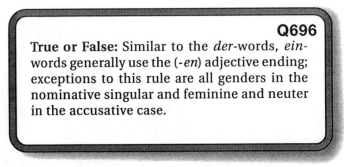

Q696

True or False: Similar to the *der*-words, *ein*-words generally use the (*-en*) adjective ending; exceptions to this rule are all genders in the nominative singular and feminine and neuter in the accusative case.

*Your Own Answer*_____

Correct Answers

A694

heiße

A695

kaltes

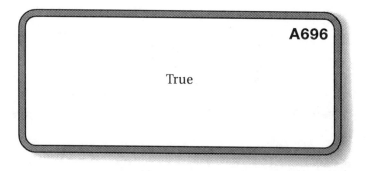

A696

True

Questions

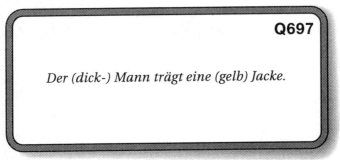

Q697

Der (dick-) Mann trägt eine (gelb) Jacke.

Your Own Answer_____

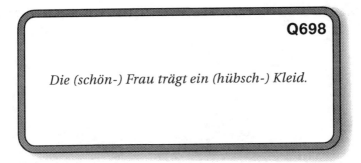

Q698

Die (schön-) Frau trägt ein (hübsch-) Kleid.

Your Own Answer_____

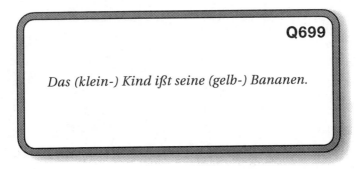

Q699

Das (klein-) Kind ißt seine (gelb-) Bananen.

Your Own Answer_____

Correct Answers

A697

dicke... gelbe

A698

schöne... hübsches

A699

kleine... gelbe

Questions

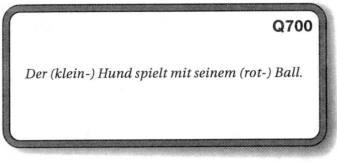

Q700

Der (klein-) Hund spielt mit seinem (rot-) Ball.

Your Own Answer_____

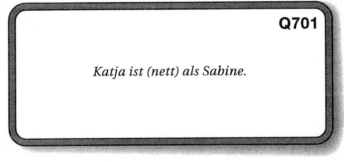

Q701

Katja ist (nett) als Sabine.

Your Own Answer_____

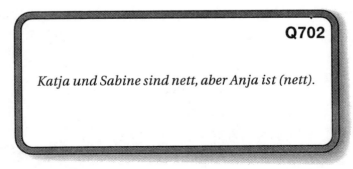

Q702

Katja und Sabine sind nett, aber Anja ist (nett).

Your Own Answer_____

Correct Answers

A700

kleine... roten

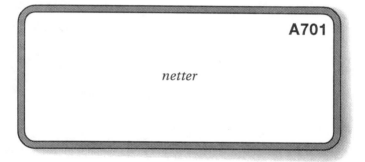

A701

netter

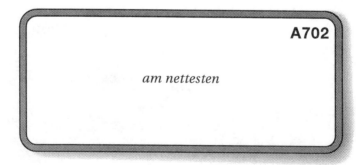

A702

am nettesten

Questions

Frank ist intelligent, aber Mark ist (intelligent).

Your Own Answer

Frank und Mark sind intelligent, aber Thomas ist (intelligent).

Your Own Answer

Ich trink Milch gern, aber ich trinke (gern) Cola.

Your Own Answer

Correct Answers

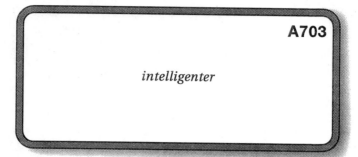

A703

intelligenter

A704

am intelligentesten

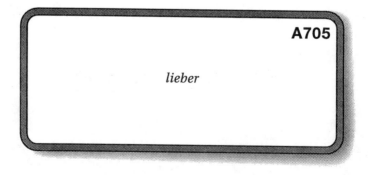

A705

lieber

Questions

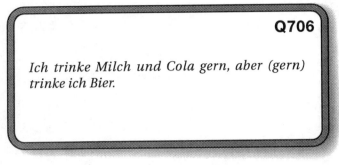

Q706

Ich trinke Milch und Cola gern, aber (gern) trinke ich Bier.

Your Own Answer_____

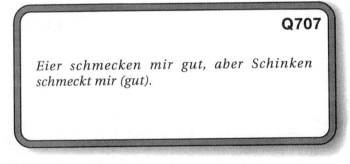

Q707

Eier schmecken mir gut, aber Schinken schmeckt mir (gut).

Your Own Answer_____

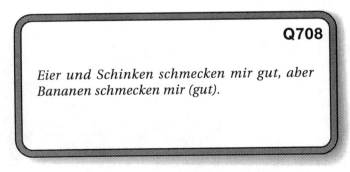

Q708

Eier und Schinken schmecken mir gut, aber Bananen schmecken mir (gut).

Your Own Answer_____

Correct Answers

am liebsten

besser

am besten

Questions

Q709

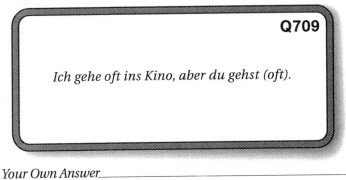

Ich gehe oft ins Kino, aber du gehst (oft).

*Your Own Answer*_____

_____

Q710

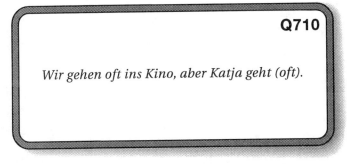

Wir gehen oft ins Kino, aber Katja geht (oft).

*Your Own Answer*_____

_____

Q711

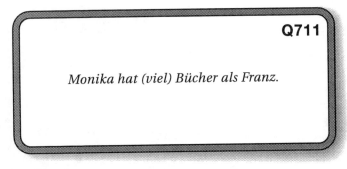

Monika hat (viel) Bücher als Franz.

*Your Own Answer*_____

_____

Correct Answers

A709

öfter

A710

am öftesten

A711

mehr

Questions

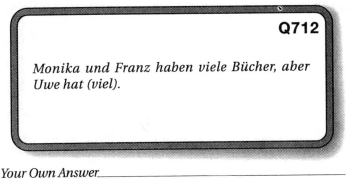

Q712

Monika und Franz haben viele Bücher, aber
Uwe hat (viel).

*Your Own Answer*_____

_____

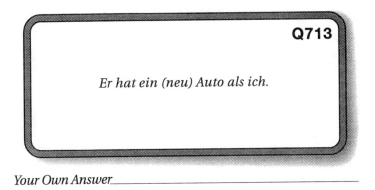

Q713

Er hat ein (neu) Auto als ich.

*Your Own Answer*_____

_____

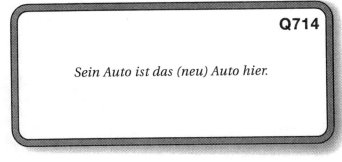

Q714

Sein Auto ist das (neu) Auto hier.

*Your Own Answer*_____

_____

Correct Answers

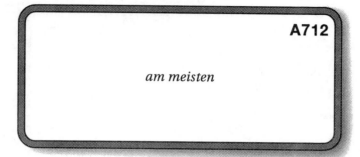

A712

am meisten

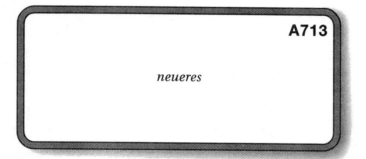

A713

neueres

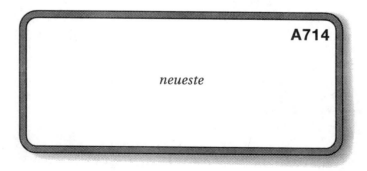

A714

neueste

Questions

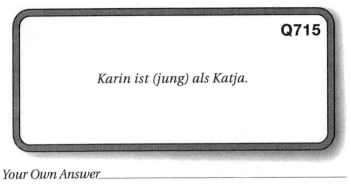

Q715

Karin ist (jung) als Katja.

*Your Own Answer*_____

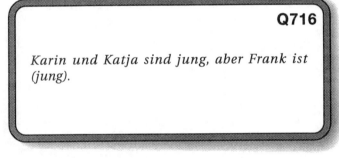

Q716

Karin und Katja sind jung, aber Frank ist (jung).

*Your Own Answer*_____

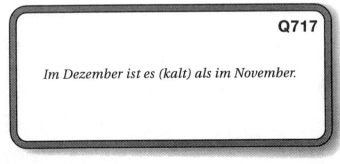

Q717

Im Dezember ist es (kalt) als im November.

*Your Own Answer*_____

Correct Answers

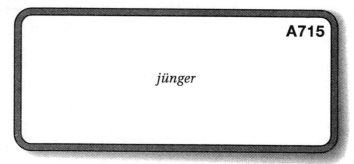

A715

jünger

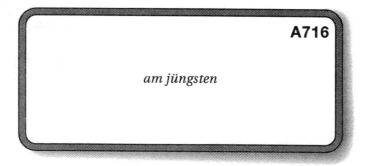

A716

am jüngsten

A717

kälter

Questions

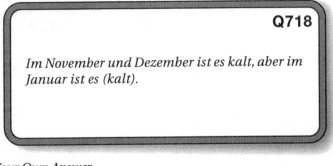

Q718

Im November und Dezember ist es kalt, aber im Januar ist es (kalt).

*Your Own Answer*_____

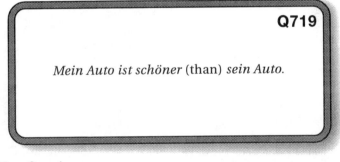

Q719

Mein Auto ist schöner (than) *sein Auto.*

*Your Own Answer*_____

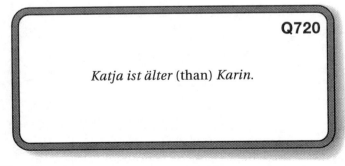

Q720

Katja ist älter (than) *Karin.*

*Your Own Answer*_____

Correct Answers

A718

am kältesten

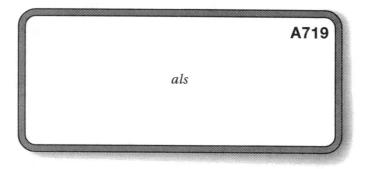

A719

als

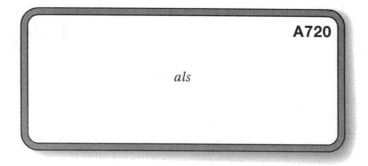

A720

als

Questions

Q721

_____ reicher wir werden, _____ weniger arbeiten wir.

Your Own Answer_____

Q722

_____ mehr wir lesen, _____ mehr verstehen wir.

Your Own Answer_____

Q723

Wenn wir viel lesen, werden wir _____ intelligenter.

Your Own Answer_____

Correct Answers

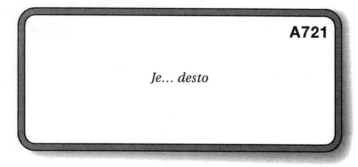

A721

Je… desto

A722

Je… desto

A723

immer

Questions

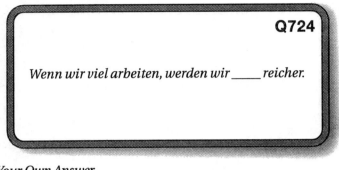

Q724

Wenn wir viel arbeiten, werden wir _____ reicher.

Your Own Answer_____

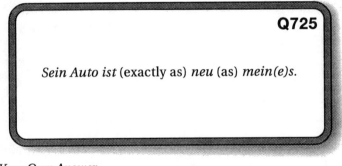

Q725

Sein Auto ist (exactly as) *neu* (as) *mein(e)s.*

Your Own Answer_____

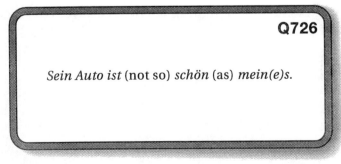

Q726

Sein Auto ist (not so) *schön* (as) *mein(e)s.*

Your Own Answer_____

Correct Answers

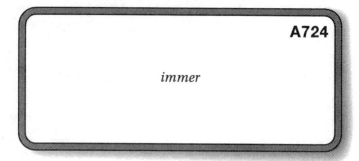

A724

immer

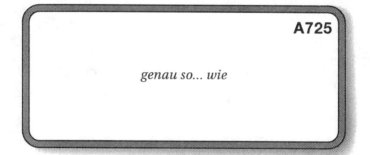

A725

genau so... wie

A726

nicht so... wie

Questions

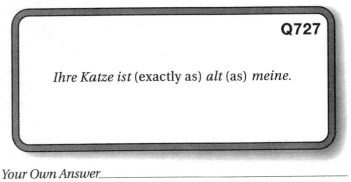

Q727

Ihre Katze ist (exactly as) *alt* (as) *meine.*

*Your Own Answer*_____

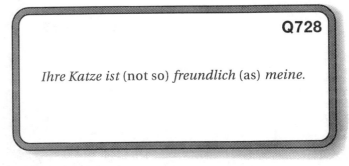

Q728

Ihre Katze ist (not so) *freundlich* (as) *meine.*

*Your Own Answer*_____

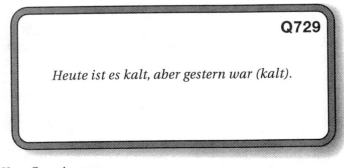

Q729

Heute ist es kalt, aber gestern war (kalt).

*Your Own Answer*_____

Correct Answers

A727

genau... wie

A728

nicht so... wie

A729

kälter

Questions

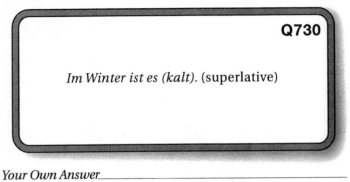

Q730

Im Winter ist es (kalt). (superlative)

*Your Own Answer*_____

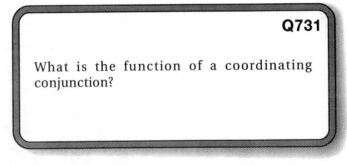

Q731

What is the function of a coordinating conjunction?

*Your Own Answer*_____

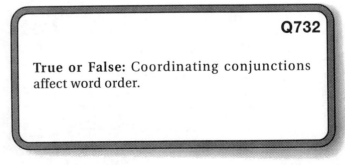

Q732

True or False: Coordinating conjunctions affect word order.

*Your Own Answer*_____

Correct Answers

A730

am kältesten

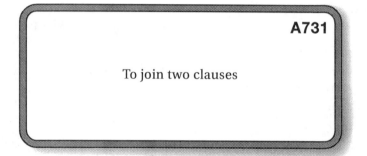

A731

To join two clauses

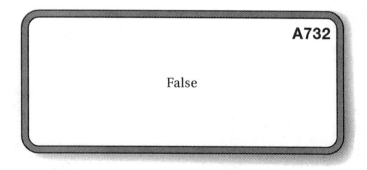

A732

False

Questions

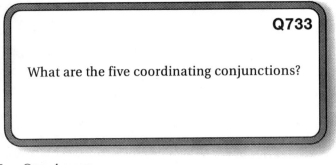

Q733

What are the five coordinating conjunctions?

*Your Own Answer*_____

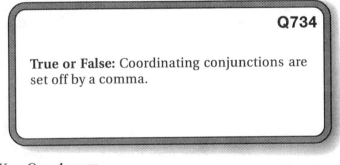

Q734

True or False: Coordinating conjunctions are set off by a comma.

*Your Own Answer*_____

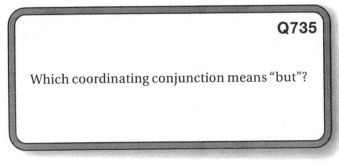

Q735

Which coordinating conjunction means "but"?

*Your Own Answer*_____

Correct Answers

aber, denn, oder, sondern, und

False. Reformed grammar no longer makes this obligatory.

aber

Questions

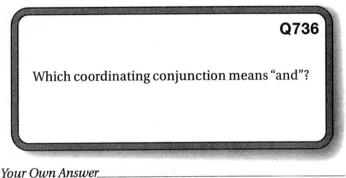

Q736

Which coordinating conjunction means "and"?

*Your Own Answer*_____

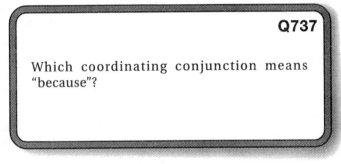

Q737

Which coordinating conjunction means "because"?

*Your Own Answer*_____

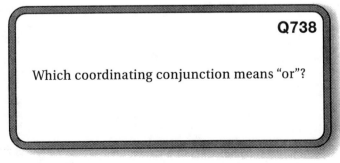

Q738

Which coordinating conjunction means "or"?

*Your Own Answer*_____

Correct Answers

A736

und

A737

denn

A738

oder

Questions

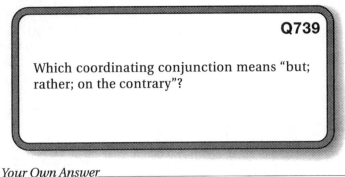

Q739

Which coordinating conjunction means "but; rather; on the contrary"?

*Your Own Answer*_____

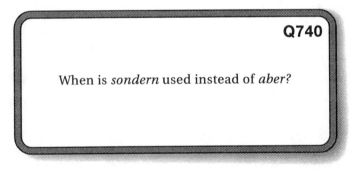

Q740

When is *sondern* used instead of *aber?*

*Your Own Answer*_____

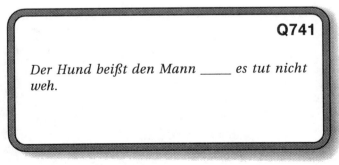

Q741

Der Hund beißt den Mann _____ *es tut nicht weh.*

*Your Own Answer*_____

Correct Answers

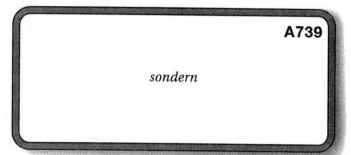

A739

sondern

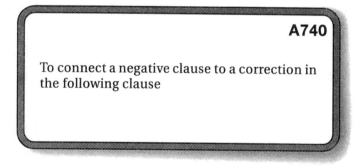

A740

To connect a negative clause to a correction in the following clause

A741

aber

Questions

Q742

Der Mann muß still bleiben _____ der Hund wird ihn beißen.

*Your Own Answer*_____

Q743

Der Hund beißt den Mann _____ er bleibt nicht still.

*Your Own Answer*_____

Q744

Der Mann bleibt nicht still _____ der Hund beißt ihn.

*Your Own Answer*_____

Correct Answers

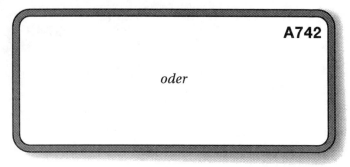

A742

oder

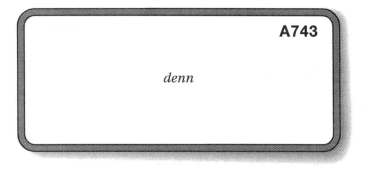

A743

denn

A744

und

Questions

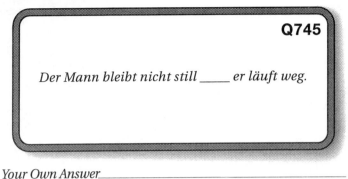

Q745

Der Mann bleibt nicht still _____ er läuft weg.

*Your Own Answer*_____

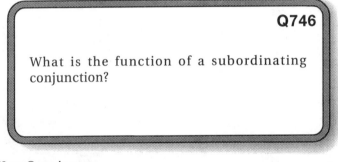

Q746

What is the function of a subordinating conjunction?

*Your Own Answer*_____

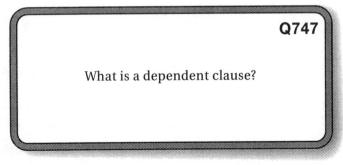

Q747

What is a dependent clause?

*Your Own Answer*_____

Correct Answers

A745

sondern

A746

To join an independent and a dependent clause

A747

A clause that can't stand alone as a sentence

Questions

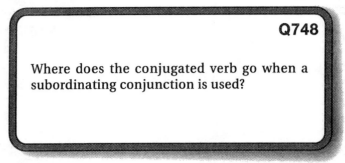

Q748

Where does the conjugated verb go when a subordinating conjunction is used?

*Your Own Answer*_____

_____

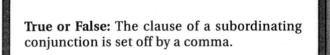

Q749

True or False: The clause of a subordinating conjunction is set off by a comma.

*Your Own Answer*_____

_____

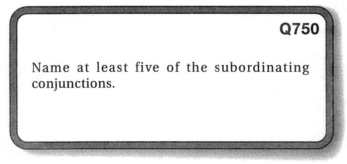

Q750

Name at least five of the subordinating conjunctions.

*Your Own Answer*_____

_____

Correct Answers

A748

At the end of the clause

A749

True

A750

als, bevor, bis, da, damit, daß, ehe, falls, indem, nachdem, ob, obwohl, seit(dem), sobald, solange, sowie, während, wie, wenn

Questions

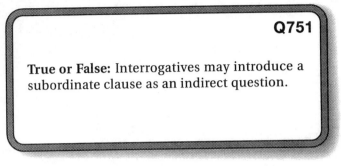

Q751

True or False: Interrogatives may introduce a subordinate clause as an indirect question.

*Your Own Answer*_____

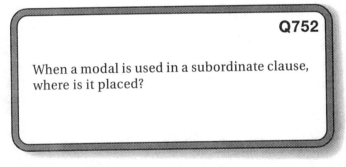

Q752

When a modal is used in a subordinate clause, where is it placed?

*Your Own Answer*_____

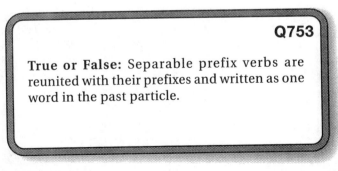

Q753

True or False: Separable prefix verbs are reunited with their prefixes and written as one word in the past particle.

*Your Own Answer*_____

Correct Answers

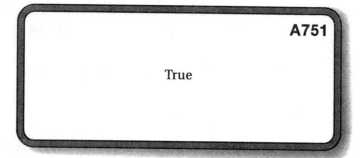

A751

True

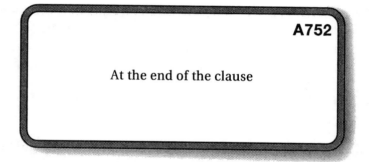

A752

At the end of the clause

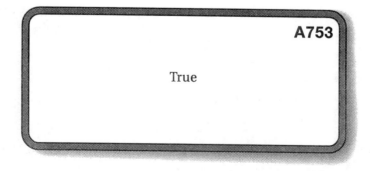

A753

True

Questions

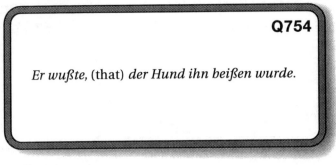

Q754

Er wußte, (that) *der Hund ihn beißen wurde.*

Your Own Answer_____

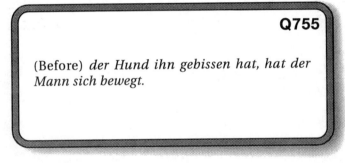

Q755

(Before) *der Hund ihn gebissen hat, hat der Mann sich bewegt.*

Your Own Answer_____

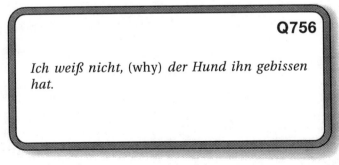

Q756

Ich weiß nicht, (why) *der Hund ihn gebissen hat.*

Your Own Answer_____

Correct Answers

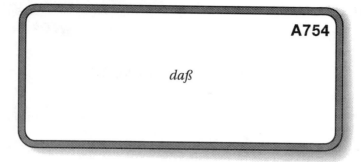

A754

daß

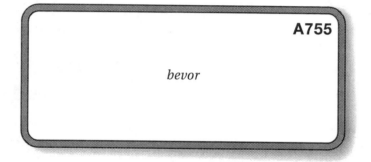

A755

bevor

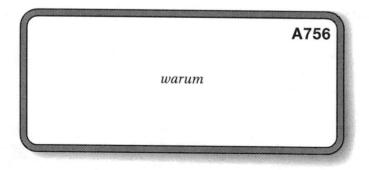

A756

warum

Questions

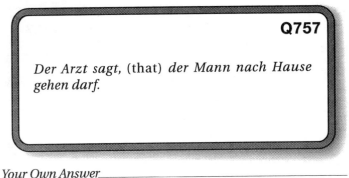

Q757

Der Arzt sagt, (that) *der Mann nach Hause gehen darf.*

Your Own Answer_____

Q758

(When) *der Mann im Krankenhaus ankam, war seine Frau schon da.*

Your Own Answer_____

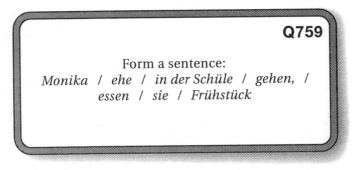

Q759

Form a sentence:
Monika / ehe / in der Schüle / gehen, / essen / sie / Frühstück

Your Own Answer_____

Correct Answers

A757

daß

A758

als

A759

Ehe Monika in die Schüle geht, ißt sie Frühstück.

Questions

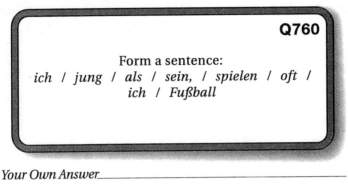

Q760

Form a sentence:
*ich / jung / als / sein, / spielen / oft /
ich / Fußball*

*Your Own Answer*_____

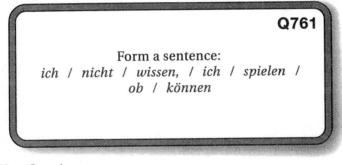

Q761

Form a sentence:
*ich / nicht / wissen, / ich / spielen /
ob / können*

*Your Own Answer*_____

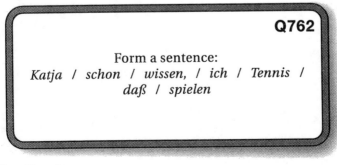

Q762

Form a sentence:
*Katja / schon / wissen, / ich / Tennis /
daß / spielen*

*Your Own Answer*_____

Correct Answers

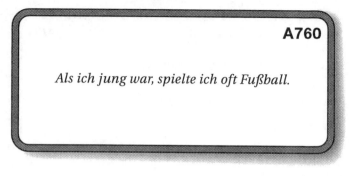

A760

Als ich jung war, spielte ich oft Fußball.

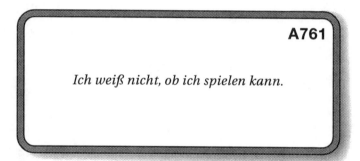

A761

Ich weiß nicht, ob ich spielen kann.

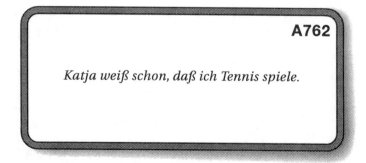

A762

Katja weiß schon, daß ich Tennis spiele.

Questions

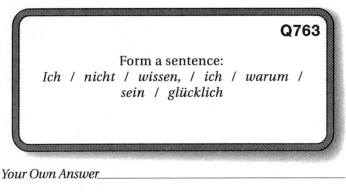

Q763

Form a sentence:
*Ich / nicht / wissen, / ich / warum /
sein / glücklich*

*Your Own Answer*_____

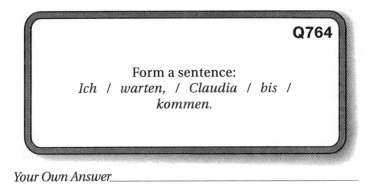

Q764

Form a sentence:
*Ich / warten, / Claudia / bis /
kommen.*

*Your Own Answer*_____

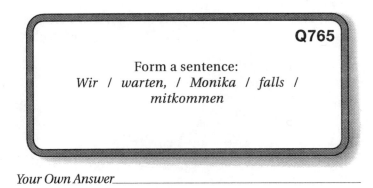

Q765

Form a sentence:
*Wir / warten, / Monika / falls /
mitkommen*

*Your Own Answer*_____

Correct Answers

A763

Ich weiß nicht, warum ich glücklich bin.

A764

Ich warte, bis Claudia kommt.

A765

Wir warten, falls Monika mitkommt.

Questions

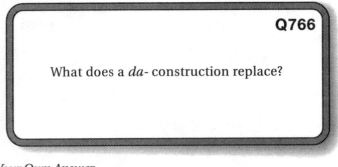

Q766

What does a *da-* construction replace?

*Your Own Answer*_____

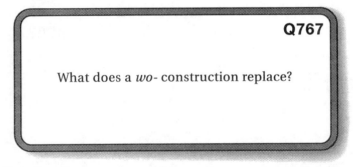

Q767

What does a *wo-* construction replace?

*Your Own Answer*_____

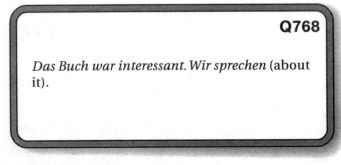

Q768

Das Buch war interessant. Wir sprechen (about it).

*Your Own Answer*_____

Correct Answers

A preposition and a pronoun referring to a thing

A preposition and a pronoun; forms a question word

darüber

Questions

Der Ball macht Spaß. Wir spielen _____ (with it)

*Your Own Answer*_____

Sie spielen mit dem Ball. _____ spielen sie? (with what)

*Your Own Answer*_____

Wir sprechen über das Buch. _____ sprechen wir? (about what)

*Your Own Answer*_____

Correct Answers

A769

damit

A770

womit

A771

worüber

Questions

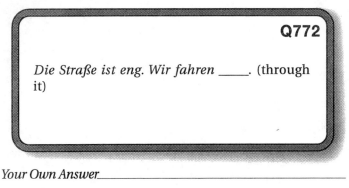

Q772

Die Straße ist eng. Wir fahren _____. (through it)

Your Own Answer_____

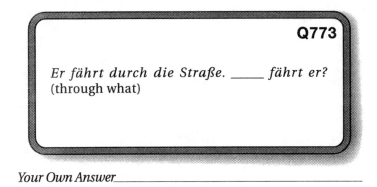

Q773

Er fährt durch die Straße. _____ fährt er? (through what)

Your Own Answer_____

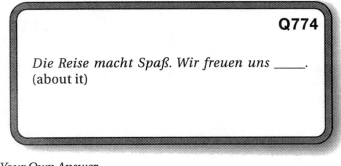

Q774

Die Reise macht Spaß. Wir freuen uns _____. (about it)

Your Own Answer_____

Correct Answers

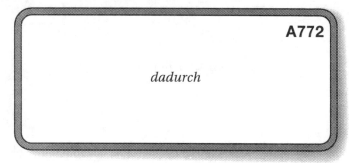

A772

dadurch

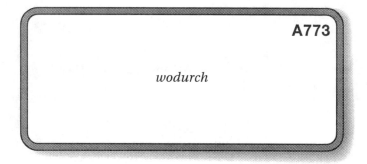

A773

wodurch

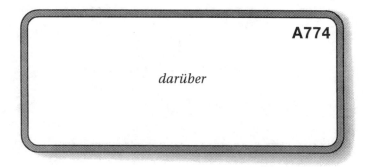

A774

darüber

Questions

Q775

Monika freut sich über die Reise. _____ freut sie sich? (about what)

*Your Own Answer*_____

Q776

Die Musik ist schön. Rolf freut sich _____. (about it)

*Your Own Answer*_____

Q777

Rolf freut sich über die Musik. _____ freut er sich? (about what)

*Your Own Answer*_____

Correct Answers

A775

worüber

A776

darüber

A777

worüber

Questions

Q778

Der Bus ist spät. Wir fahren ____ (with it)

Your Own Answer_____

Q779

Thomas fährt mit dem Bus. ____ fährt er?

Your Own Answer_____

Q780

Meine Note ist gut. Ich freue mich ____. (about it)

Your Own Answer_____

Correct Answers

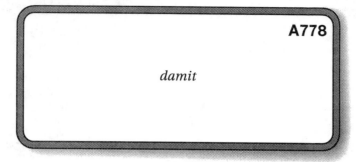

A778

damit

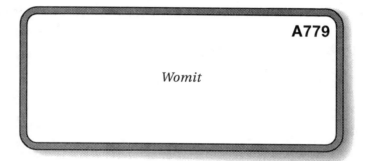

A779

Womit

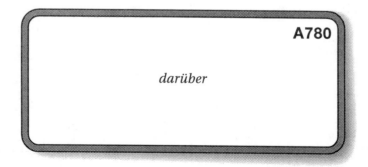

A780

darüber

Questions

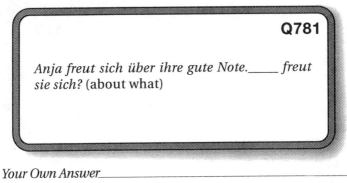

Q781

Anja freut sich über ihre gute Note.____ freut sie sich? (about what)

Your Own Answer_____

Q782

Das Auto ist kaputt. Monika wollte ____ fahren. (with it)

Your Own Answer_____

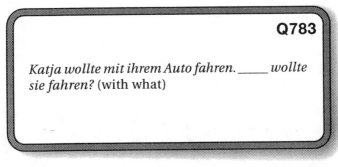

Q783

Katja wollte mit ihrem Auto fahren. ____ wollte sie fahren? (with what)

Your Own Answer_____

Correct Answers

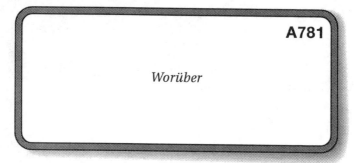

A781

Worüber

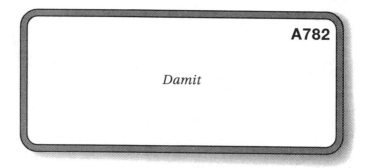

A782

Damit

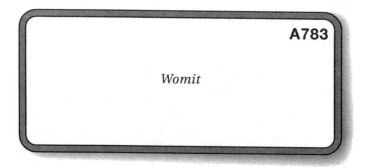

A783

Womit

Questions

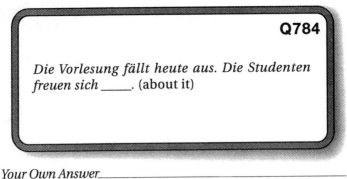

Q784

Die Vorlesung fällt heute aus. Die Studenten freuen sich _____. (about it)

*Your Own Answer*_____

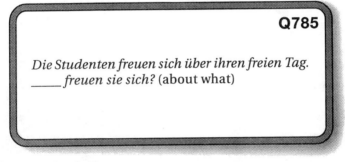

Q785

Die Studenten freuen sich über ihren freien Tag. _____ freuen sie sich? (about what)

*Your Own Answer*_____

Q786

Ich habe _____ Interesse für Musik. (keine or nicht)

*Your Own Answer*_____

Correct Answers

Questions

Q787

Ich glaube Sabine _____ (kein or nicht)

Your Own Answer_____

Q788

Ich gehe heute Abend _____ ins Kino. (kein or nicht)

Your Own Answer_____

Q789

Katja trinkt _____ Kaffee. (keinen or nicht)

Your Own Answer_____

Correct Answers

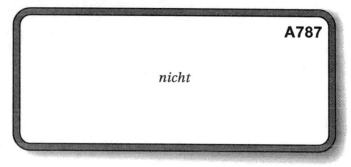

A787

nicht

A788

nicht

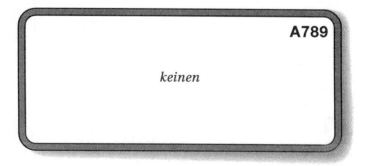

A789

keinen

Questions

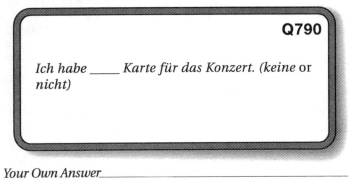

Q790

Ich habe _____ Karte für das Konzert. (keine or *nicht)*

Your Own Answer_____

Q791

der Kopf

Your Own Answer_____

Q792

der Mund

Your Own Answer_____

Correct Answers

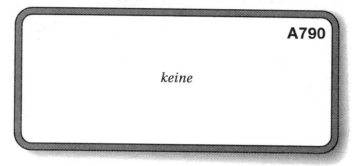

A790

keine

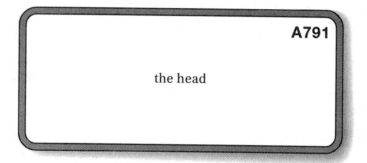

A791

the head

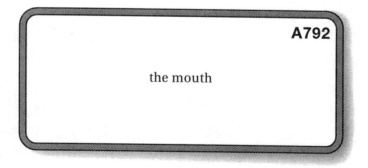

A792

the mouth

Questions

Q793

der Bauch

*Your Own Answer*_____

Q794

der Finger

*Your Own Answer*_____

Q795

der Arm

*Your Own Answer*_____

Correct Answers

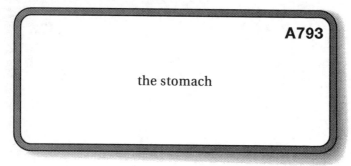

A793

the stomach

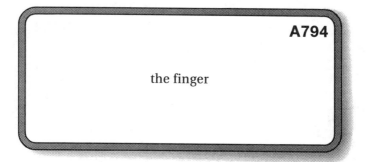

A794

the finger

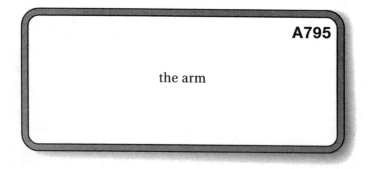

A795

the arm

Questions

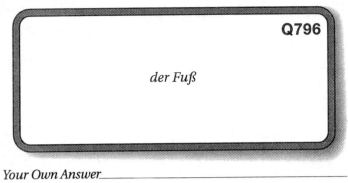

Q796

der Fuß

*Your Own Answer*_____

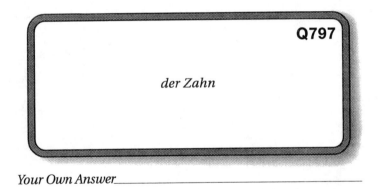

Q797

der Zahn

*Your Own Answer*_____

Q798

die Nase

*Your Own Answer*_____

Correct Answers

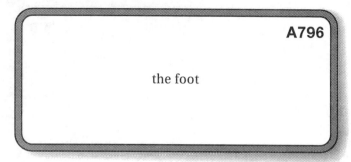

A796

the foot

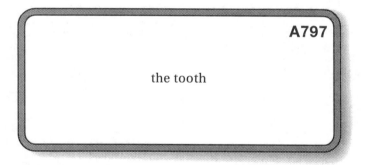

A797

the tooth

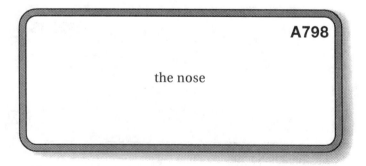

A798

the nose

Questions

Q799

die Hand

Your Own Answer_____

Q800

das Gesicht

Your Own Answer_____

Q801

das Knie

Your Own Answer_____

Correct Answers

A799

the hand

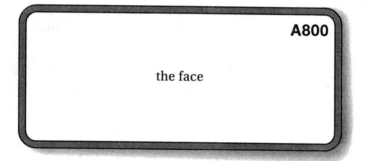

A800

the face

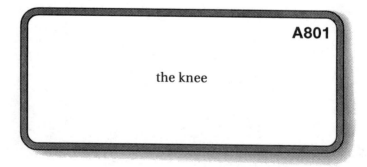

A801

the knee

Questions

Q802

das Auge

*Your Own Answer*_____

Q803

das Ohr

*Your Own Answer*_____

Q804

das Haar

*Your Own Answer*_____

Correct Answers

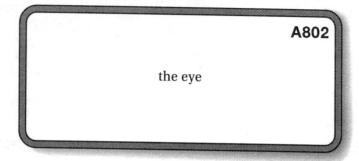

A802

the eye

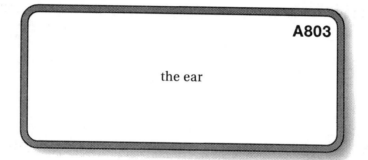

A803

the ear

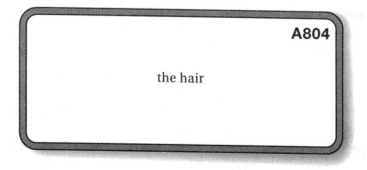

A804

the hair

Questions

Q805

das Bein

Your Own Answer_____

Q806

die Bluse

Your Own Answer_____

Q807

die Hose

Your Own Answer_____

Correct Answers

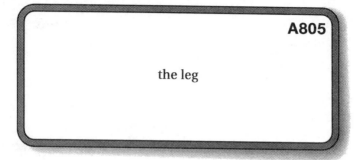

A805

the leg

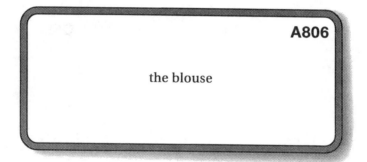

A806

the blouse

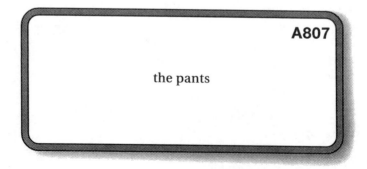

A807

the pants

Questions

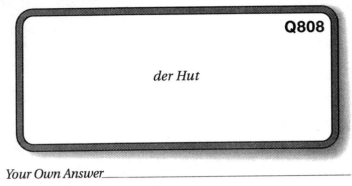

Q808

der Hut

*Your Own Answer*_____

Q809

das Kleid

*Your Own Answer*_____

Q810

der Mantel

*Your Own Answer*_____

Correct Answers

A808

the hat

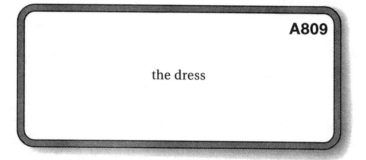

A809

the dress

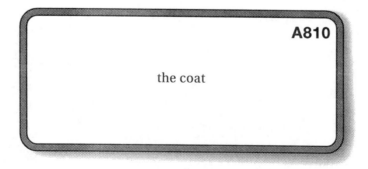

A810

the coat

Questions

der Rock

*Your Own Answer*_____

der Anzug

*Your Own Answer*_____

das Hemd

*Your Own Answer*_____

Correct Answers

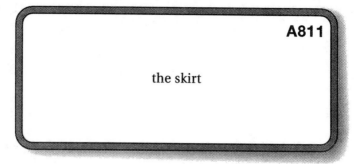

A811

the skirt

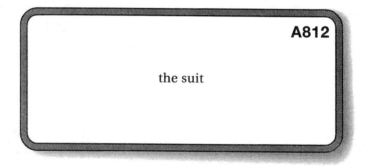

A812

the suit

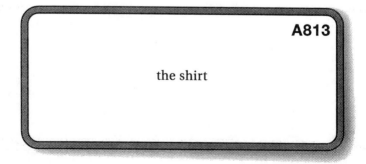

A813

the shirt

Questions

die Krawatte

*Your Own Answer*_____

die Socken

*Your Own Answer*_____

blau

*Your Own Answer*_____

Correct Answers

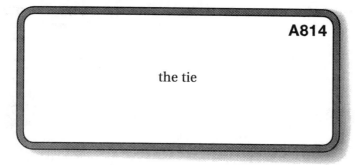

A814

the tie

A815

the socks

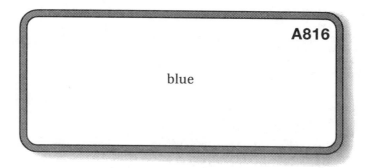

A816

blue

Questions

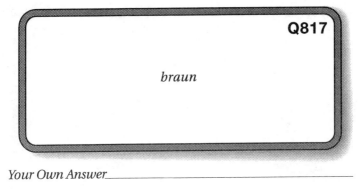

Q817

braun

*Your Own Answer*_____

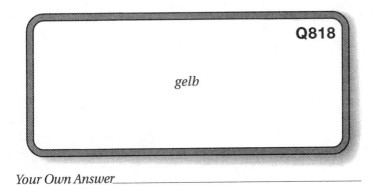

Q818

gelb

*Your Own Answer*_____

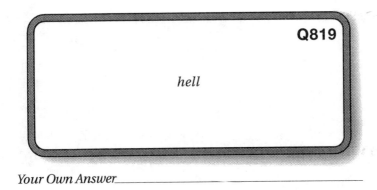

Q819

hell

*Your Own Answer*_____

Correct Answers

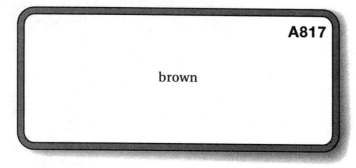

A817

brown

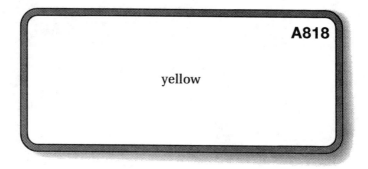

A818

yellow

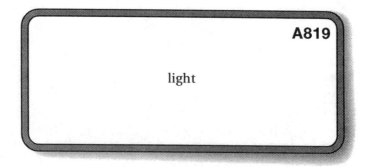

A819

light

Questions

Q820

dunkel

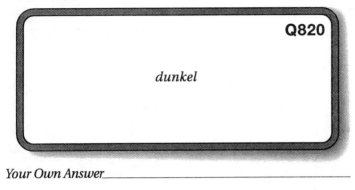

*Your Own Answer*_____

Q821

grau

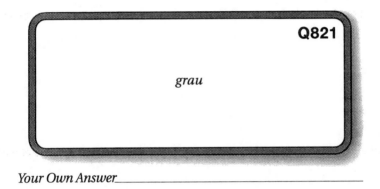

*Your Own Answer*_____

Q822

grün

*Your Own Answer*_____

Correct Answers

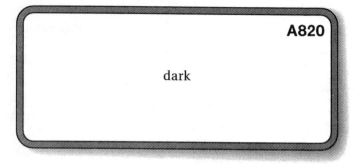

A820

dark

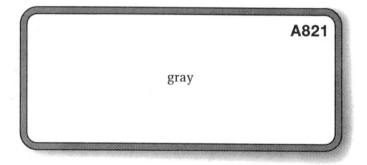

A821

gray

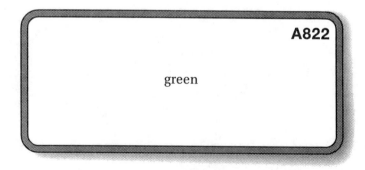

A822

green

Questions

orange

*Your Own Answer*_____

bunt

*Your Own Answer*_____

weiß

*Your Own Answer*_____

Correct Answers

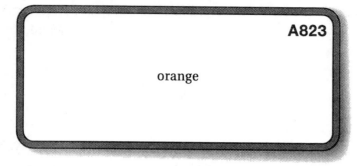

A823

orange

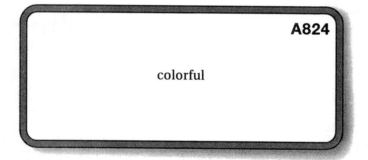

A824

colorful

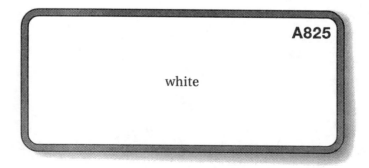

A825

white

Questions

rot

*Your Own Answer*_____

schwarz

*Your Own Answer*_____

der Vater

*Your Own Answer*_____

Correct Answers

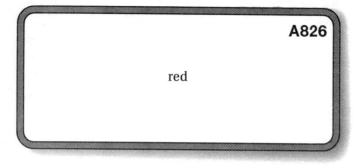

A826

red

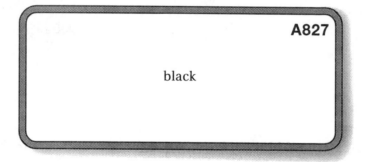

A827

black

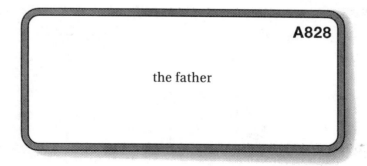

A828

the father

Questions

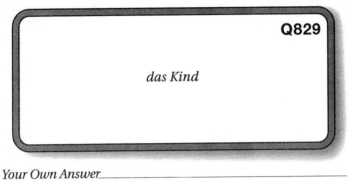

Q829

das Kind

Your Own Answer_____

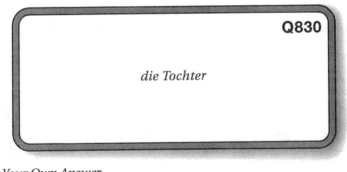

Q830

die Tochter

Your Own Answer_____

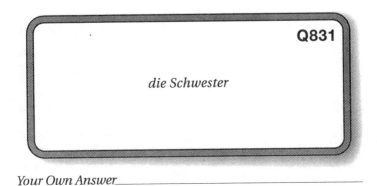

Q831

die Schwester

Your Own Answer_____

Correct Answers

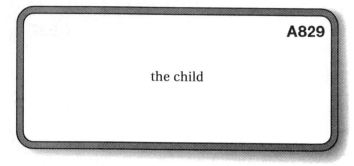

A829

the child

A830

the daughter

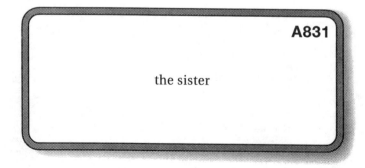

A831

the sister

Questions

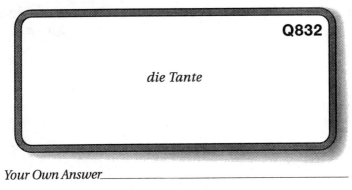

Q832

die Tante

*Your Own Answer*_____

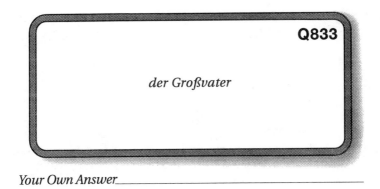

Q833

der Großvater

*Your Own Answer*_____

Q834

die Großmutter

*Your Own Answer*_____

Correct Answers

A832

the aunt

A833

the grandfather

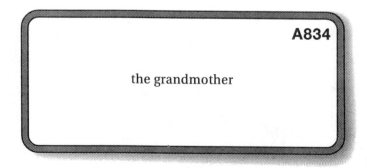

A834

the grandmother

Questions

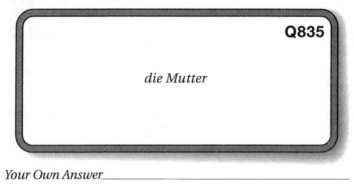

Q835

die Mutter

*Your Own Answer*_____

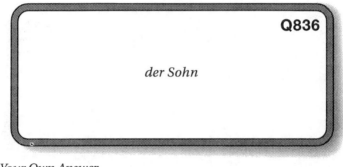

Q836

der Sohn

*Your Own Answer*_____

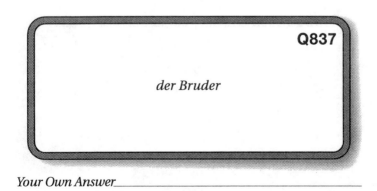

Q837

der Bruder

*Your Own Answer*_____

Correct Answers

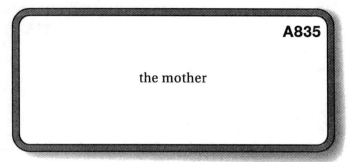

A835

the mother

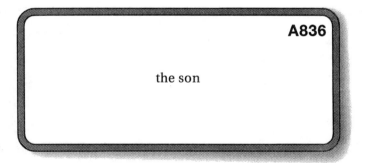

A836

the son

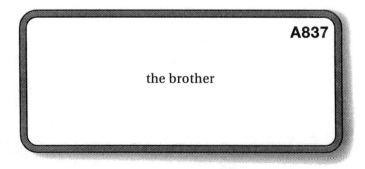

A837

the brother

Questions

Q838

der Onkel

Your Own Answer_____

Q839

das Brot

Your Own Answer_____

Q840

der Kuchen

Your Own Answer_____

Correct Answers

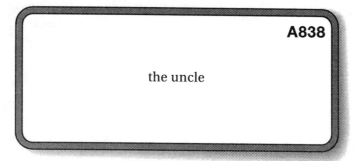

A838

the uncle

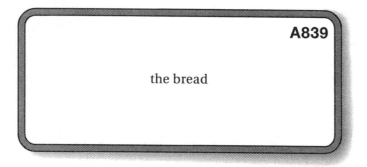

A839

the bread

A840

the cake

Questions

Q841

der Fisch

Your Own Answer_____

Q842

die Wurst

Your Own Answer_____

Q843

die Butter

Your Own Answer_____

Correct Answers

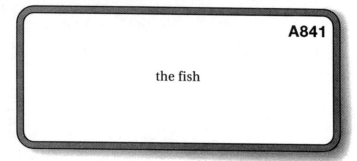

A841

the fish

A842

the sausage

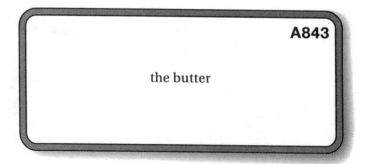

A843

the butter

Questions

Q844

der Käse

Your Own Answer_____

Q845

die Kartoffel

Your Own Answer_____

Q846

die Tomate

Your Own Answer_____

Correct Answers

A844

the cheese

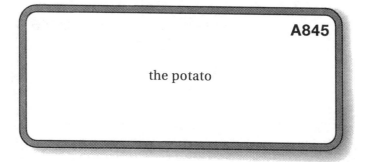

A845

the potato

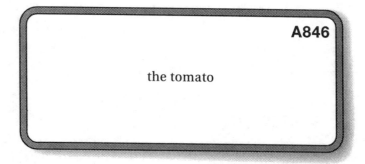

A846

the tomato

Questions

Q847

die Milch

Your Own Answer_____

Q848

die Cola

Your Own Answer_____

Q849

das Wasser

Your Own Answer_____

Correct Answers

A847

the milk

A848

the cola (soft drink)

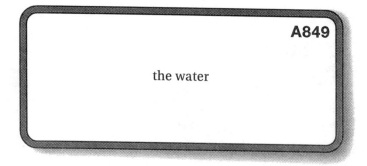

A849

the water

Questions

Q850

der Kaffee

Your Own Answer_____

Q851

die Limonade

Your Own Answer_____

Q852

der Apfel

Your Own Answer_____

Correct Answers

A850

the coffee

A851

the lemonade

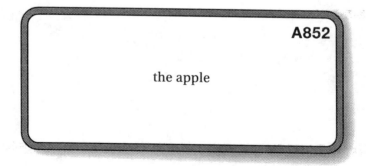

A852

the apple

Questions

Q853

die Orange

Your Own Answer_____

Q854

der Kirsch

Your Own Answer_____

Q855

der Pfirsisch

Your Own Answer_____

Correct Answers

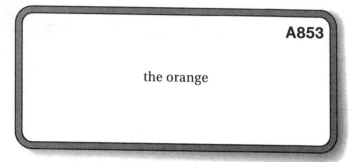

A853

the orange

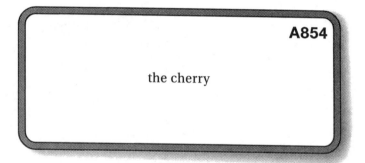

A854

the cherry

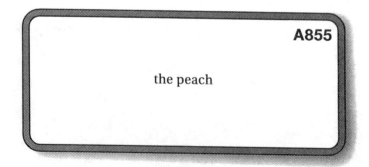

A855

the peach

Questions

Q856

Q856

Guten Morgen!

*Your Own Answer*_____

Q857

Guten Tag!

*Your Own Answer*_____

Q858

Guten Abend!

*Your Own Answer*_____

Correct Answers

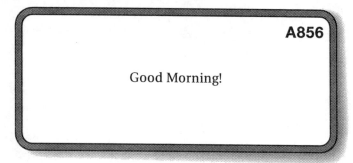

A856

Good Morning!

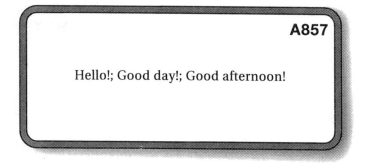

A857

Hello!; Good day!; Good afternoon!

A858

Good Evening!

Questions

Q859

Gute Nacht!

*Your Own Answer*_____

Q860

Wie geht es Ihnen?

*Your Own Answer*_____

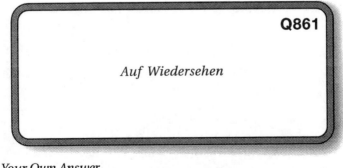

Q861

Auf Wiedersehen

*Your Own Answer*_____

Correct Answers

A859

Good Night!

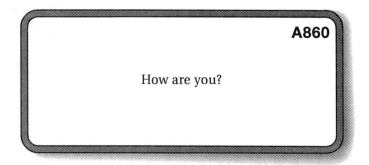

A860

How are you?

A861

Goodbye

Questions

Q862

gleichfalls

*Your Own Answer*_____

Q863

aber

*Your Own Answer*_____

Q864

abfahren

*Your Own Answer*_____

Correct Answers

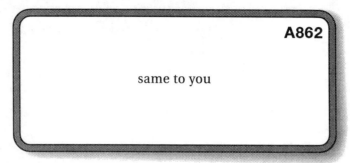

A862

same to you

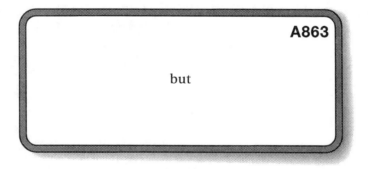

A863

but

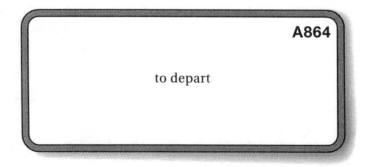

A864

to depart

Questions

Q865

die Adresse

Your Own Answer_____

Q866

alle

Your Own Answer_____

Q867

alt

Your Own Answer_____

Correct Answers

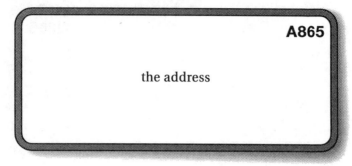

A865

the address

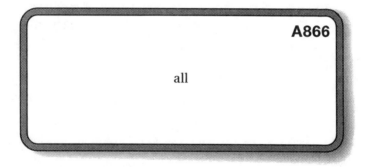

A866

all

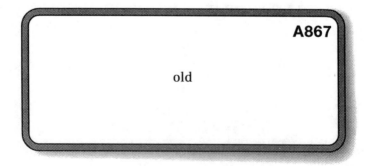

A867

old

Questions

jung

Your Own Answer_____

---

die Angst

Your Own Answer_____

(an)statt

Your Own Answer_____

Correct Answers

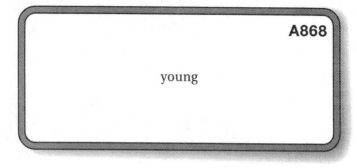

A868

young

A869

the fear

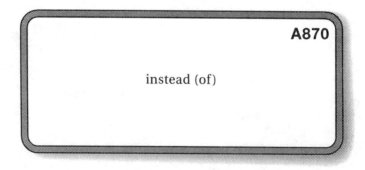

A870

instead (of)

Questions

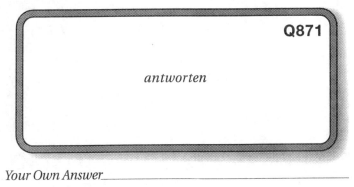

Q871

antworten

*Your Own Answer*_____

Q872

der Tag

*Your Own Answer*_____

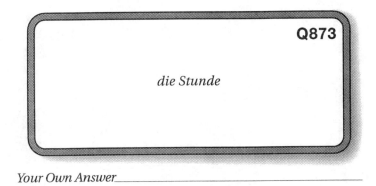

Q873

die Stunde

*Your Own Answer*_____

Correct Answers

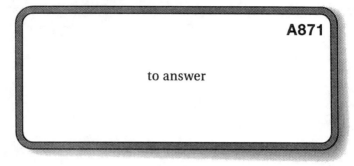

A871

to answer

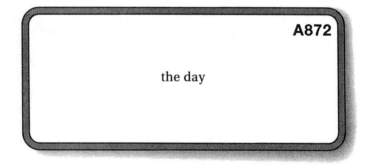

A872

the day

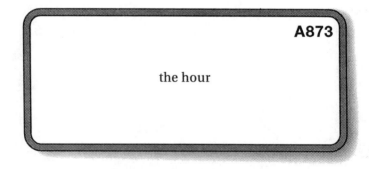

A873

the hour

Questions

Q874

die Minute

*Your Own Answer*_____

Q875

die Sekunde

*Your Own Answer*_____

Q876

die Woche

*Your Own Answer*_____

Correct Answers

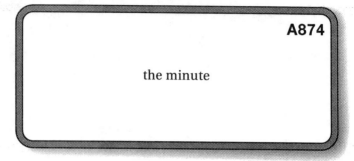

A874

the minute

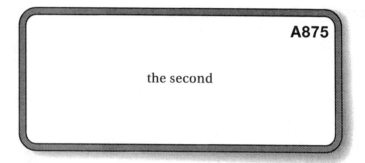

A875

the second

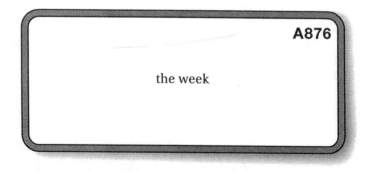

A876

the week

Questions

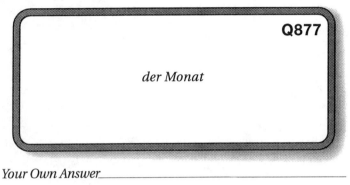

Q877

der Monat

*Your Own Answer*_____

Q878

das Jahr

*Your Own Answer*_____

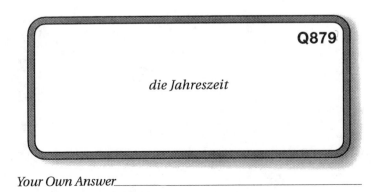

Q879

die Jahreszeit

*Your Own Answer*_____

Correct Answers

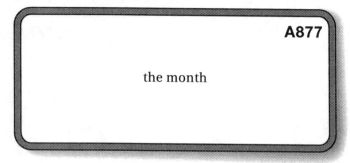

A877

the month

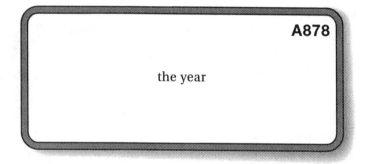

A878

the year

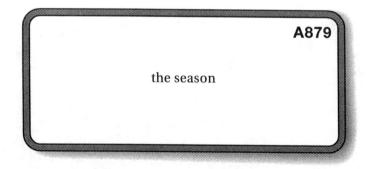

A879

the season

Questions

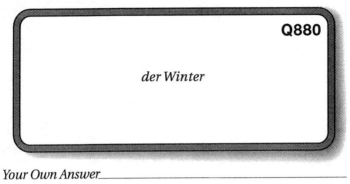

Q880

der Winter

*Your Own Answer*_____

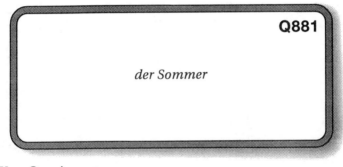

Q881

der Sommer

*Your Own Answer*_____

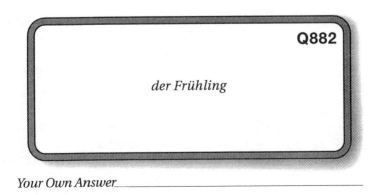

Q882

der Frühling

*Your Own Answer*_____

Correct Answers

A880

the winter

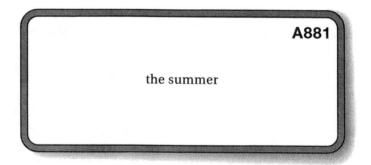

A881

the summer

A882

the spring

Questions

Q883

der Herbst

*Your Own Answer*_____

Q884

der Januar

*Your Own Answer*_____

Q885

der Februar

*Your Own Answer*_____

Correct Answers

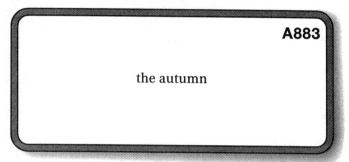

A883

the autumn

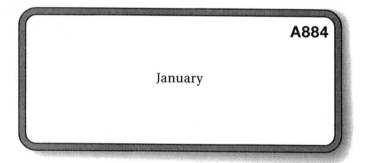

A884

January

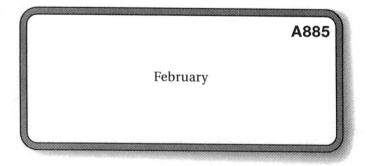

A885

February

Questions

Q886

der März

*Your Own Answer*_____

Q887

der April

*Your Own Answer*_____

Q888

der Mai

*Your Own Answer*_____

Correct Answers

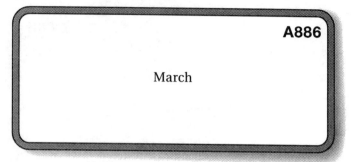

A886

March

A887

April

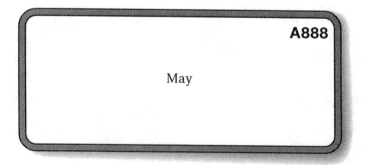

A888

May

Questions

Q889

der Juni

Your Own Answer_____

Q890

der Juli

Your Own Answer_____

Q891

der August

Your Own Answer_____

Correct Answers

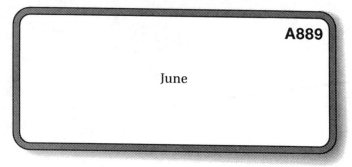

A889

June

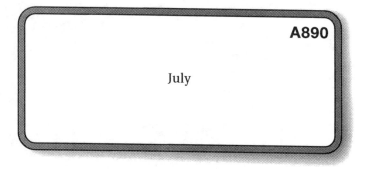

A890

July

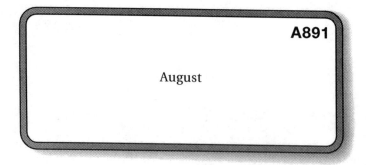

A891

August

Questions

Q892

der September

*Your Own Answer*_____

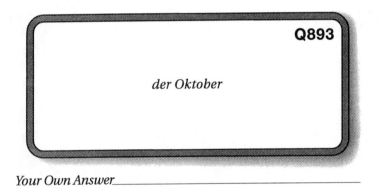

Q893

der Oktober

*Your Own Answer*_____

Q894

der November

*Your Own Answer*_____

Correct Answers

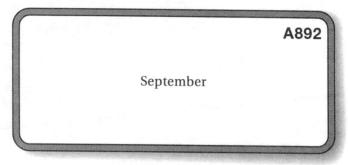

A892

September

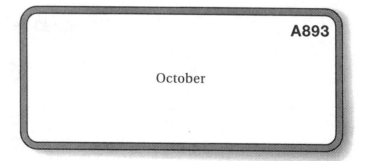

A893

October

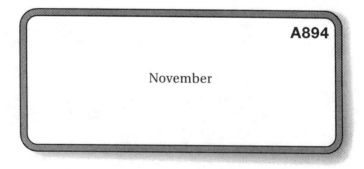

A894

November

Questions

Q895

der Dezember

*Your Own Answer*_____

Q896

arbeiten

*Your Own Answer*_____

Q897

das Auto

*Your Own Answer*_____

Correct Answers

December

to work

the car

Questions

beginnen

*Your Own Answer*_____

der Freund

*Your Own Answer*_____

der Bekannte

*Your Own Answer*_____

Correct Answers

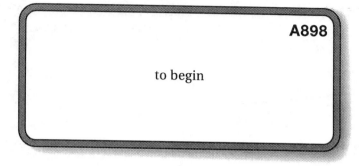

A898

to begin

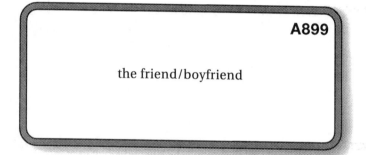

A899

the friend/boyfriend

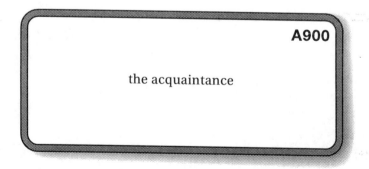

A900

the acquaintance

Questions

bestellen

*Your Own Answer*_____

bevor

*Your Own Answer*_____

das Bild

*Your Own Answer*_____

Correct Answers

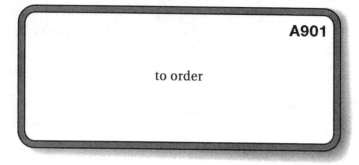

A901

to order

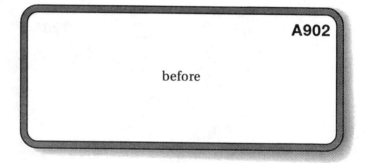

A902

before

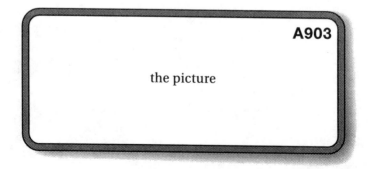

A903

the picture

Questions

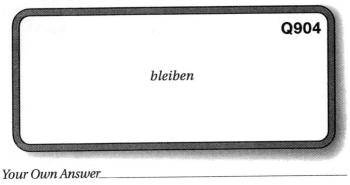

Q904

bleiben

*Your Own Answer*_____

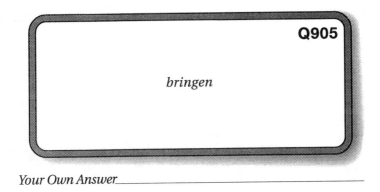

Q905

bringen

*Your Own Answer*_____

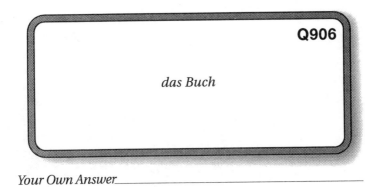

Q906

das Buch

*Your Own Answer*_____

Correct Answers

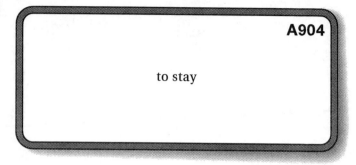

A904

to stay

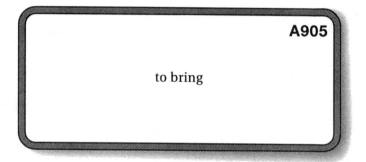

A905

to bring

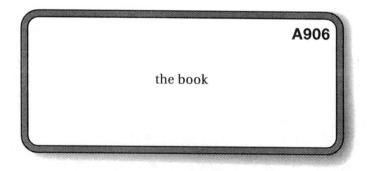

A906

the book

Questions

Q907

danken

*Your Own Answer*_____

Q908

denken

*Your Own Answer*_____

Q909

deutsch

*Your Own Answer*_____

Correct Answers

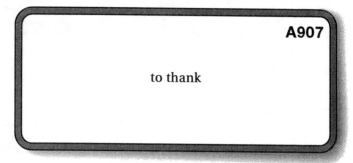

A907

to thank

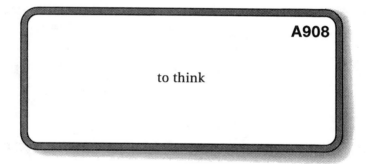

A908

to think

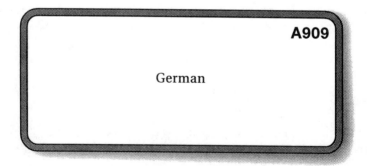

A909

German

Questions

Q910

der Deutsche

*Your Own Answer*_____

Q911

dick

*Your Own Answer*_____

Q912

schlank

*Your Own Answer*_____

Correct Answers

A910

the German

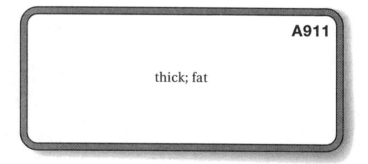

A911

thick; fat

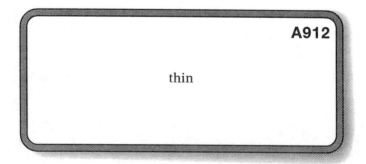

A912

thin

Questions

der Montag

*Your Own Answer*_____

der Dienstag

*Your Own Answer*_____

der Mittwoch

*Your Own Answer*_____

Correct Answers

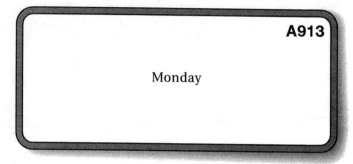

A913

Monday

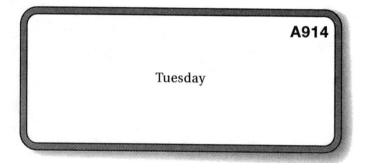

A914

Tuesday

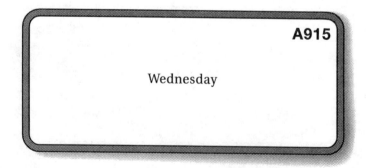

A915

Wednesday

Questions

Q916

der Donnerstag

*Your Own Answer*_____

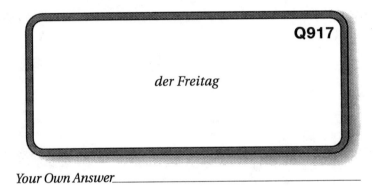

Q917

der Freitag

*Your Own Answer*_____

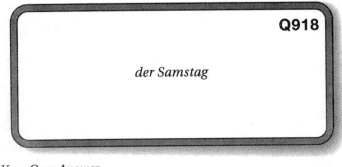

Q918

der Samstag

*Your Own Answer*_____

Correct Answers

A916

Thursday

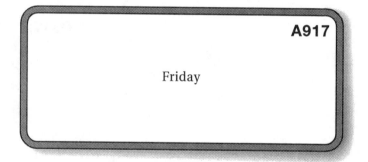

A917

Friday

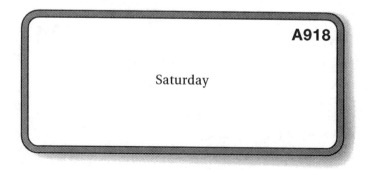

A918

Saturday

Questions

der Sonntag

*Your Own Answer*_____

durch

*Your Own Answer*_____

ehe

*Your Own Answer*_____

Correct Answers

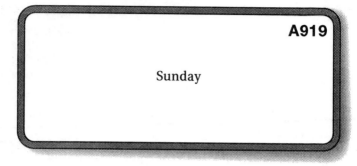

A919

Sunday

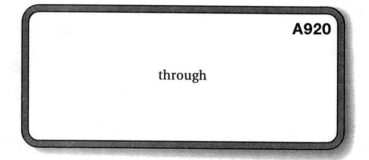

A920

through

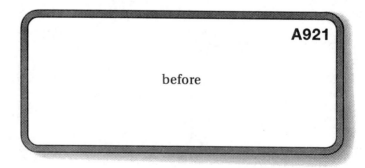

A921

before

Questions

Q922

endlich

*Your Own Answer*_____

Q923

erzählen

*Your Own Answer*_____

Q924

essen

*Your Own Answer*_____

Correct Answers

A922

finally

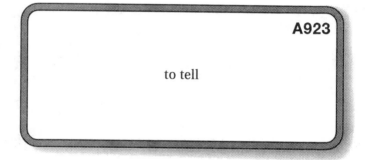

A923

to tell

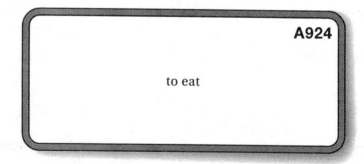

A924

to eat

Questions

etwas

*Your Own Answer*_____

euch

*Your Own Answer*_____

euer

*Your Own Answer*_____

Correct Answers

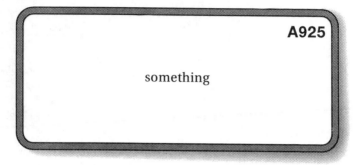

A925

something

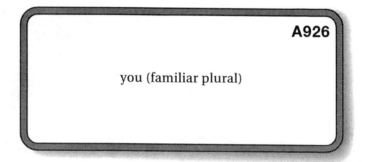

A926

you (familiar plural)

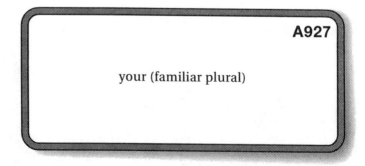

A927

your (familiar plural)

Questions

Q928

fahren

*Your Own Answer*_____

Q929

die Farbe

*Your Own Answer*_____

Q930

finden

*Your Own Answer*_____

Correct Answers

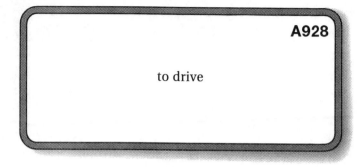

A928

to drive

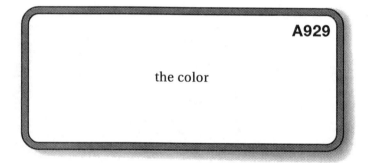

A929

the color

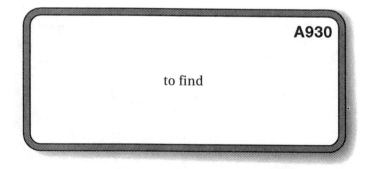

A930

to find

Questions

fliegen

*Your Own Answer*_____

fragen

*Your Own Answer*_____

freundlich

*Your Own Answer*_____

Correct Answers

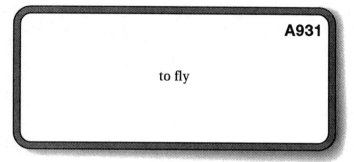

A931

to fly

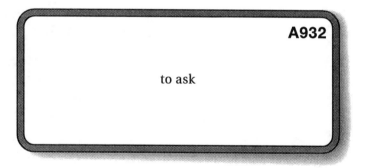

A932

to ask

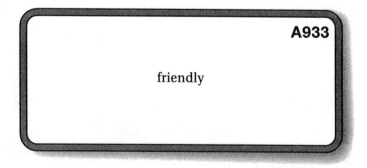

A933

friendly

Questions

Q934

zu Fuß

*Your Own Answer*_____

Q935

geben

*Your Own Answer*_____

Q936

gefallen

*Your Own Answer*_____

Correct Answers

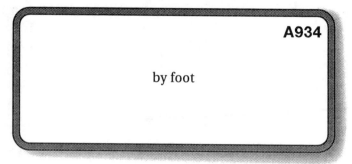

A934

by foot

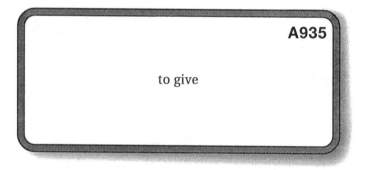

A935

to give

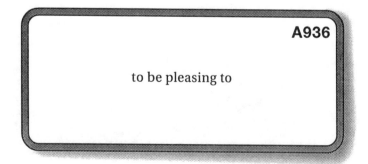

A936

to be pleasing to

Questions

Q937

der Geburtstag

*Your Own Answer*_____

Q938

gestern

*Your Own Answer*_____

Q939

heute

*Your Own Answer*_____

Correct Answers

A937

the birthday

A938

yesterday

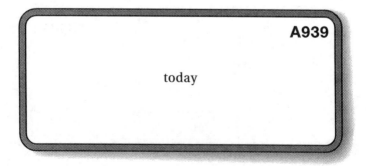

A939

today

Questions

morgen

*Your Own Answer*_____

gehen

*Your Own Answer*_____

glauben

*Your Own Answer*_____

Correct Answers

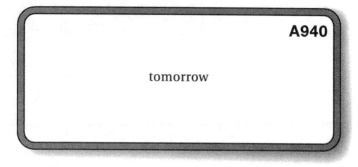

A940

tomorrow

A941

to go

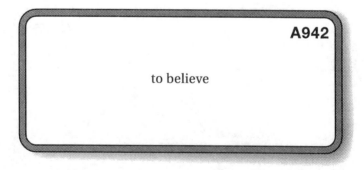

A942

to believe

Questions

Q943

glücklich

*Your Own Answer*_____

Q944

böse

*Your Own Answer*_____

Q945

groß

*Your Own Answer*_____

Correct Answers

A943

happy; lucky

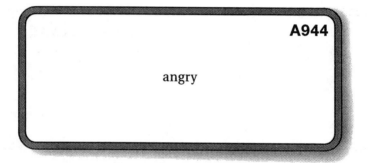

A944

angry

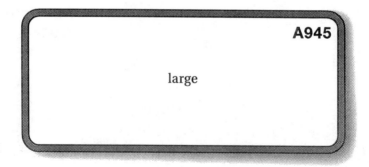

A945

large

Questions

klein

Your Own Answer_____

haben

Your Own Answer_____

heiß

Your Own Answer_____

Correct Answers

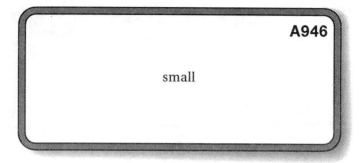

A946

small

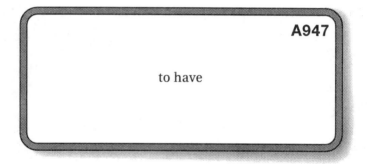

A947

to have

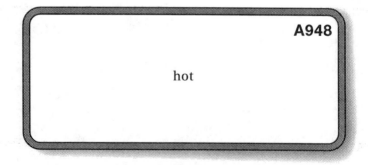

A948

hot

Questions

kalt

Your Own Answer_____

heißen

Your Own Answer_____

hoch

Your Own Answer_____

Correct Answers

A949

cold

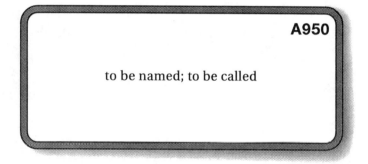

A950

to be named; to be called

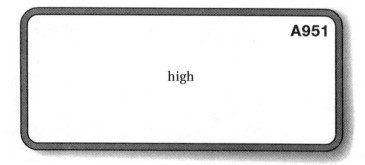

A951

high

Questions

Q952

kaufen

*Your Own Answer*_____

Q953

kennen

*Your Own Answer*_____

Q954

wissen

*Your Own Answer*_____

Correct Answers

A952

to buy

A953

to be acquainted with

A954

to know

Questions

Q955

leben

Your Own Answer_____

Q956

lesen

Your Own Answer_____

Q957

machen

Your Own Answer_____

Correct Answers

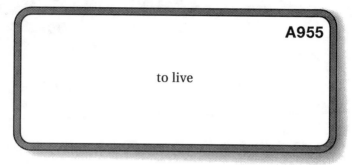

A955

to live

A956

to read

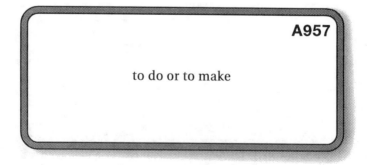

A957

to do or to make

Questions

Q958

nehmen

*Your Own Answer*_____

Q959

sagen

*Your Own Answer*_____

Q960

schreiben

*Your Own Answer*_____

Correct Answers

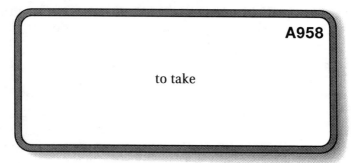

A958

to take

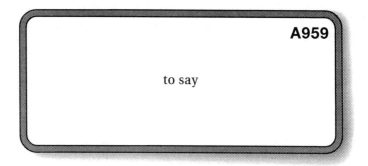

A959

to say

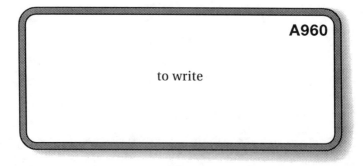

A960

to write

Questions

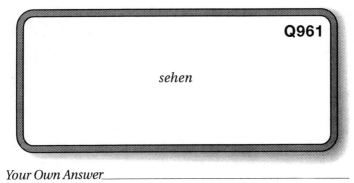

Q961

sehen

*Your Own Answer*_____

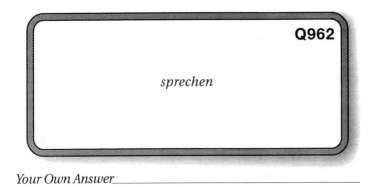

Q962

sprechen

*Your Own Answer*_____

Q963

werden

*Your Own Answer*_____

Correct Answers

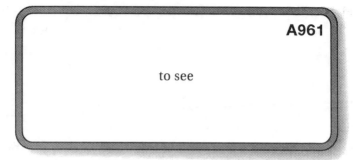

A961

to see

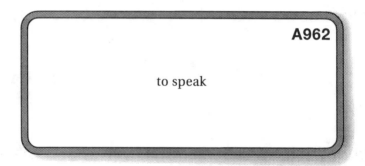

A962

to speak

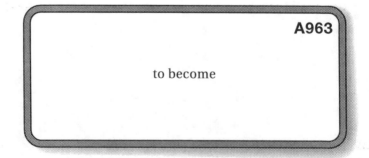

A963

to become

Questions

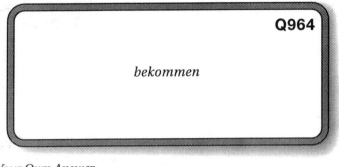

Q964

bekommen

Your Own Answer_____

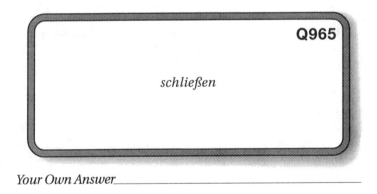

Q965

schließen

Your Own Answer_____

Q966

das Wetter

Your Own Answer_____

Correct Answers

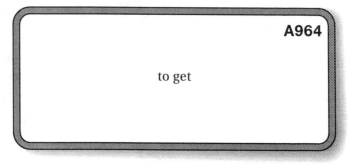

A964

to get

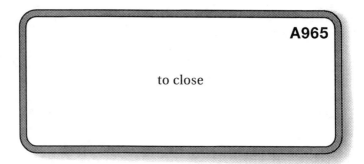

A965

to close

A966

the weather

Questions

der Regen

*Your Own Answer*_____

die Arbeit

*Your Own Answer*_____

tun

*Your Own Answer*_____

Correct Answers

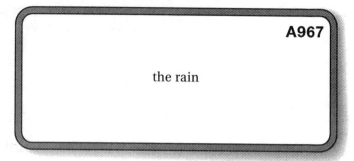

A967

the rain

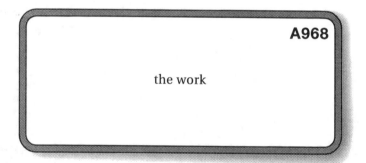

A968

the work

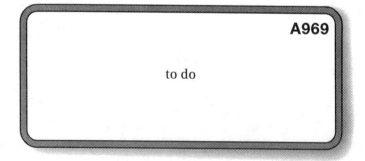

A969

to do

Questions

die Jacke

*Your Own Answer*_____

das Restaurant

*Your Own Answer*_____

die Straße

*Your Own Answer*_____

Correct Answers

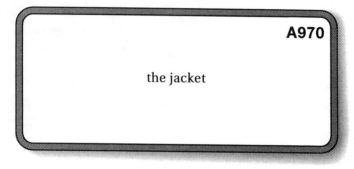

A970

the jacket

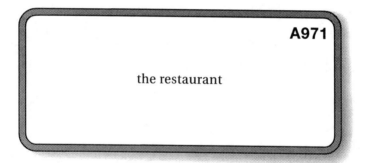

A971

the restaurant

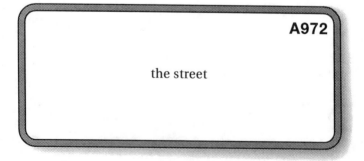

A972

the street

Questions

Q973

der Wagen

*Your Own Answer*_____

Q974

krank

*Your Own Answer*_____

Q975

gesund

*Your Own Answer*_____

Correct Answers

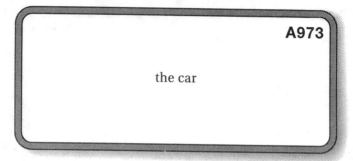

A973

the car

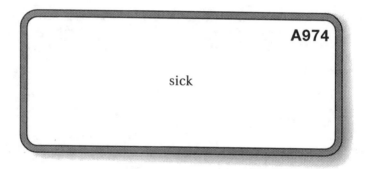

A974

sick

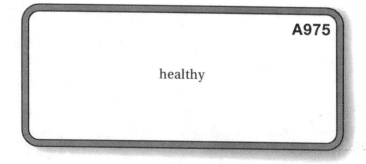

A975

healthy

Questions

Q976

unglücklich

*Your Own Answer*_____

Q977

die Kleidung

*Your Own Answer*_____

Q978

links

*Your Own Answer*_____

Correct Answers

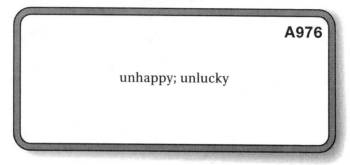

A976

unhappy; unlucky

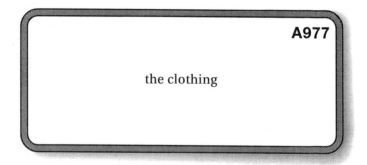

A977

the clothing

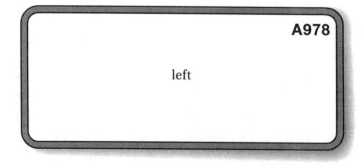

A978

left

Questions

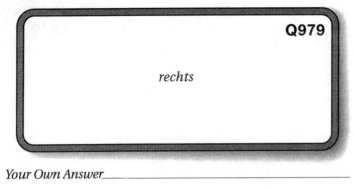

Q979

rechts

*Your Own Answer*_____

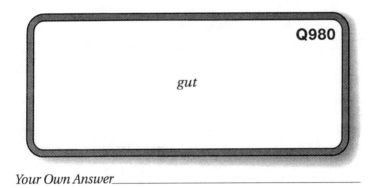

Q980

gut

*Your Own Answer*_____

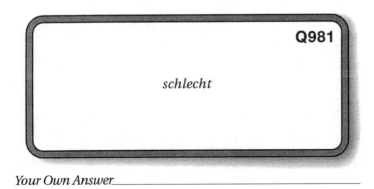

Q981

schlecht

*Your Own Answer*_____

Correct Answers

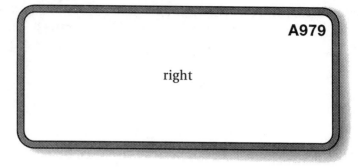

A979

right

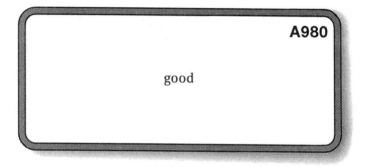

A980

good

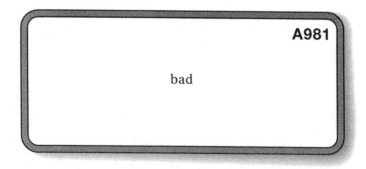

A981

bad

Questions

teuer

*Your Own Answer*_____

billig

*Your Own Answer*_____

frisch

*Your Own Answer*_____

Correct Answers

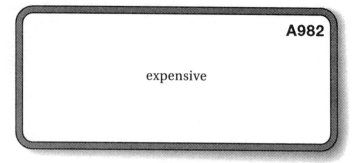

A982

expensive

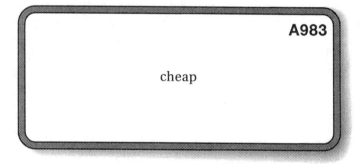

A983

cheap

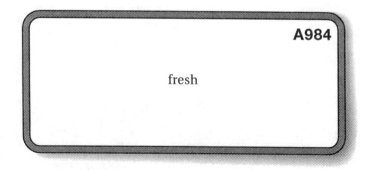

A984

fresh

Questions

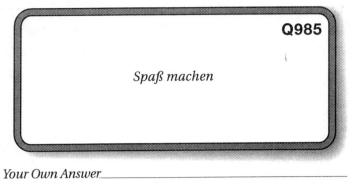

Q985

Spaß machen

*Your Own Answer*_____

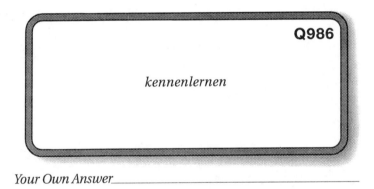

Q986

kennenlernen

*Your Own Answer*_____

Q987

Wieviel Uhr ist es?

*Your Own Answer*_____

Correct Answers

A985

to be fun

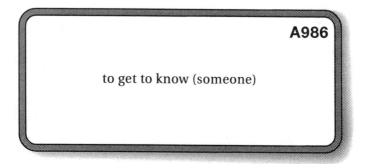

A986

to get to know (someone)

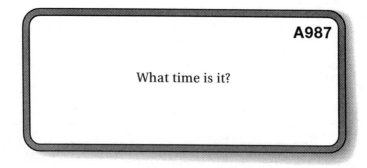

A987

What time is it?

Questions

Q988

Wieviel kostet das?

*Your Own Answer*_____

Q989

schreien

*Your Own Answer*_____

Q990

das Ei

*Your Own Answer*_____

Correct Answers

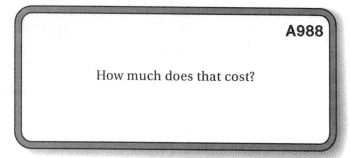

A988

How much does that cost?

A989

to scream

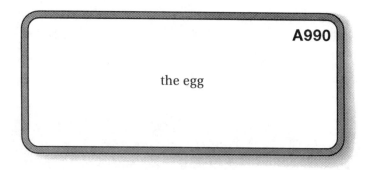

A990

the egg

Questions

Q991

der Angestellte

*Your Own Answer*_____

Q992

hilfsbereit

*Your Own Answer*_____

Q993

der Tisch

*Your Own Answer*_____

Correct Answers

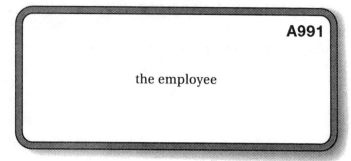

A991

the employee

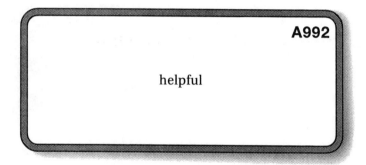

A992

helpful

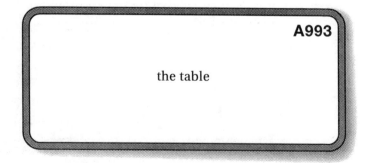

A993

the table

Questions

Q994

die Wand

*Your Own Answer*_____

Q995

die Lampe

*Your Own Answer*_____

Q996

fressen

*Your Own Answer*_____

Correct Answers

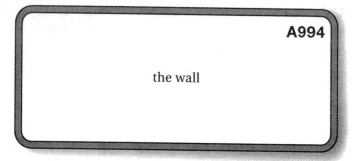

A994

the wall

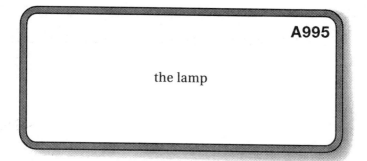

A995

the lamp

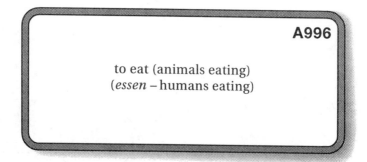

A996

to eat (animals eating)
(*essen* – humans eating)

BLANK CARDS
To Make Up Your Own Questions

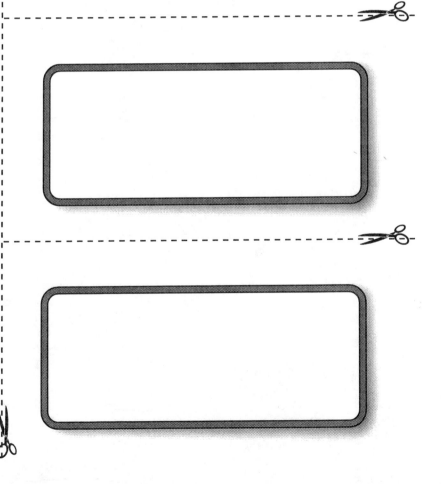

CORRECT ANSWERS

for

Your Own Questions

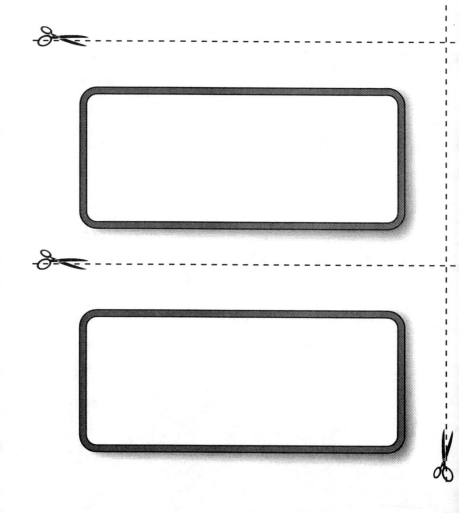

Blank Cards for
Your Own Questions

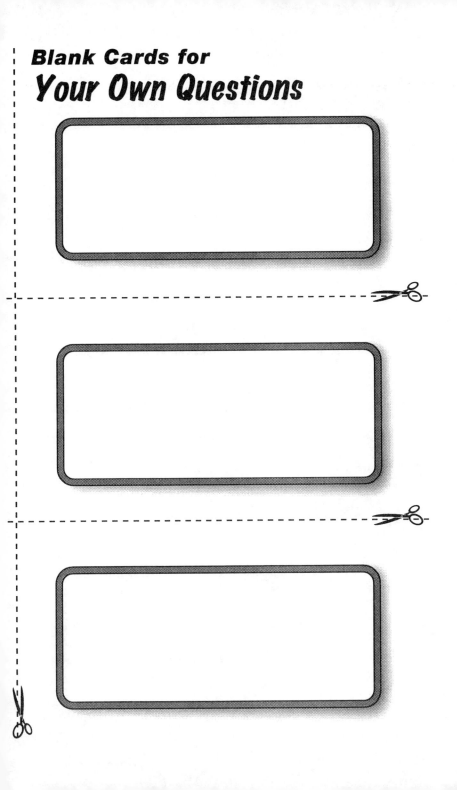

Correct Answers

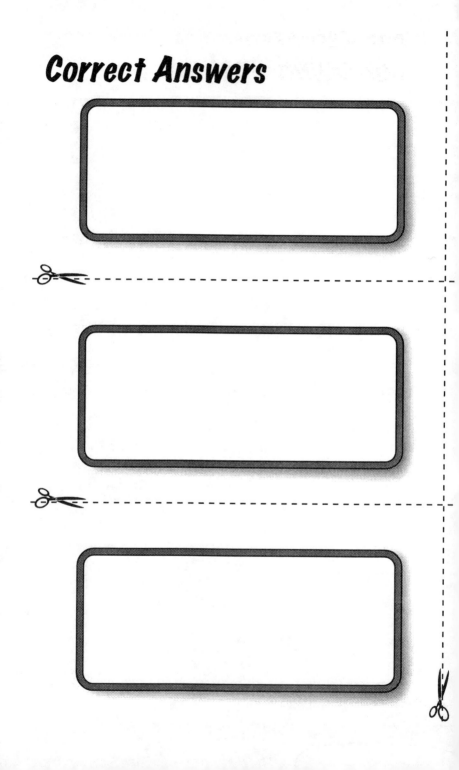

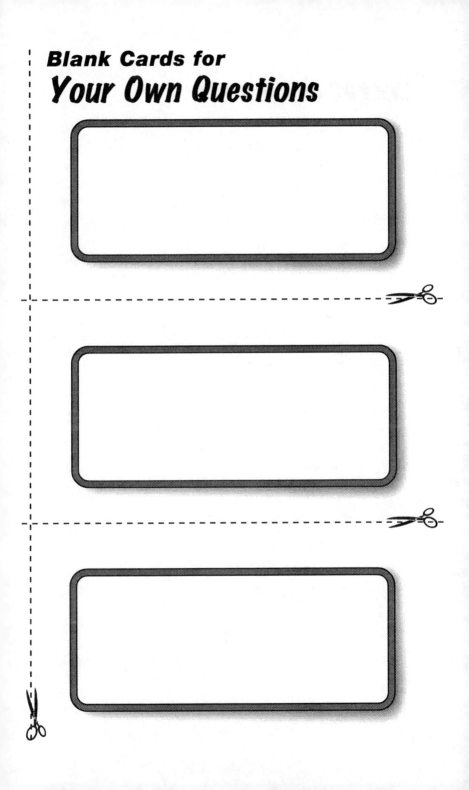

Blank Cards for
Your Own Questions

Correct Answers

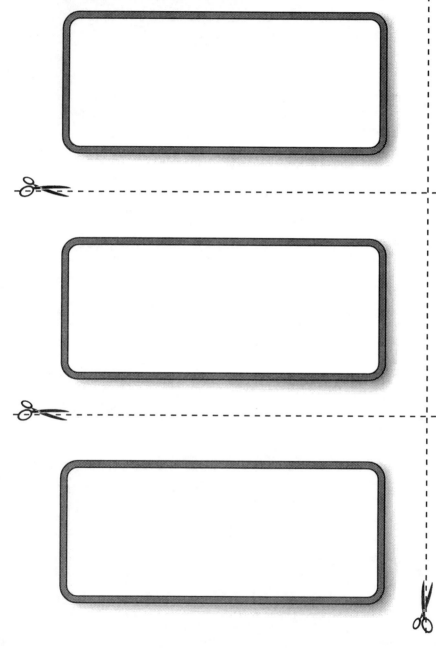

Blank Cards for
Your Own Questions

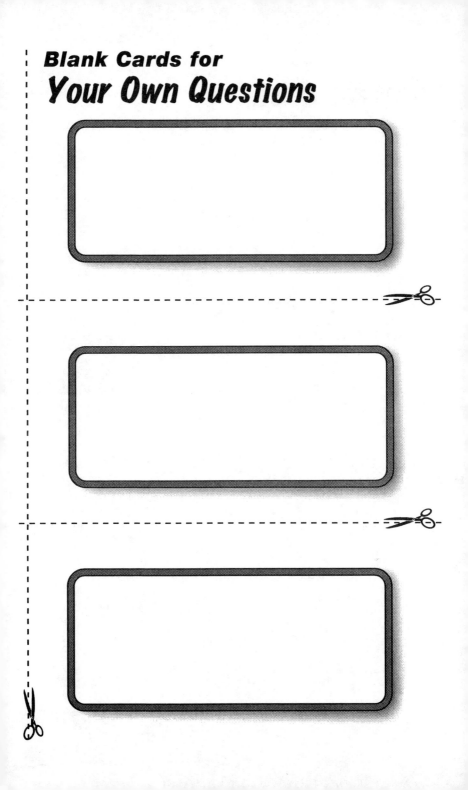

Correct Answers

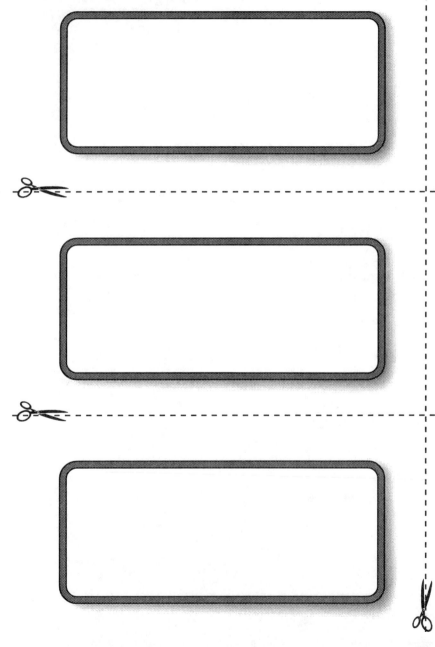

Blank Cards for *Your Own Questions*

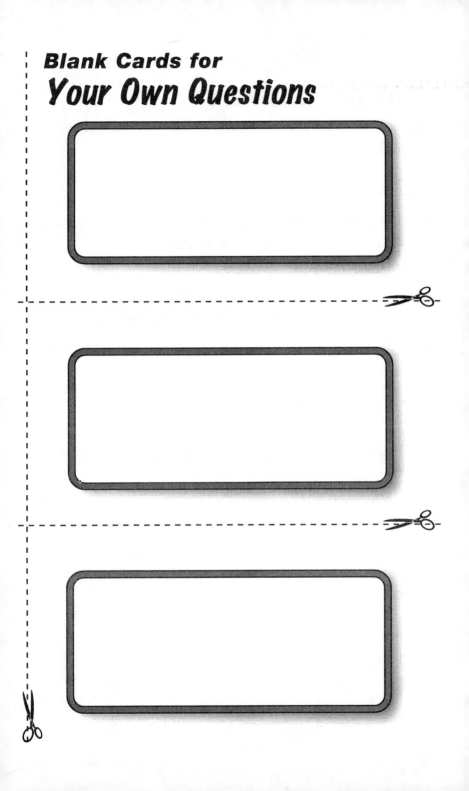

Correct Answers

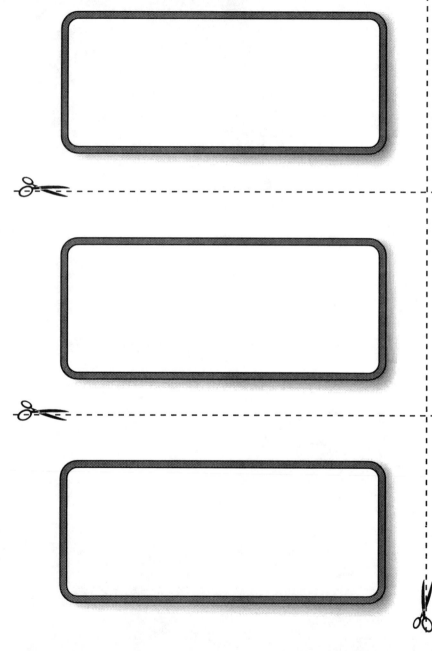

Blank Cards for *Your Own Questions*

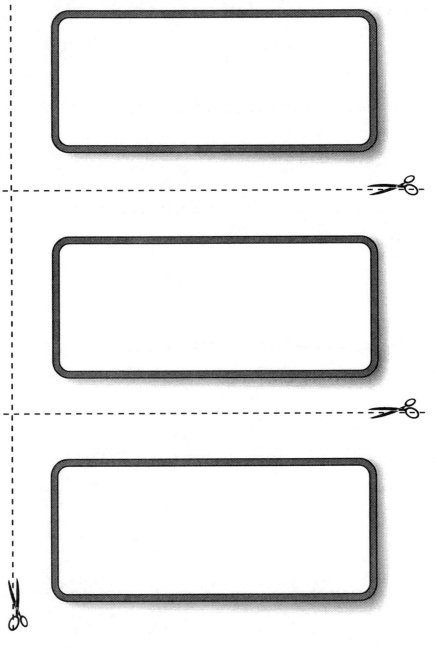

Correct Answers

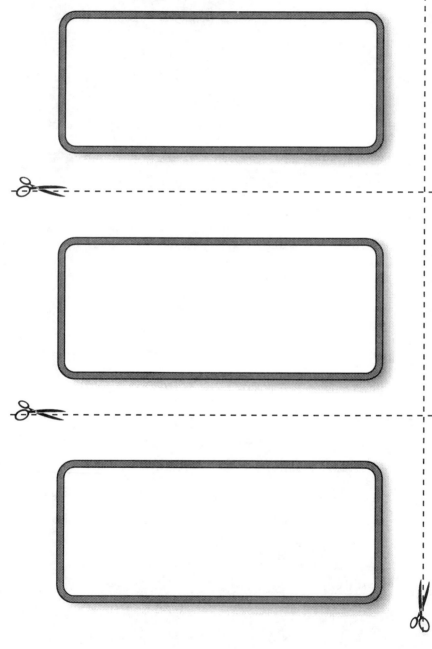

Blank Cards for
Your Own Questions

Correct Answers

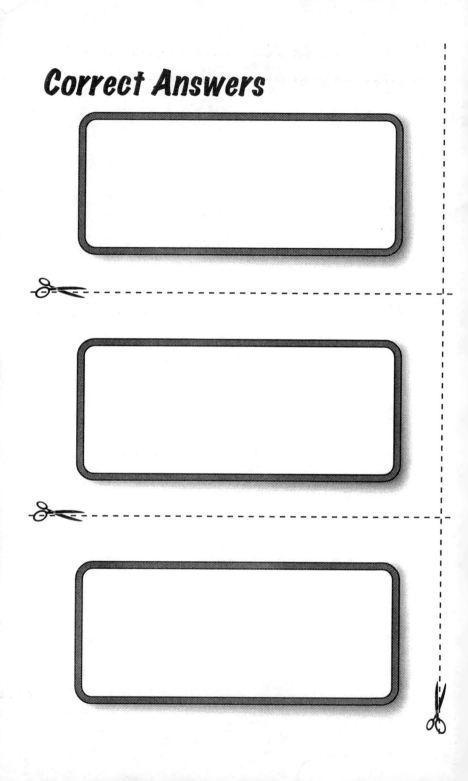

Blank Cards for *Your Own Questions*

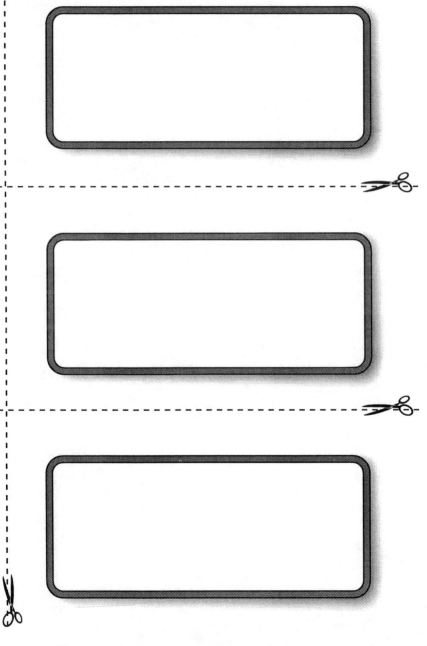

Correct Answers

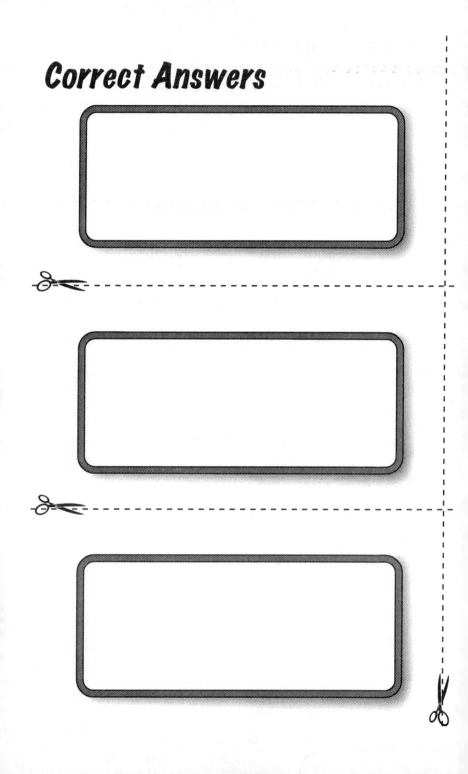

Blank Cards for
Your Own Questions

Correct Answers

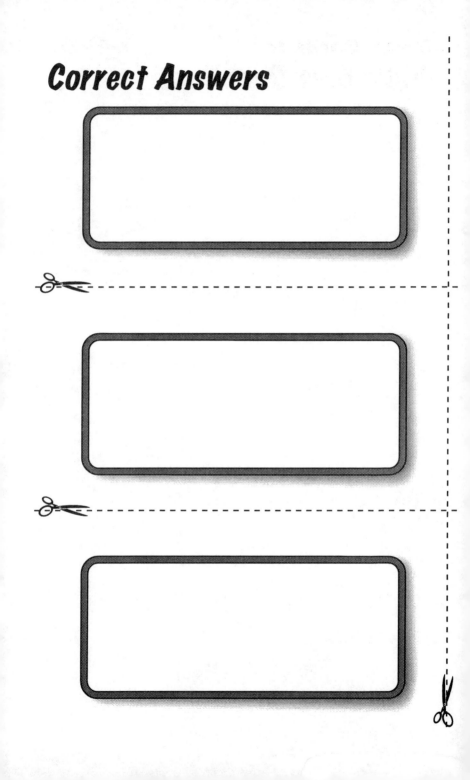

Blank Cards for *Your Own Questions*

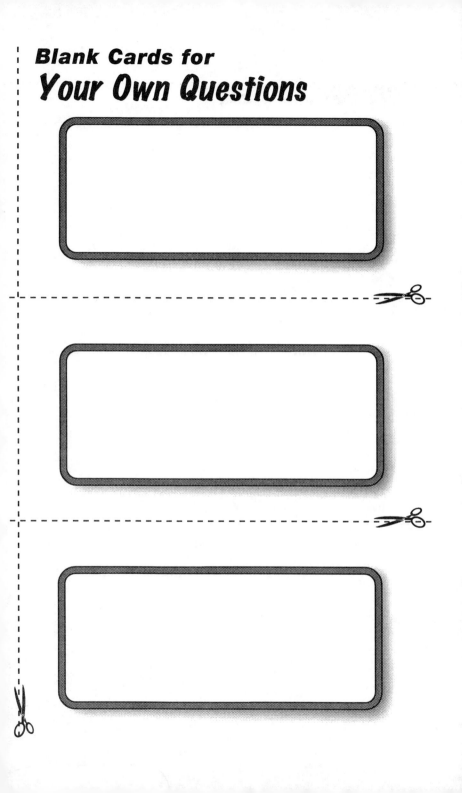

Correct Answers

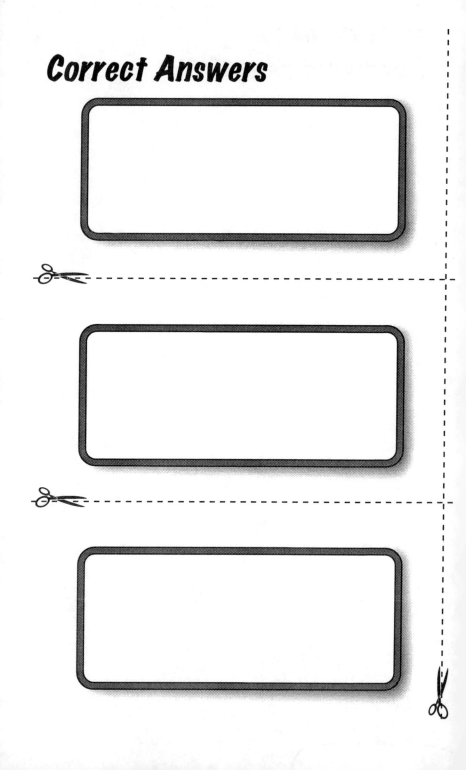

Blank Cards for
Your Own Questions

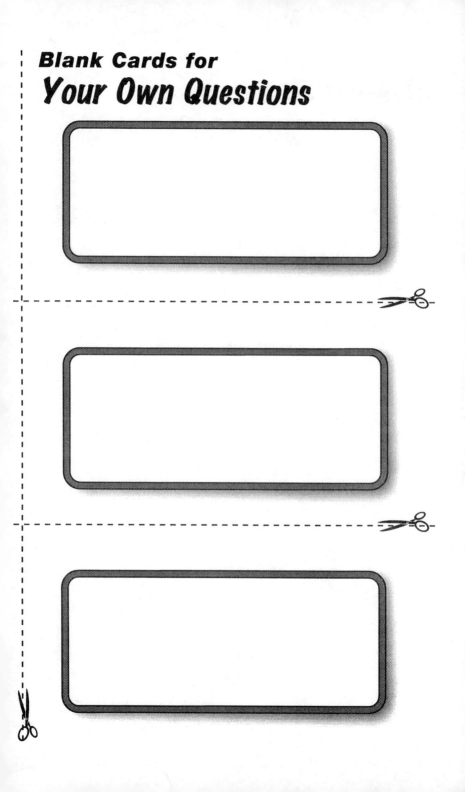

Correct Answers

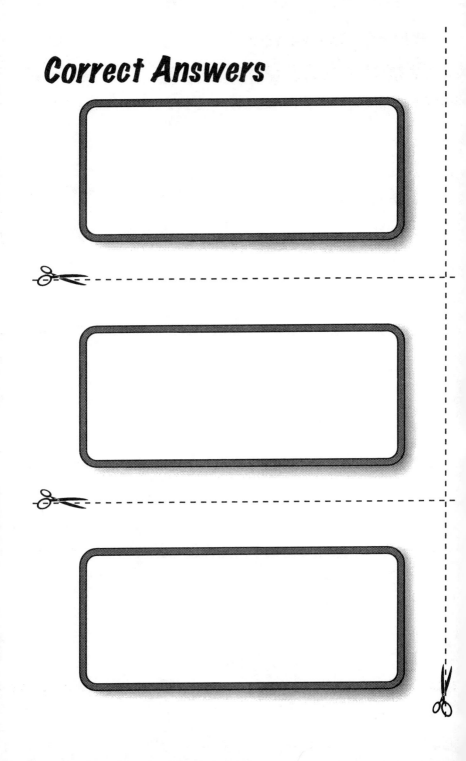

Blank Cards for *Your Own Questions*

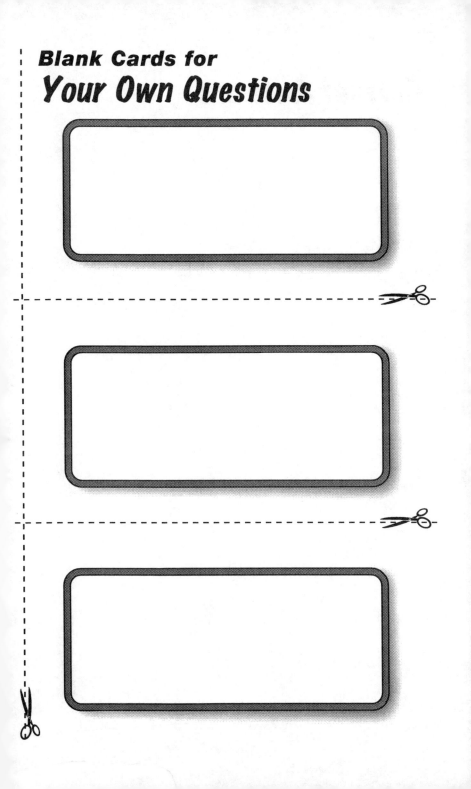

Correct Answers

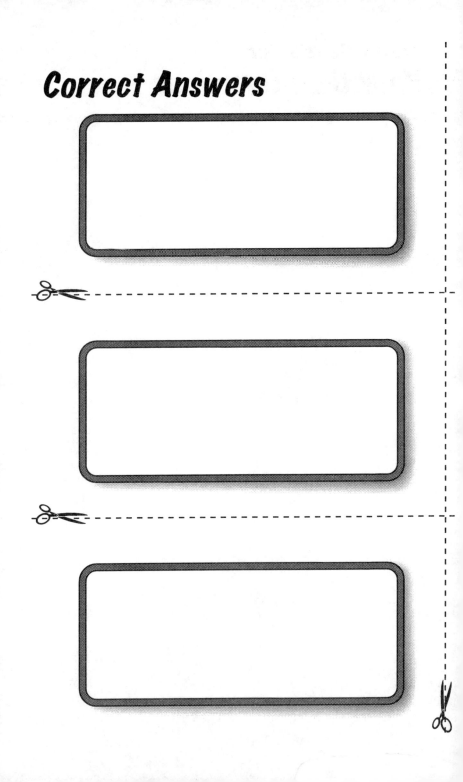

Blank Cards for *Your Own Questions*

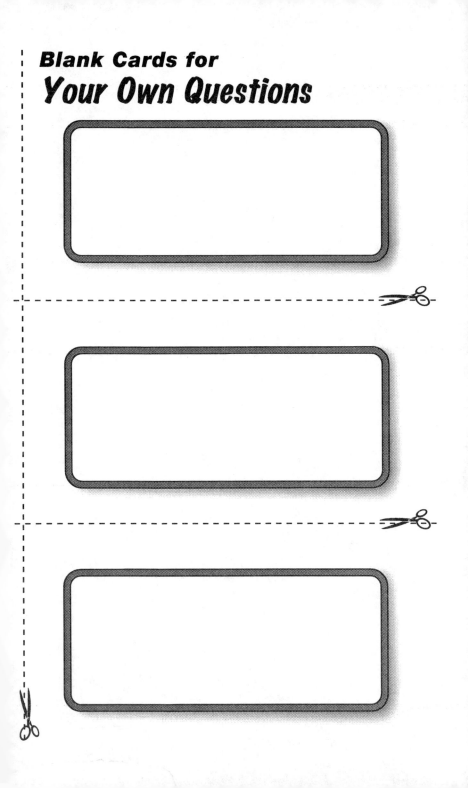

Correct Answers

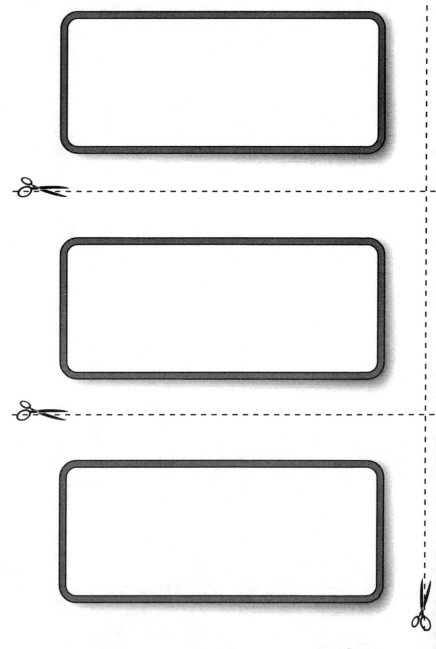

Blank Cards for
Your Own Questions

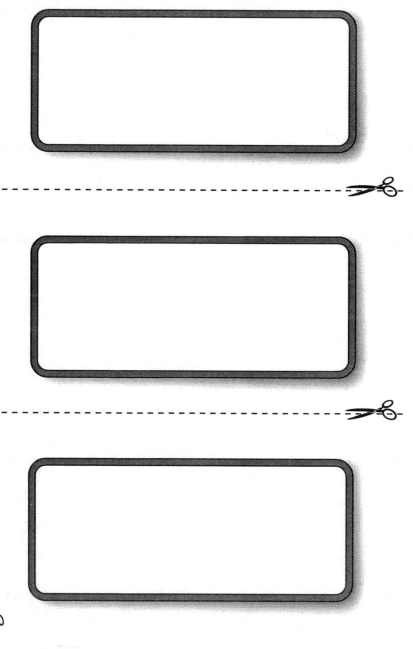

Correct Answers

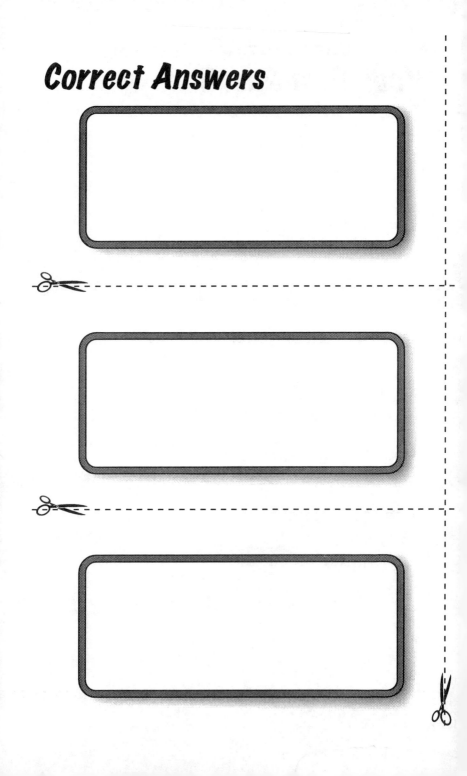

Blank Cards for
Your Own Questions

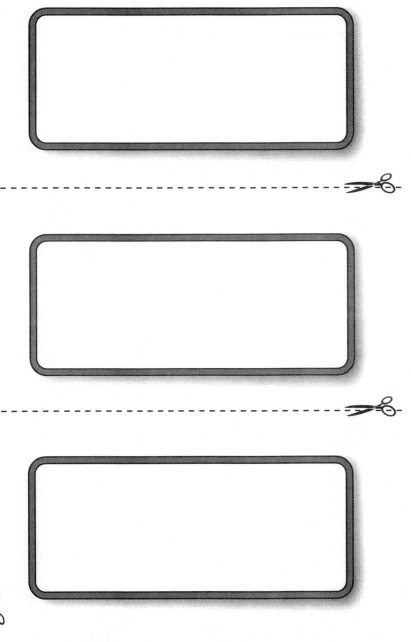

Correct Answers

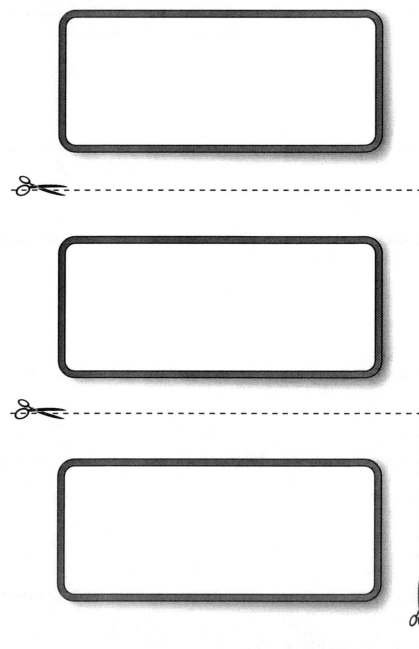

Blank Cards for
Your Own Questions

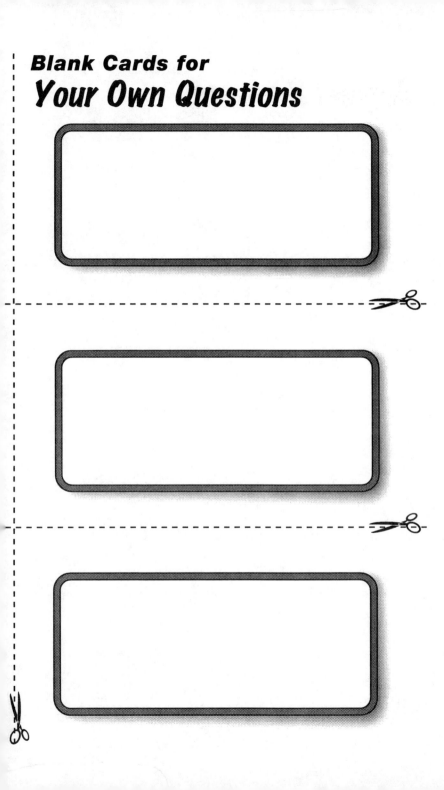

Correct Answers

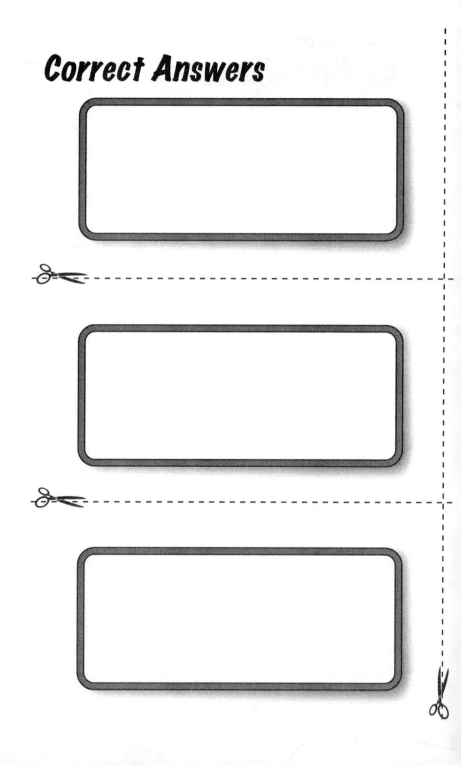

Correct Answers

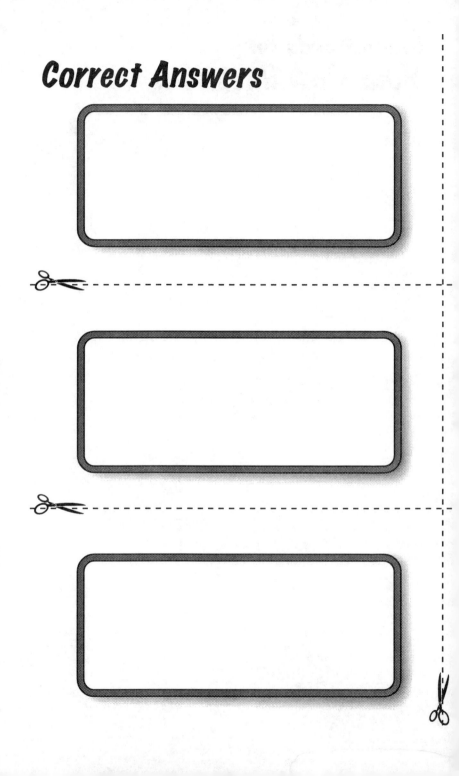

Blank Cards for
Your Own Questions

Correct Answers

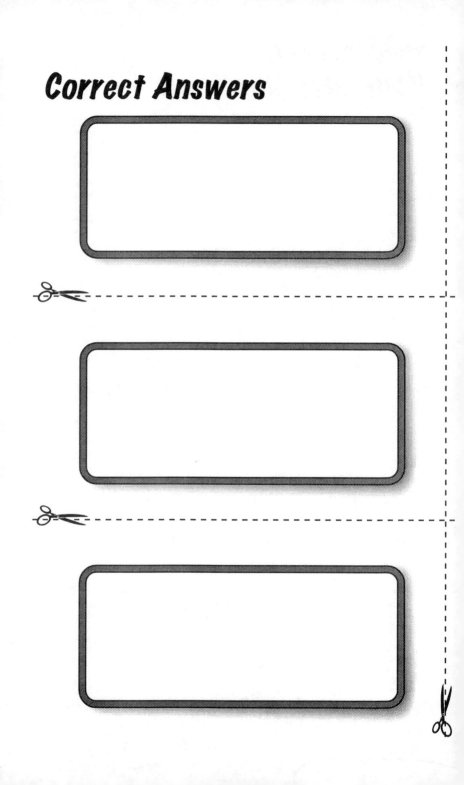

Blank Cards for
Your Own Questions

Correct Answers

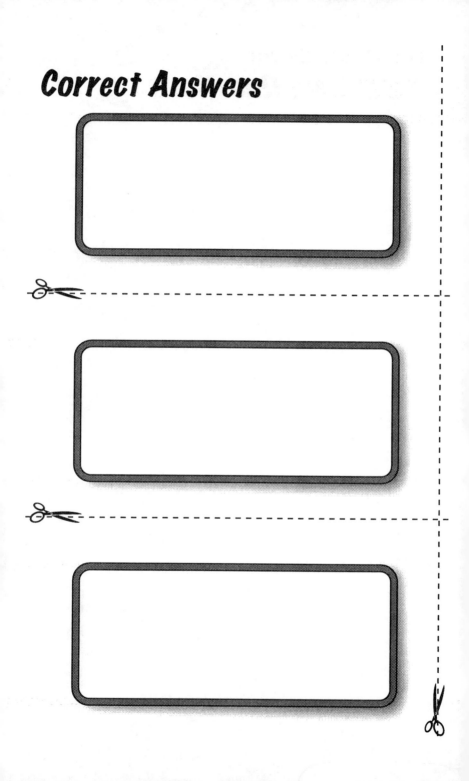

Blank Cards for *Your Own Questions*

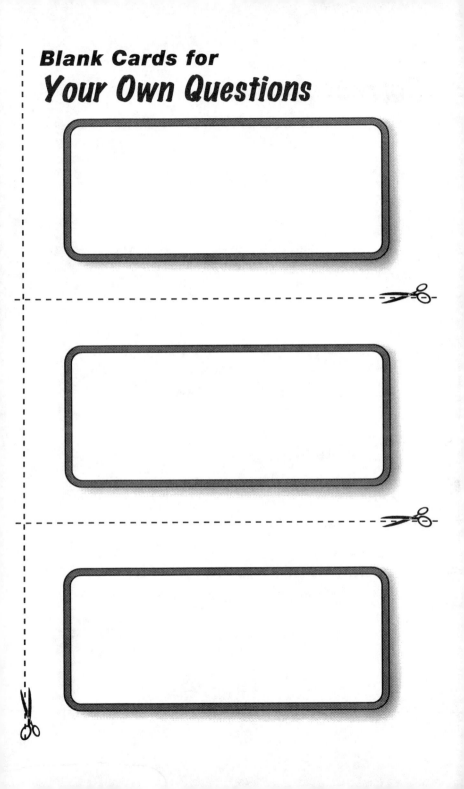

Correct Answers

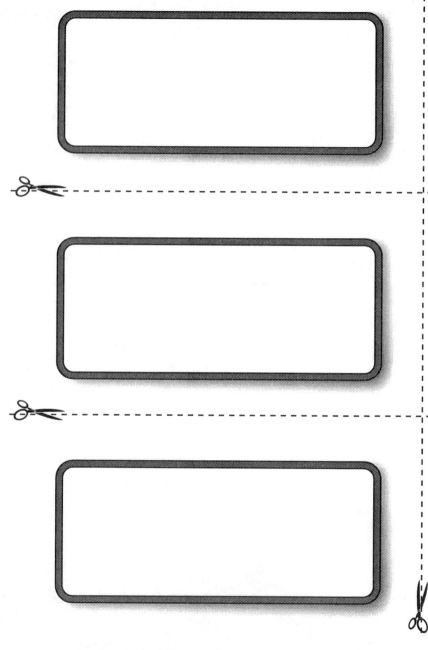

Blank Cards for
Your Own Questions

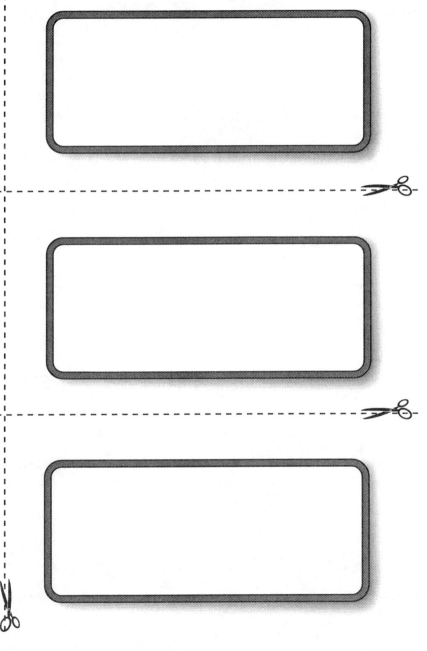

Correct Answers

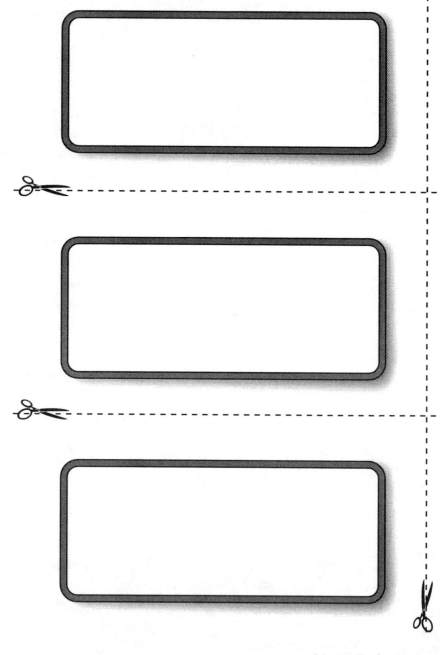

Blank Cards for *Your Own Questions*

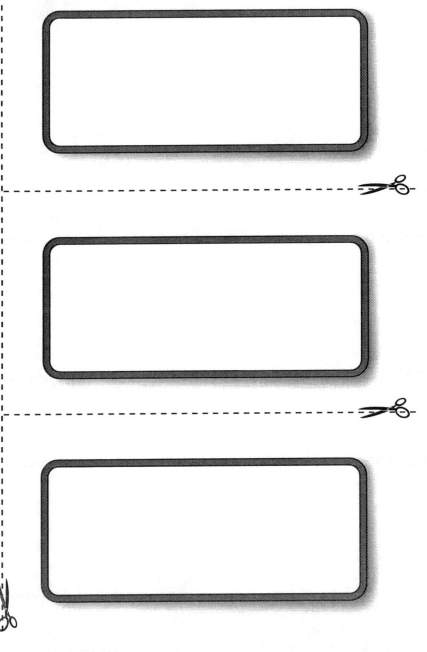

Correct Answers

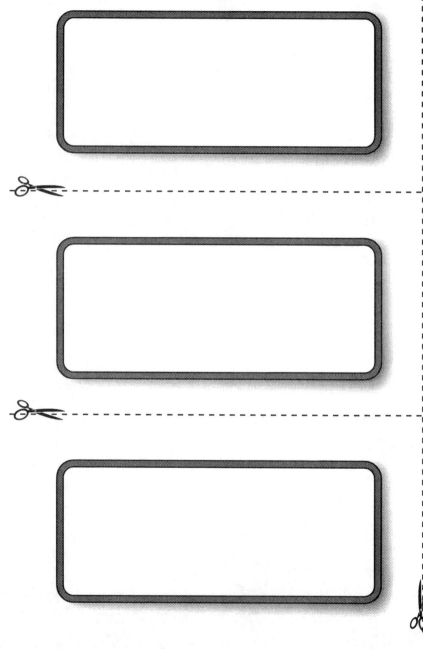

Blank Cards for
Your Own Questions

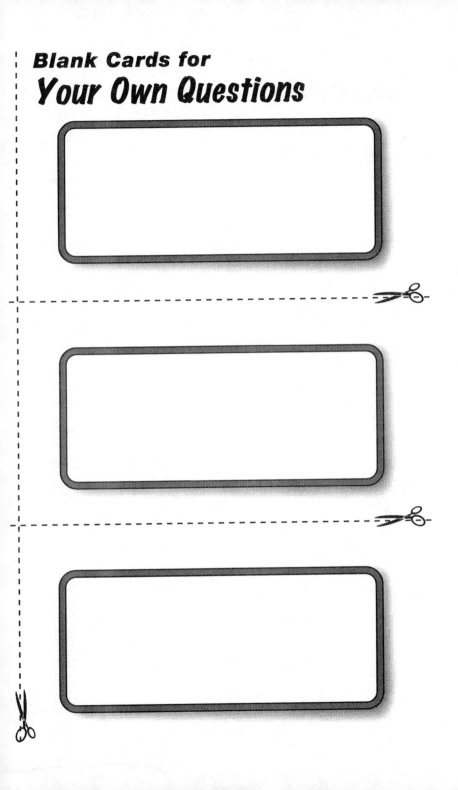

Correct Answers

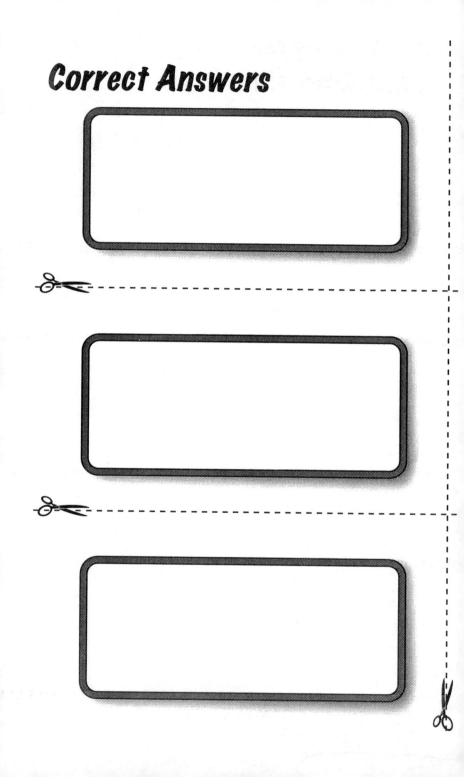

Blank Cards for *Your Own Questions*

Correct Answers

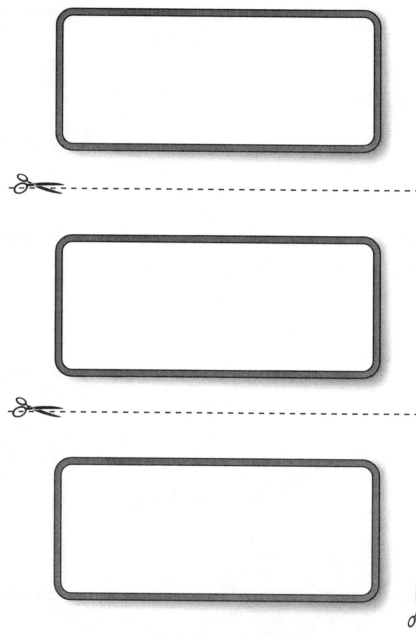

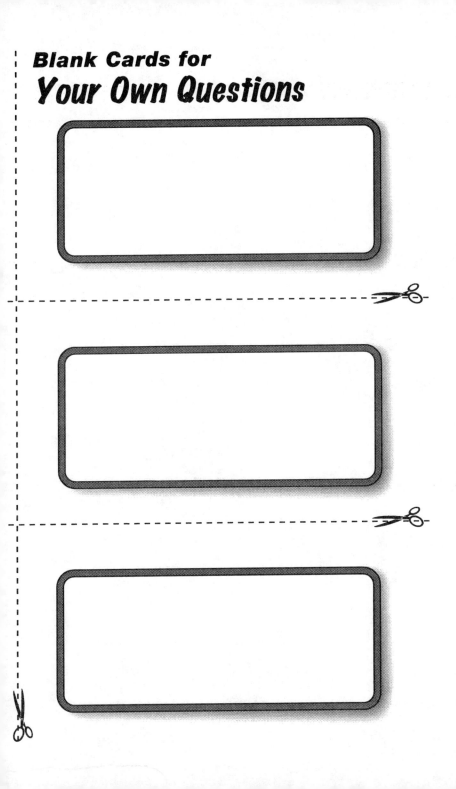

Blank Cards for
Your Own Questions

Correct Answers

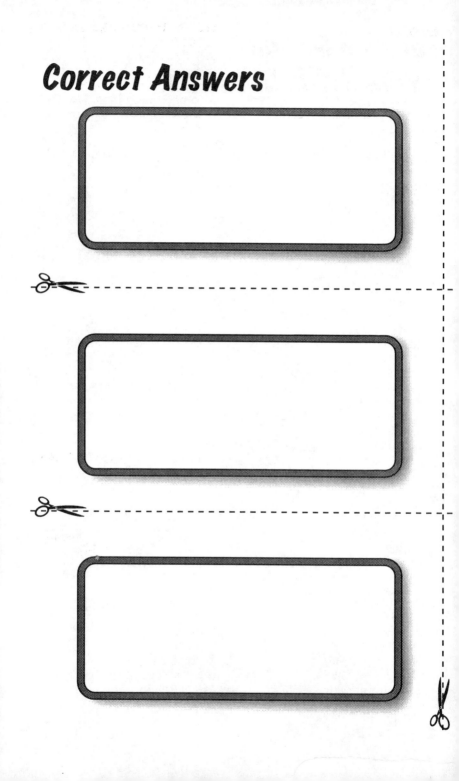

INDEX